Cold War Refugees

COLD WAR REFUGEES

*Connected Histories of Displacement
and Migration across Postcolonial Asia*

Edited by Yumi Moon

STANFORD UNIVERSITY PRESS
Stanford, California

Stanford University Press
Stanford, California

© 2025 by the Board of Trustees of the Leland Stanford Jr. University. All rights reserved.

This book has been published with the assistance of the Laboratory Program for Korean Studies through the Ministry of Education of the Republic of Korea and Korean Studies Promotion Service of the Academy of Korean Studies (AKS-2020-LAB-2230o1).

No part of this book may be reproduced or transmitted in any form or by any means, electronic or mechanical, including photocopying and recording, or in any information storage or retrieval system, without the prior written permission of Stanford University Press.

Printed in the United States of America

Library of Congress Cataloging-in-Publication Data
Names: Moon, Yumi editor
Title: Cold War refugees : connected histories of displacement and migration across postcolonial Asia / edited by Yumi Moon.
Description: Stanford, California : Stanford University Press, [2025] | Includes bibliographical references and index.
Identifiers: LCCN 2025003422 (print) | LCCN 2025003423 (ebook)
 | ISBN 9781503642638 cloth | ISBN 9781503643130 paperback |
 ISBN 9781503643147 epub
Subjects: LCSH: Political refugees—Asia—History—20th century | Cold War—Social aspects—Asia | Asia—History—1945-
Classification: LCC DS35.2 .C637 2025 (print) | LCC DS35.2 (ebook) | DDC 950.4/2—dc23/eng/20250326

LC record available at https://lccn.loc.gov/2025003422
LC ebook record available at https://lccn.loc.gov/2025003423

Cover design: Michele Wetherbee
Cover photograph: SuperStock / Alamy Stock Photo, Dachen Refugees, 1955

The authorized representative in the EU for product safety and compliance is: Mare Nostrum Group B.V. | Mauritskade 21D | 1091 GC Amsterdam | The Netherlands | Email address: gpsr@mare-nostrum.co.uk | KVK chamber of commerce number: 96249943

To the loving memory of Carter J. Eckert.

Contents

	Contributors	ix
	Notes on Romanization	xi
	INTRODUCTION YUMI MOON	1
ONE	Vietnam's 1954 Partition and Displacement in a Global Perspective PHI-VÂN NGUYEN	22
TWO	The Cold War, Anti-Communist Propaganda, and the Resettlement of Dachen Refugees from Coastal Zhejiang to Taiwan DOMINIC MENG-HSUAN YANG	43
THREE	Northern Refugees and the Rise of Cold War Nationalism in South Korea, 1945–1950 YUMI MOON	74

FOUR	Rethinking Spatial Politics and the Legacy of the Cold War in Karachi IJLAL MUZAFFAR	110
FIVE	Afghan Refugees as Political Actors SABAUON NASSERI *and* ROBERT D. CREWS	135
EPILOGUE	After Cruelty: The Last Subject of Cold War Humanism AISHWARY KUMAR	158

Notes — 197

Index — 241

Contributors

ROBERT D. CREWS is professor of history at Stanford University. He is the author of *Afghan Modern: The History of a Global Nation* (Harvard University Press, 2015) and *For Prophet and Tsar: Islam and Empire in Russia and Central Asia* (Harvard University Press, 2006), as well as coeditor of *Under the Drones: Modern Lives in the Afghanistan-Pakistan Borderlands* (Harvard University Press, 2012) and *The Taliban and the Crisis of Afghanistan* (Harvard University Press, 2008).

AISHWARY KUMAR is associate professor of history and director of the Democracy Institute at Cal Poly Pomona, where he heads the GIFT (Global Inquiries in Freedom and Tyranny) Project and the American Institutions Common Core. He is also director of the Ahimsa Center for the study of political nonviolence. He is the author of *Radical Equality: Ambedkar, Gandhi, and the Risk of Democracy* (Stanford University Press, 2015).

YUMI MOON is associate professor of history at Stanford University. She is the author of *Populist Collaborators: The Ilchinhoe and the Japanese Colonization of Korea, 1896–1910* (Cornell University Press, 2013).

IJLAL MUZAFFAR is professor of modern architectural history at the Rhode Island School of Design. He is the author of *Modernism's Magic Hat: Architecture and the Illusion of Development without Capital* (University of Texas Press, 2024).

SABAUON NASSERI holds a PhD in history from Stanford University. His research focuses on the political and cultural history of Afghanistan, the broader Middle East, and South and Central Asia in the twentieth and twenty-first centuries. He has taught courses on Islam and literature, globalization, intellectual history, and environmental history at Beloit College.

PHI-VÂN NGUYEN is associate professor of history at the University of Saint-Boniface in Winnipeg, Canada. She is the author of *A Displaced Nation: The 1954 Evacuation and Its Political Impact on the Vietnam Wars* (Cornell University Press, 2024).

DOMINIC MENG-HSUAN YANG is associate professor of East Asian history at the University of Missouri–Columbia. His book *The Great Exodus from China: Trauma, Memory, and Identity in Modern Taiwan* (Cambridge University Press, 2020) won the Memory Studies Association First Book Award in 2020.

Notes on Romanization

This book uses the McCune-Reischauer system to romanize Korean. Exceptions include names of prominent historical figures known by alternate spellings (e.g., Syngman Rhee and Kim Il Sung), as well as Korean authors and places with widely recognized English names.

The romanization of Chinese characters in chapter 2 follows the Hanyu Pinyin system. The exceptions are the names of prominent historical figures known by alternate spellings (e.g., Chiang Kai-shek), as well as the names of Taiwanese authors (Chen Jen-ho and Dominic Meng-Hsuan Yang), places (e.g., Keelung, Kaohsiung, and Taitung), organizations, etc. Wade-Giles is used for all Taiwanese individuals in the chapter, with the Pinyin provided in parentheses.

All words in Urdu in chapter 4 have been italicized with translations in parentheses except for proper names of individuals and locations.

Cold War Refugees

INTRODUCTION

YUMI MOON

Chinese mainlanders crossing into Hong Kong, escaping Mao Zedong's Great Leap Forward; the desperate exodus of the "boat people" from Vietnam to the People's Army of Vietnam after the fall of Saigon; the US Navy's winter evacuation of North Koreans from Hŭngnam Harbor during the Korean War—called the "Christmas Miracle": such scenes of refugees escaping Communist countries are some of the most iconic images of Asia's Cold War. Consider the 1950 "Miracle," which—as was recently claimed by the *National Interest*, a conservative magazine that covers US foreign affairs—was the largest wartime rescue of civilians undertaken by the US military until the evacuation from Afghanistan in the summer of 2021.[1] Meanwhile, Amnesty International attributes the origins of the current Afghanistan refugee crisis to the violence of the leftist government established in 1978 and the Soviet invasion of Afghanistan in 1979.[2] Clearly, these Asian refugees remain symbolically prominent in Cold War ideology and imagery. And yet their experiences and trajectories have been relatively obscure in the history of the Cold War and in global refugee studies.[3]

Scholars of refugee studies have criticized the sensationalist depictions of these refugees and the objectification of their identities to uphold the narratives promoted by the Cold War's power holders. Yến Lê Espiritu et al.'s October 2022 volume, *Departures: An Introduction to Critical Refugee Studies*, explores an alternative framework and methodology, which foregrounds the agency and the life stories of refugees themselves.[4] The authors of the book critically review the existing literature on refugees with regard to legal issues, state and international institutions, humanitarianism, and cultural studies. However, the book's discussion of historical cases of refugees and their implications for refugee studies is still scanty. The authors of *Departures* should not be faulted for this lack; rather, it stems from historians' relative neglect of the subject of refugees, especially in the field of Cold War studies. For example, the multivolume series *The Cambridge History of the Cold War* covers a comprehensive range of topics and regions yet contains only one chapter on global migration and population control.[5]

Recent publications on Cold War refugees have started to address this neglect.[6] However, we are still in the early stages of understanding the extent of population displacement caused by Cold War conflicts and the larger significance of refugee stories across many countries. One reason for this delay is Western countries' migration policies and their interests in restraining the influx of Asian refugees to their countries. In her 2016 book, *Elusive Refuge: Chinese Migrants in the Cold War*, Laura Madokoro analyzes the positions of Western countries toward Chinese refugees in Hong Kong, referring to these nations as "white settler societies" to highlight their colonial past and racial discrimination against Asian immigrants. Specifically, the leaders of these countries sought to make sure humanitarian assistance for refugees did not undermine their strict immigration regulations on Asians. In such a context, the reality of refugee lives was simplified: either portrayed as helpless and in dire need of aid or categorized into certain personality or occupational types, deemed deserving or undeserving of immigration rights.[7]

A fundamental reason for this invisibility of refugees can be found in the main paradigms in Cold War studies, which have overwhelmingly focused on the decisions of great powers and the narratives of elite state leaders, metropolitan and local, involved in those decisions. The stateless or homeless status of refugees and their experiences did not easily fit into state- or nation-centered narratives, even when some refugee groups supported or were mobilized to defend the ideologies of the states or nations. Meanwhile, our understanding of non-Western regions has been fragmented under the Cold War–rubric of area studies. This condition has led scholars to overlook the continental scale of refugee displacements during the Cold War and the significance of their connected experiences across Asia.

In order to overcome such limitations in studying Cold War refugees, the current book proposes a transnational and transimperial approach, investigating the five cases of Vietnam, Taiwan, Korea, Pakistan, and Afghanistan. Here, "Cold War refugees" refers to the people who forcibly or voluntarily deserted their hometowns as a result of ongoing revolutions or war, subsumed under the bipolar conflicts between the United States and the Union of Soviet Socialist Republics (USSR).

The number of refugees in this category is large, as we see in the cases covered in this book alone. (Later, this introduction will discuss why the term "refugees" is used to characterize these people who crossed borders when Cold War conflicts affected them.) Dominic Meng-Hsuan Yang counts one million Chinese refugees to Taiwan and another million to Hong Kong during Mao's takeover of the mainland. Phi-Vân Nguyen investigates the history of more than eight hundred thousand Vietnamese civilians who moved to southern Vietnam in 1954 when the Geneva ceasefire divided Vietnam along the seventeenth parallel. When the United States and the USSR divided Korea in 1945, more than one million northern Koreans left for US-occupied South Korea even before the outbreak of the Korean War (1950–1953). According to Sabauon Nasseri and Robert D. Crews, the United Nations classified over six million Afghans living outside Afghanistan as refugees by 1990, one-third of the country's prewar population.

By exploring the history of these refugee groups together, this book provides several observations that should be more thoroughly investigated in the history of the Cold War. The first theme is the trans-Asian connections: The displacements of refugees during the Cold War conflicts occurred continuously across Asia. The case in any given country was not isolated but chronologically and diachronically linked to the cases in other countries. For example, the influx of Korean refugees from the Soviet-occupied zone transformed how the United States perceived migrants from the Communist side of the peninsula and beyond. In turn, this altered perception subsequently influenced US negotiations over the repatriation of Korean War prisoners, as well as the 1954 Geneva Convention that granted Vietnamese civilians the right to choose their preferred residence following Vietnam's division. The control of refugee movements was both transimperial and transnational.

The second theme is the importance of partitions and artificial borders in shaping the course of the Cold War. Partition served as a convenient solution for great powers to redefine the balance of power and redistribute their economic and security interests. Such partitions occurred across Asia in less than a decade: in Korea in 1945, in India and Pakistan in 1947, in Taiwan (the island was divided from the mainland when the defeated Chinese Nationalists relocated their government there at the end of the Chinese Civil War) in 1949, and in Vietnam in 1954. Partitions not merely were the result of great powers' decisions but also became independent factors that reshaped societies that were previously unified. These forced partitions provoked widespread violence among local populations, deepened hostilities among communities divided by the new borders, and, ultimately, served as direct or indirect catalysts for civil wars and prolonged military conflicts in these regions. While similar artificial borders were built in postwar Europe, as will be discussed later, the movements of people across them were more carefully managed there than in Asia. Consequently, partitions in Asia resulted in larger scales of population displacements, with refugees responding to them through heightened mobility.

The third and final theme is that the agency and experiences of refugees are complex and should be identified in their historical contexts rather than being assumed in theoretical, governmental, or humanitarian discourses. Drawing from multilingual archival sources, the chapters of this book examine the agendas, identities, and cultures of the refugees and investigate the local, regional, and global contexts of their displacements. Centering refugee experiences and agency, each chapter revisits and challenges the established historical accounts of the key Cold War events in Asia: Korea's partition in 1945, the 1954 Geneva Agreement on Vietnam, the First Taiwan Strait Crisis, the 1978 leftist coup in Afghanistan and the subsequent Soviet invasion of the country, and the transformation of Karachi into a Cold War city with the influx and resettlement of refugees.

In what follows, this introduction offers a preliminary study of how the notion of the Cold War refugees emerged, first, in the process of relocating "displaced persons" after the Second World War. It is preliminary because it focuses only on the documents of the United States without fully investigating the positions of the British, French, and other powers responsible for the displaced persons within their jurisdictions. Nevertheless, the American plans remain central because the US military played a primary role in ending the war in the Pacific and negotiated with its allies to manage displaced persons and refugees in Asia, concurrent with their decisions in Europe.[8]

This introduction will first analyze the American guidelines for displaced persons and refugees in Asia after the defeat of the Japanese Empire. It will then discuss a few differences in refugee administration taken by the United States and the Allied forces in Asia and Europe as the notion of Cold War refugees emerged in the postwar milieu. Next, it will present the editor's standpoint on the concept of refugees and discuss the significance of examining the history of the Cold War from the perspective of refugees. Finally, it will provide a brief summary of the chapters to follow.

Nation, Race, and Displaced Persons in the Aftermath of the Japanese Empire

The Cold War refugees who emerged in the aftermath of World War II were part of an ongoing phenomenon of migration and displacement within imperial contexts, and they intermingled with various types of individuals displaced by the war both in Europe and Asia. Peter Gatrell argues that the refugee crises in twentieth-century Europe were closely intertwined with the collapse of multinational and multicultural empires and their replacement with modern nation-states. During and after World War II, the United States and Allied forces applied a similar approach of "unmixing of peoples" to relocate displaced populations.[9] The notion of nationality imposed a semblance of order amid the chaotic movements of people for repatriation, migration, and resettlement. Still, while extensive research exists on the European context, the United States' approach to displaced persons in Asia remains relatively understudied (with the exception of studies on European Jews in China and their repatriation).[10]

Toward the end of the Pacific War, the US State Department organized the Special Committee on Migration and Resettlement (hereafter, the Special Committee).[11] Lori Watt, a historian of the Japanese Empire, provides a thorough study of how multiple US government agencies during the war debated policies regarding "Japanese civilians" across Japan-occupied regions and ultimately chose to classify them as "displaced persons" without segregation.[12] The Special Committee, in collaboration with the War and Navy Departments, drafted a series of papers about displaced groups in Asia, whose final versions were sent to the highest-ranking commanders of the US military.[13] The regions included in such recommendations were Taiwan (Formosa), Japan's mandated islands, Japan, the Philippines, Korea, and the Dutch East Indies. Outlining the geographical features and population groups within these areas, it estimated the potential displacement of diverse ethnic, national, and tribal groups in the case of the Allied forces engaging in conflict against Japan in these regions.[14] The United States did not create such plans for the British and French colonies in Asia or for China's territory, assuming China's sovereignty. The United States along with the United Kingdom signed the Treaty for the Relinquishment of Extraterritorial Rights in China in January 1943 and endorsed China's recovery of Taiwan and Manchuria through the Cairo Declaration in November 1943.[15] Though research was being prepared on Manchuria, Thailand, Burma, coastal China, and the Pacific, the Special Committee did not end up issuing papers on these areas.

In May 1944, the Special Committee approved a program for Taiwan, which served as a prototype for subsequent papers. Throughout its deliberations, the Special Committee separated the Japanese from Koreans, Chinese, and other indigenous groups, cautioning against inflaming tensions that existed between the Japanese and others. Indeed, the committee consistently recommended that military commanders prevent conflicts among different ethnic or national groups and protect the Japanese from the potential violence they anticipated would target them, evidently viewing such efforts as a necessary first step toward restoring order in Asia.[16] Accordingly, the military authorities were advised to congregate Japanese civilians in major cities or specific key islands until their repatriation to Japan and to provide protective custody to local collaborators with the Japanese if they sought refuge from violence.[17] According to the program on Taiwan, the Special Committee initially contemplated interning certain Japanese civilians and moving the majority of Japanese in Taiwan to several large Japanese settlements in the secluded east-coast valley between the cities of Karenkō (known as Keelung today) and Taitō (now Taitung).[18] However, proposals for internment or large-scale camps were inconspicuous or absent in the reports on other regions of Asia. Overall, the US program for displaced groups in Asia prioritized the repatriation of Japanese without any punitive restrictions on Japanese colonial settlers and their local collaborators.

The United States adopted nationality as the primary criterion for administering displaced groups and their repatriation. This policy presented numerous challenges in Asia because nationality of certain ethnic and racial groups in the Japan-occupied regions was defined as Japanese by the Japanese Empire or was highly complex. For example, in Taiwan or Japan, the Special Committee did not identify Koreans as "foreigners," recognizing them instead as Japanese nationals holding Japanese registration cards.[19] Similarly, classifying Chinese residents in these regions into a single national category was challenging and arbitrary. In Korea and Japan, the Special Committee classified most Chinese (70,000 in Korea and 225,000 in Japan) as "foreigners."[20] In the Dutch East Indies, it was difficult to fully differentiate between Chinese and Dutch nationals: Chinese people born in the Dutch East Indies were considered Dutch citizens while residing in the colony but would become Chinese citizens if they moved back to China according to a 1911 convention between the Netherlands and China.[21] Without further addressing such ambiguity, the Special Committee recommended that military authorities register all Chinese nationals. The registrations recorded their addresses in China, including province, district (*xian*), village, or city, as well as the length of their stay in the Dutch Indies since their last arrival. If requested, this information was to be delivered to the Chinese government.[22]

In addition to the complexities of Asian identities, another issue was that the US conception of race and racial hierarchy influenced its approach to displaced persons in Asia. Examining the condition of the Dutch East Indies, the Special Committee was troubled that here the racial category of "Europeans" referred to all people with the legal rights of Europeans, thus including those the United States did not consider as such: Americans, Armenians, Japanese, and Turks, as well as their Indonesian wives and children. Moreover, in the Indies, the terms "Indo-European" or "Eurasian" were applied to children born from these interracial marriages. This definition of "Europeans" in the Dutch Indies changed in 1943 when the Japanese reclassified residents of Java, designating all the individuals of "Indonesian blood" as "original inhabitants," who were separated from Japan's "enemy nationals" and "nationals with hostile feelings." Japan proceeded to intern Europeans who were "enemy nationals" and impose restrictions on the residency and travel of certain population groups.[23] The Special Committee highlighted this hybridity of Europeans in the Dutch East Indies and did not recommend granting all Dutch nationals and Indo-Europeans the choice to repatriate to the Netherlands.[24]

Such racial bias was deeply ingrained in the US guidelines on locally displaced people in Asia. The Special Committee acknowledged the displacement of local Asians resulting from Japan's wartime mobilization, forced migration by Western colonial powers to plantations, and combat activities in the area. However, the committee's recommendations were mainly to direct the local people's movements only for military expediency and to provide minimal relief for them only to avoid short-term local disorder. In the Japanese mandated islands, for example, the committee ascribed the displacement of native people to the militarization of the islands and the arrival of Japanese settlers for the sugar industry. However, the committee did not consider this displacement to be a significant problem, arguing that native people would be taken care of by their clan relatives.[25] In the Dutch Indies, the United States had to address the Chinese government's request to allow overseas Chinese to either return home or stay in liberated areas. Without fully respecting this request, the Special Committee left the responsibility for aiding Chinese repatriation to the Chinese themselves, claiming that Chinese workers had savings to cover their travel expenses and that the Chinese associations in the Dutch Indies were capable of assisting those who wished to return home to other islands or repatriate to China.[26]

The Special Committee concluded its work on November 3, 1944, and its meeting minutes on that date reveal the shortcomings of the recommendations described above.[27] The committee member George L. Warren believed, for example, that it would be confusing and arduous for military authorities to clearly distinguish between people displaced by war and minority groups in the region who had historically migrated from one place to another.[28] The committee also noted that addressing the consequences of wartime displacement would require long-term policies regarding the migration and settlement of both displaced groups and other minority populations after the end of the war. The Special Committee's reports set the initial stage for the US administration of the displaced persons in Asia, but further research is needed to gain a comprehensive understanding of exactly how these programs may have affected the actual policies taken by the United States and the Allied forces as well as how those policies influenced the subsequent movements of Cold War refugees across Asia.

The following section briefly discusses how the United States implemented polices on displaced people in its early stage. It also notes how they influenced the local migration from the Soviet zone, drawing a comparison with their administration in Europe.

From Displaced Persons to Cold War Refugees: the US Refugee Administration in Asia

In Asia, the US guidelines on displaced persons became a significant tool for reclassifying culturally, racially, and politically diverse Asians into distinct nationalities, as well as encouraging their relocation to their ancestral or ethnic homelands. The United States implemented this policy—that is, grouping war refugees based on nationality—when controlling the movements of the displaced groups in Asia, as well as when operating quarantine or relief centers for them. This monumental process quickly collapsed the demographic foundation of the Japanese Empire and repopulated Asians within the system of nation-states.

Despite this shared process of national regroupings, notable differences exist regarding how the United States and Allied forces administered displaced persons (DPs) in Europe and in Asia. According to a study on Jewish refugees in postwar Shanghai, the Working Committee on Displaced Persons identified DPs as "United Nations nationals, stateless persons" and "enemy or ex-enemy nationals who are [not] certain Italian nationals, and found in liberated territories and who have been intruded into the homes of United Nation nationals."[29] In Europe, "displaced persons" primarily referred to the people who had been seized by the Nazis from occupied Europe to work as forced laborers and who were expected to repatriate after the war.[30] Indeed, the United States coined this term, according to Gerard Daniel Cohen, and made it central in the relief and rehabilitation operations of the Allied forces.[31] Even so, Cohen states that between nine and twelve million ethnic Germans were expelled from east Central Europe after the war but that these expellees fell outside the category of displaced persons eligible for Allied relief. Several hundred thousand died during this displacement process.[32] Germans thus were not the central focus of the Allied relief efforts for DPs. In Asia, by contrast, the United States effectively identified Japanese civilians as DPs at the expense of other Asian groups. They did so by, on the one hand, prioritizing the repatriation of the Japanese and, on the other hand, providing only minimal relief to non-Japanese Asians, leaving them to rely on their own resources and local assistance. As mentioned earlier, Lori Watt indicates that the US government engaged in focused discussions on "overseas Japanese" and formulated policies based on careful considerations of the postwar order and decolonization in Asia.[33]

In Europe, the United States and the Allied forces accommodated displaced persons in camps and strictly regulated their movements.[34] Between spring and fall of 1945, military and United Nations Relief and Rehabilitation Administration (UNRRA) officials facilitated the return of six to seven million displaced persons in Europe to their countries of origin. Some of them, especially citizens of the USSR, were compelled to repatriate against their will. Even so, as Cohen notes, around 1.2 million individuals remained in the DPs camps. Among the DPs, a portion opted not to return home and sought refugee status and the opportunity to migrate to a third country. To determine their eligibility for immigration rights to the West, these displaced persons who refused repatriation were interrogated by camp administrators.[35] As their status changed—from that of persons displaced by World War II to what we may call Cold War refugees—the process was a controlled one. In these years before the mass migration following the 1948 Communist coup in Czechoslovakia and the establishment of the German Democratic Republic in October 1949,[36] the United States and Allied forces in Europe imposed restrictions on the DPs' migration to the West in order to uphold wartime agreements with the USSR and to prevent an influx of new migrants from hindering the recovery of Western Europe.

In Asia, such careful control of population movements between the West and the East did not exist. While the United States and the USSR in principle prohibited the transportation of people and goods between their respective zones, they initially allowed large-scale movements of local refugees across national borders. Soon the "problem" of Cold War refugees in Asia emerged as a crisis of mass migration, commencing from the Korean peninsula in August 1945. This mass migration resulted from the fact that the United States, the USSR, and other Allied forces concluded the war by establishing artificial borders in geopolitically important regions and in the areas ruled by the Western and Japanese Empires. The forced divisions, without any caution to mitigate their impacts on local populations, triggered massive migration, violence, and displacement within local society. In the case of the divided Korean peninsula (which will be analyzed more in chapter 3), the resettlement process for displaced groups was soon overshadowed by the migration of people from the Soviet-controlled North to the US-occupied South. While some people from South Korea did move to the North, their numbers were smaller and remain unverified due to limited historical sources.

As the number of migrants from the Soviet zone of Korea increased, the US military took steps to separate the North Korean people from other displaced groups and sought to determine their motivations for migration. Through interviews and interrogation, the US military gradually developed a narrative that portrayed northern Korean refugees as "dissidents of the regime" arising under Soviet occupation. This shift in perspective likely developed in tandem with the US government's perception of migrants from Eastern Europe as a general notion of "refugees from the Soviet world" took shape. This new conception of refugees would have implications for the US negotiations with China and North Korea over prisoners of war during the Korean War and for subsequent international agreements pertaining to similar types of refugees in Asia.

Given the perception that refugees were escaping from the Communist countries due to their opposition to those regimes, the United States supported voluntary rather than mandatory repatriation of prisoners of war during the Korean War. South Korean president Syngman Rhee went further, releasing North Korean prisoners of war without the approval of the United States.[37] Meanwhile, China and North Korea demanded mandatory repatriation of prisoners in accordance with Article 118 of the 1949 Geneva Convention. According to David Chang, the United States and China's prolonged negotiations and conflicts over these issues delayed the ceasefire in the Korean War.[38] This conflict surrounding prisoners of war likely impacted the stance of the United States and other Western powers during the negotiations over the 1954 Geneva Convention, particularly the provision that allowed Vietnamese citizens to select their preferred side of the divided Vietnam for their residence (as analyzed by Phi-Vân Nguyen in chapter 1).

The US military in Korea accepted refugees from the Soviet zone without restrictions, partly because it was not obligated to grant them immigration rights to the West or to establish long-term camps for their relief. In comparison to Europe, where the Allied forces had more direct control, many Asian refugees during the early Cold War period operated outside the purview of the US and USSR occupation forces and pursued their own initiatives and movements, advancing various agendas—an agency of refugees that will be further discussed below and throughout the chapters that follow.

Because some groups of Cold War refugees pursued immigration to the West, leading scholars in refugee studies have frequently discussed the history of refugees in terms of legal regulations of immigration, humanitarian relief, and the culture and identities of refugees after their immigration to the West or a third country. However, prior to the Vietnam War, Cold War refugees in Asia primarily moved between the divided sides of their country or resettled in neighboring regions. While some eventually migrated to the West, many chose to stay closer to home and organized movements to bring about change in their hometowns or improve their own situations in the places where they had resettled. Therefore, when examining the history of Cold War refugees in Asia, it is important to consider the agency and experiences of refugees beyond the question of immigration rights and the changes that came along with resettlement in the West. These refugees played a transformative role in shaping the ideological, political, cultural, and spatial landscape of their own countries and of their places of resettlement within the region.

Definitions of Refugees, Violence, and "Refugeetude" in Cold War History

The present-day legal concept of refugees was formalized after World War II with the adoption of the 1951 Refugee Convention and the establishment of the Office of the United Nations High Commissioner for Refugees (UNHCR).[39] The convention defined "refugees" as individuals who had a "well-founded fear of being persecuted on grounds of race, religion, nationality, membership of a particular social group or political opinion."[40] This definition became widely accepted and served as the basis for determining refugee status and refugees' corresponding rights within their new host communities.

However, during the Cold War, the legal protections of the Refugee Convention were not consistently extended to Asian refugees. Initially, the convention solely applied to individuals displaced by events in Europe before 1951. It was not until the 1967 Protocol Relating to the Status of Refugees expanded the temporal and regional scope of the convention that its provisions were made applicable to a broader range of refugees, including those affected by conflicts in Asia.[41]

Despite this exclusion from the initial application of the Refugee Convention, Western governments, humanitarian and religious organizations, and think tanks selectively provided financial, material, and technical assistance to Asian refugees during the Cold War.[42] Scholars have raised valid concerns regarding the limitations of legal and international conventions and resolutions in defining "refugees." Rebecca Hamlin, for instance, criticizes the conceptual dichotomy that distinguishes refugees from other types of migrants—a distinction based on the assumption that refugee migration is forced and politically motivated, while other forms of migration are mostly voluntary and driven by economic motivations. Hamlin calls this binary categorization "fictional" and argues that its reinforcement by international law and the immigration laws of receiving states justifies excluding many border crossers from the rights and privileges afforded to refugees.[43] In fact, determining whether a person's decision to migrate was forced or voluntary can be difficult because people in similar situations often make different choices.

At its core, the refugee population is part of a spectrum of migrants who have left their homes because of threats to life and livelihood, which can be climatic, economic, political, or military. We can identify refugees based on the urgency of the crises they have faced, which have displaced them and made them rely on external relief. Scholars of critical refugee studies call this situation "forcible displacement" and offer the following definition of "refugees": "Refugees are human beings forcibly displaced within or outside of their land of origin as a result of persecution, conflict, war, conquest, settler/colonialism, militarism, occupation, empire, and environmental and climate-related disasters, regardless of their legal status. Refugees can be self-identified and are often unrecognized within the limited definitions proffered by international and state laws."[44] This definition underlines the multiple sources of violence that lead to the displacement of refugees from their homes, and it recognizes the agency of refugees in identifying their experiences as a form of violent displacement. It also prompts a reconsideration of the wartime categories of displaced persons and refugees, as well as the blurred boundaries between the two terms before the nationality principle was introduced for defining "refugees."

During World War II, the United States and Allied forces used both "displaced persons" and "refugees" to refer to people who had been dislocated from their homes by the war and required external assistance to either return home or find a new place for resettlement. The two terms were often used interchangeably. However, toward the end of the war, the United States, in preparation for occupying Europe, began to differentiate the term "displaced persons" from "refugees." This distinction aimed to clarify the relationship between war refugees and their home governments: displaced persons were refugees but with a nationality that could presumably be entrusted to their home governments for repatriation; refugees, meanwhile, were either stateless or fleeing from their own home governments.

For instance, the US State Department initially described all of those who had fled to Spain from territories under Axis control in the summer of 1943 as refugees. According to the State Department's estimates, most of these escapees were French nationals, while the rest were citizens of Allied countries, Axis nationals, or stateless. The United States decided to relocate all refugees in Spain elsewhere and to make the Spanish government keep the channel open for additional escapees from Axis-controlled areas.[45] A refugee camp was opened in Philippeville, Algeria, to place the French refugees under the care of French North African authorities, while refugees of other Allied nationalities were to be sent to their respective governments for assistance.[46] As the US State Department took into consideration future coordination with the refugees' respective governments, it made a distinction between displaced persons—who had been uprooted from their homes due to war but were deemed capable of being repatriated by their home governments—and refugees—who were stateless or escaping persecution by their own government. This division of displaced persons and refugees was driven by administrative and political objectives rather than reflecting intrinsic differences between the two groups. In fact, the two categories would be defined differently at different times.

The ambiguity of the terms can be observed in the documents drafted by the United States outlining suggestions for the Allied occupation of Germany. A top-secret memorandum from Supreme Headquarters, dated August 12, 1944,[47] defined "displaced persons" as "civilians outside the national boundaries of their country by reason of the war who are 1) desirous but unable to return home, or find homes without assistance and 2) to be returned to enemy or ex-enemy territory." In comparison, "refugees" were defined as "civilians not outside the national boundaries of their country who desire to return to their home but require assistance to do so: they are 1) temporarily homeless because of military operations or 2) at some distance from their homes for reasons related to the war."[48] This revised definition of "refugees"—that is, "civilians displaced inside of their country"—coexisted in US usage with the more conventional meaning of the term.[49]

Yet even the US State Department expressed concern about Supreme Headquarters' perplexing usage of "refugees," writing, "The use of the word 'Refugees' to define persons displaced within their own countries will prove confusing. The word 'Refugees' is accepted international usage to identify those who have left their homes and countries for reasons of race, religion, or political belief, cannot return to them and lack the protection of any government. In contrast those displaced within their own countries have homes to which they can return, and they enjoy the protection of their governments. They are more correctly defined as the 'Internally Displaced.'"[50] In explaining the varied definitions of "refugees" found in wartime documents, Gatrell argues that policymakers, wanting to identify different conditions of displacement, created multiple categories to name those who were uprooted, ranging from "war fugitive" to "refugees."[51] Gatrell also highlights Hannah Arendt's statement that the category of displaced persons "was invented during the war for the purpose of liquidating statelessness once and for all by ignoring its existence." In other words, the term "displaced persons"—by emphasizing DPs' belonging to a certain nation and presumed suitability for repatriation—effectively erased their experiences of displacement and confinement, which they shared with refugees.[52] By acknowledging the historical and political context in which refugees were distinguished from DPs, a broader definition of "refugees" can be restored, as advocated by critical refugee studies—a definition that underlines forcible displacement by violent crises and the stateless condition experienced by refugees.

In studying migration during the Cold War, scholars have been hesitant to label the people who crossed the borders between the Communist and capitalist zones as refugees. Using the term "refugees" in this context may evoke stereotypes of victims or helpless people reliant on assistance. Moreover, employing the term "refugees" to examine the movements of the people affected by Cold War conflicts can carry ideological implications, potentially portraying the regimes they fled from as zones of disaster or humanitarian crisis. Notwithstanding these connotations, this volume uses the term "refugees" because it more accurately captures the sense of crisis, deprivation, and psychological complexity experienced by those displaced by the Cold War. Hannah Arendt graphically depicts the political, psychological, and identity crises faced by Jewish refugees who migrated to America before and during World War II, writing, "A refugee used to be a person driven to seek refuge because of some act committed or some political opinion held. . . . [B]ut we committed no acts and most of us never dreamt of having any radical political opinion. With us the meaning of the term 'refugee' has changed. Now 'refugees' are those of us who have been so unfortunate as to arrive in a new country without means and have to be helped by refugee committees."[53] As exemplified in this context, refugees are not solely defined by their escape from crises but also associated with certain administrative conceptions of being rescued from those crises. Hence, Edward Said characterizes refugees as a political category of twentieth-century states and contrasts them with exiles. The term "refugees" conjures images of "large herds of innocent and bewildered people requiring urgent international assistance," Said argues; the term "exiles," meanwhile, evokes individuals who, in solitude, possess the spiritual capacity to cultivate an intellectual vision for a future outside the mass institutions of the modern era.[54] However, this distinction between refugees and exiles does not hold up in historical studies; a central question explored in the cases here is refugees' agency in defining their own identities and struggles to solve their own agendas, often in conflict with legal or institutionalized definitions of "refugees" and their needs.

Some cases explored in this volume delve into the contentious nature of defining "refugees," examining the conflicting views of different historical actors and institutions regarding who qualified for relief and what entitlements they deserved. The institutions responsible for providing aid and relief did not merely adhere to the legal concept of refugees but instead competed with other political actors to shape the definition of "refugees" and determine the course of refugee administration. Within this volume, Phi-Vân Nguyen illustrates such competition concerning displaced Vietnamese civilians in 1954. At that time, it was India, claiming to represent neutral countries, that chaired a crucial committee that oversaw migration within Vietnam. Yet as the 1951 Refugee Convention did not apply to the Vietnamese moving to southern Vietnam, India called the movements of the displaced Vietnamese a domestic or bilateral matter. India's Third Worldism prioritized avoiding Western intervention in the region, including the violence caused by India's partition over addressing the grievances of the displaced civilians. In comparison, the United States, other governments, and international organizations claimed to support the "refugees" fleeing Communism. Nguyen interprets these contrasting conceptions as ideological or political choices made by the actors involved in the conflict rather than as a reflection of the positions of displaced Vietnamese or as altruistic responses to a humanitarian crisis.

Similarly, in a chapter on Afghanistan, Nasseri and Crews investigate how multiple actors participated in shaping the "Cold War conceptions" of refugees and promoted distinct definitions of the term to serve their own interests. Nasseri and Crews argue that in Afghanistan, *all* the parties involved in the conflict—the Soviets, Americans, Pakistanis, Iranians, international organizations, and even most Afghan rebel groups—agreed that the refugee population should not be treated as substantive political actors with a say in determining their political destiny. What distinguished the Cold War refugees from other migrant groups was the ideological context of their displacement. Indeed, the refugees in this volume have often been stereotyped as "heroes" or "victims" of ideologies. Paradoxically, the refugees' own narratives have been suppressed in public memory, precisely because they could compromise the mythologies of state building in the countries where they sought resettlement.

For example, Yang, the author of *The Great Exodus from China* and a contributor to this volume, highlights that serious historical works on Chinese refugees in Taiwan did not emerge until the early 2010s. The memories of refugees themselves also changed over time. Yang calls such changes the "mnemonic regime," through which Chinese mainlanders in Taiwan recollected their traumas of exodus and subsequent events.[55] As such, the refugees developed a new political awareness through their experiences during and after their flight and pursued new roles in their resettlement societies. The scholar of Asian diasporic literature Vinh Nguyen calls this awareness or positionality "refugeetude," arguing that it "takes refugee experiences as constitutive of a significant subject position, giving rise to or shaping modes of critical existence and politics."[56] This positionality of "refugeetude" can illuminate the limitations of Cold War ideologies and contextualize their local receptions.[57] Nguyen's article introduces the story of a Vietnamese refugee in the United States and discusses the incongruency with the US discourses about refugee migrants that lean on concepts of American rescue and benevolence, liberalism, and the American Dream.[58]

This subversive orientation is not prevalent in every refugee group discussed in this volume, however. Some refugees exhibited a high degree of conformity with the ideologies of nation-states or Cold War powers. Nevertheless, the conservatism or anti-Communism observed in their refugee consciousness did not merely indicate assimilation to the dominant ideology but mirrored their experience of displacement in the society they had fled. In other words, the refugees internalized and localized Cold War ideology, either substantiating or criticizing it on their own terms. While the notion of refugeetude suggests the agency of refugees and their political possibilities, moral and ideological consciousness in refugee politics took multiple forms in different historical contexts. The cases examined in this volume present diverse scenarios in terms of whether Cold War refugees introduced a new and relatively cohesive ideological consciousness to their host societies or pursued heterogeneous and multifaceted strategies to navigate the challenging circumstances of resettlement. Refugees distinguish themselves from other groups of migrants due to their transient and stateless status. Until they obtain formal residency in a country, their lives exist in a precarious state: outside the protection of the law and without affiliation to any state that could protect their rights and meet their basic needs. Displaced from their original homes, they navigate toward new locations, reimagining them for their new settlement.

The significance of such dislocation in refugee politics prompts a reconsideration of spatiality and topography in the context of the Cold War.[59] In his chapter on the development of Karachi as a Cold War city, Ijlal Muzaffar argues that the Cold War can be seen as a war over space rather than territory and that control over space is a question not so much of changing the physical world as of having the ability to change its meaning, turning stable into unstable, visible into invisible, and vice versa. This insight helps us acknowledge the value of exploring how particular groups of refugees tried to "construct, remember, and lay claim" to their original homelands as well as the new places they moved to for survival.[60] Some theorists have gone so far as to suggest that refugees can embody a new political space that does not align with "homogeneous national territory" or with a "*topographical* sum" of such territories.[61] It remains unclear whether the Cold War refugees discussed in this book truly developed a deterritorialized sense of space and challenged postcolonial states in such a way. Nonetheless, it is evident that their conceptions of spatiality contradicted the artificial boundaries introduced violently by great powers, privileging their own geopolitics and interests.

It is important to mention that the cases presented in this volume do not include refugees from the capitalist countries to the Communist zone. This is primarily because it is difficult to find historical sources on such groups, and many of the available cases are anecdotal. However, this book hopes to invite further exploration into the history of refugees who departed their homes to join the Communist side. These people were officially portrayed as revolutionaries or patriots by the Communist countries rather than refugees fleeing crises. There remains a dearth of knowledge regarding the number of refugees who went from the capitalist side to the Socialist countries, their experiences following their flight, and how they were perceived in the Communist society upon resettlement.

Since the dissolution of the USSR in 1991, studies of the Cold War have undergone a shift, moving away from investigating its origins and the diplomatic and military decisions made in Washington and Moscow. Instead, scholars have embraced the use of multiarchival sources, explored cultural and discursive transformations, and sought to understand the Cold War through the lens of a "dialectic" relationship among the superpowers and their local allies on the periphery. Notably, Odd Arne Westad proposes that the decisions of the superpowers be understood in terms of the ideological origins of Cold War interventionism but also of the specific contexts of the Third World that facilitated the involvement of the superpowers there.[62] With this paradigm shift, an increasing number of studies have acknowledged the importance of local factors—such as peripheral initiatives and regional agendas—that could override the intentions and objectives of the superpowers.

This emphasis on local factors, however, has still fixated on elite politics rather than looking for the Cold War's impacts on the broader population living on the periphery. As the Cold War unfolded in Asia, the violence inherent in bipolar conflicts disrupted people's ways of life, permeating "their most immediate, intimate domains."[63] Displaced from their homes, the refugees depicted in this volume bore witness to and experienced the visceral effects of such violence and political polarization. The complexity of refugee politics and ideologies explored in this volume compels us to reexamine key conceptual categories in the study of postcolonial Asia, including revolution, territory, ideology, and decolonization.

Chapter Summaries

In chapter 1, "Vietnam's 1954 Partition and Displacement in a Global Perspective," Phi-Vân Nguyen studies the 1954 Geneva conference, which established a ceasefire in Indochina and split Vietnam into two temporary zones on each side of the seventeenth parallel. Article 14(d) of the Geneva Agreement allowed civilians to join the zone of their choice within a grace period of three hundred days. By May 1955, around eight hundred thousand people had gone to the non-Communist zone in the South. Using American, Indian, and Vietnamese documents, Nguyen analyzes the international negotiations over Article 14(d), as well as the different interpretations of this civilian evacuation by the countries involved in the ceasefire.

In chapter 2, "The Cold War, Anti-Communist Propaganda, and the Resettlement of Dachen Refugees from Coastal Zhejiang to Taiwan," Dominic Meng-Hsuan Yang uncovers the little-known story of the Dachen refugees from the coastal islands of Zhejiang Province, China, who were forcibly resettled to Taiwan following the First Taiwan Strait Crisis (1954–1955). In 1954, a year after the conclusion of the Korean War, Chairman Mao Zedong and his generals resumed their plans to attack the Nationalists and invade Taiwan. And so, in early 1955—after an intense but ultimately futile defensive war against the Communist forces—Chiang Kai-shek ordered his army to withdraw from the Dachen Islands off the coast of Zhejiang Province and, crucially, to relocate all inhabitants of these coastal islands to Taiwan. In total, eighteen thousand local people, mostly fishermen and their families, were relocated. Yang analyzes how the Nationalist elites in Taiwan integrated the politics of refugees into their anti-Communist and irredentist ideology aimed at reclaiming the mainland. He also explores the reasons behind the failure of the joint Nationalist-US relief programs for the Dachen refugees and examines how the refugees themselves forged a path to survival.

In chapter 3, "Northern Refugees and the Rise of Cold War Nationalism in South Korea, 1945–1950," Yumi Moon studies northern Koreans who crossed the thirty-eighth parallel and entered the South between 1945 and 1950. The US occupation forces in Korea initially classified these northerners with the wartime category of "displaced persons" but soon reclassified them as "refugees" from the Soviet zone. Sharing a sense of loss as "refugees," northerners in the South organized militant and violent youth movements; meanwhile, their discourse and activism reshaped Korean Nationalism after colonialism against the backdrop of the ideological conflicts of the Cold War. This chapter discusses the combative origins of South Korean conservatism by investigating the transformation of the thirty-eighth parallel into a border and refugees' experiences of crossing it, the motivations and social characteristics of northern refugees, and the discourse and activism of northerners in the South between 1945 and 1950. In examining these subjects, Moon uses a variety of sources, including US documents, oral interviews with refugees, North Korean sources seized by the US Army during the Korean War, and *Ibuk T'ongsin*, the magazine published by northern refugees in South Korea during the time.

In chapter 4, "Rethinking Spatial Politics and the Legacy of the Cold War in Karachi," Ijlal Muzaffar examines Karachi, a major city in southern Pakistan. In the 1980s, this city became a crucial hub in the American-led proxy war against the Soviet invasion of Afghanistan. The city was inundated not only by thousands of refugees from across the border but also by ethnic Pashtuns from northern Pakistan, who had economic and familial ties in Afghanistan. With this historical context, Muzaffar analyzes a housing project proposed in 1959 by the firm of Greek architect and planner Constantinos Doxiadis, aimed at accommodating displaced populations who had arrived in Karachi after the partition of the subcontinent in 1947. In Doxiadis's rhetoric and design, Muzaffar identifies elements of instability and unpredictability woven into the city's planning and governance. Doxiadis's scheme facilitated a covert and unpredictable model of governance, enabling the military regime in Pakistan to control the physical environment, borders, neighborhoods, and even waste management, effectively extending the Cold War into the region. In Cold War–era Karachi, urban planning was not merely a projection of stability and growth; it was also an instrument for introducing unpredictability, which the governing regime wanted so as to control space and create the very conditions necessary for waging the Cold War.

Then, in chapter 5, "Afghan Refugees as Political Actors," Sabauon Nasseri and Robert D. Crews explore the Soviet invasion of Afghanistan and its aftermath to investigate Cold War conceptions of the "refugee." They show how all parties to this conflict competed to define the place of the refugee in the wider contest over the future of Afghanistan. One matter that the Soviets, Americans, Pakistanis, Iranians, international organizations, and even most Afghan rebel groups could agree on was the notion that these refugees should not be treated as substantive political actors who might have a voice in determining their political fate. Collectively, the efforts of the various authorities who oversaw refugee lives in Pakistan and Iran resembled those of the administrators of later African refugee camps, who, as Liisa

Malkki argues, sought "to depoliticize the refugee category and to construct in that depoliticized space an ahistorical, universal humanitarian subject."[64] In the Afghan setting, actors across the political spectrum worked to capitalize on the image of the doleful and defenseless refugee as one key strategy, among others, to gain advantage in the war and, for Afghan parties in particular, to monopolize political power. Preventing several million Afghans from actively participating in the political contestation of the jihad was a central, if largely unexplored, aspect of the politics of the Cold War struggle in Afghanistan. In practice, though, these efforts largely failed, and Afghan refugees remained part of the broader landscape of Afghan politics.

Finally, in the epilogue, "After Cruelty: The Last Subject of Cold War Humanism," Aishwary Kumar offers his theoretical reflections on the history of Cold War refugees, questioning how we fully comprehend the issues of statelessness, violence, dispossession, and inequality. Kumar discusses why the figure of the refugee is significant today but also questions why we remain trapped in cycles of moral indifference and political violence against them on a global scale. According to Kumar, this cycle persists because we morally and conceptually distinguish the internal frontiers and segregation within nation-states—such as racial apartheid or caste segregation—from the legal orders governing interstate or international borders, boundary lines, and partitions.

Facing the global crises of wars, climate change, and technological shifts, Kumar urges us to acknowledge that none of us are safe from displacement and that the boundaries within and among nation-states are equally arbitrary, violent, and stained by histories of colonization, sacrifice, and slavery. He argues that segregation within borders and statelessness beyond them are legally intertwined. Our indifference to this connection has led to refugees drowning just miles off the coast as these states—both imperial and postcolonial—draw artificial lines and borders, jeopardizing the future of the planet with barbaric depredations against both the earth and humanity.

One

VIETNAM'S 1954 PARTITION AND DISPLACEMENT IN A GLOBAL PERSPECTIVE

PHI-VÂN NGUYEN

Introduction

Any mention of "Cold War refugees" evokes the plight of the Vietnamese, Laotians, and Cambodians who left the region in the 1970s because of the war, an economic crisis, and the establishment of Communist governments. But many of them had already moved once, twice, or more times over the previous years. In Vietnam, some of those that left in the 1970s had first left their homeland in 1954 and, by then, felt there was no coming back. The year of 1954 was when the Geneva Accords ended the First Indochina War—a conflict where French Union Forces opposed the People's Army of Vietnam—at which point Vietnam was split at the seventeenth parallel. By May 1955—marking the end of the transition period to implement the partition—over 800,000 people went to the South, whereas only 150,000 civilians had gone to the North. Unlike what happened after 1975, this 1954 population movement was not spontaneous; instead, it was a provision of the ceasefire agreement ending the First Indochina War.

The 1954 Geneva Accords divided Vietnam and required troops to join the zone of their own political authorities within three hundred days. Soldiers of the People's Army headed to the North, whereas soldiers of the French Union, including the army of the State of Vietnam (SVN), which Paris created in 1949, went to the South. Article 14(d) also allowed civilians to move within that same period. Afterward, virtually no one would be allowed to cross the demarcation line—that is, until two years later, when a planned referendum would allow the population to reunite the country and choose their government. Given those plans, the Geneva Accords' population movement was therefore envisioned as a necessary measure to guarantee the ceasefire. But why were civilians allowed to move across the seventeenth parallel?

Virtually all books on the Vietnam War mention the 1954 evacuation because this marked a turning point in the long and convoluted history of the armed conflict. The massive movement of people allowed the United States to intervene on the ground, both to transport this population and then to resettle them.[1] After witnessing how Ngô Đình Diệm, the SVN's prime minister, overcame domestic opposition from other Nationalist groups, Washington replaced Paris as Saigon's closest ally. Thus, the ceasefire was not meant to prepare for peace but instead to transition from a military confrontation into a political and economic struggle by turning South Vietnam into a nation capable of resisting Communist expansion.[2] In other words, Vietnam became, much like Germany and Korea, a country divided by the Cold War; likewise, people who left to go to the South seemed to have "chosen the Free World." Perhaps this interpretation explains how the evacuation contributed to the future involvement of the United States in Vietnam.[3] But it still does not address the fundamental reasons why the partition was decided upon.

Rather than maintain a perspective that focuses strictly on the Cold War, this chapter situates Vietnam's territorial division within the longer history of late-colonial empires and partitions. Within the British Empire, for example, historians Arie M. Dubnov and Laura Robson explore the genealogy of the partitions in Ireland, Palestine, and India.[4] In these cases, a territorial division was what allowed the swift departure of the colonial power. This not only meant that the departing power avoided dealing with the ethnic and religious heterogeneity that had prevailed in their empire but also that this power could reasonably entertain the hope that new postcolonial authorities could remain client states. This paper claims that the division of Vietnam and its population movement can also be traced to that genealogy.

Consider the difference between the Geneva Accords as written and their intended effect. The 1954 ceasefire agreement only provided for a temporary partition, and the provision regarding population movement was drafted as a right granted to individuals so that they would receive assistance to join the zone of their choice. However, neither the partition nor the population transfer was meant to protect people. Instead, the Geneva Accords mostly served the interests of an international community concerned with different agendas: the Cold War, the end of colonial rule, and the sovereignty of newly independent states.

As might be expected, then, those concerned with the partition were not only the two competing Vietnamese states, France, and the United States. India, who had itself emerged out of a territorial division, also played an essential role in the process. As the chair of the International Control Commission, which was created to monitor the ceasefire, it limited the population movement to a pure technical matter. For example, certain people in the North sought to migrate south but clashed with local Democratic Republic of Vietnam (DRV) representatives who refused to let them evacuate. But rather than using its role as chair of the commission to solve these local issues, India instead adopted a hands-off approach. By leaving this matter unsolved, India reinforced—albeit unwittingly—the claims brought forward by Washington and Saigon that people were victims of Communist persecution and that, if they could, the entire population would "vote with their feet" and head south. This confusing situation not only drew criticism at India from within South Vietnam and beyond; it also opened up the possibility for Saigon to break free from the ceasefire agreement and refuse to organize the referendum.

Between Decolonization and the Cold War

The partition of Vietnam was far from obvious from the outset. Armies had not been stationed in predefined areas, like in Berlin, where Allied countries had agreed on the zones their troops would occupy even before war's end. Nor had the fighting settled along a line, marking two clear zones, like in Korea. Instead, the war in Vietnam was multilayered, decentralized, and messy. There was no easy solution to end the conflict.

Only months after Ho Chi Minh proclaimed the establishment of the DRV on September 2, 1945, war broke out between this new state and French Union Forces. For years, the armed conflict resembled a war of decolonization, in which the Vietminh, a mobilization front, called on all Vietnamese to join the DRV in the jungle to resist against French colonial rule. However, when the victory of the Chinese Communists became imminent further north in 1949, the armed conflict in Indochina was transformed in two ways. As a new hot spot of the Cold War, foreign support coming in escalated the conflict. This in turn inspired some Nationalist fighters to come together in the hope that they could form an alternative to the DRV. At this point, Vietnam was not engaged in a decolonial struggle but in a civil war, fueled by international tensions.[5]

The United States was concerned that the victory of the Chinese Communist revolutionary movement could spread across borders to other countries in Asia and to other decolonization movements. Hence, Washington considered the wars in Korea and in Indochina as the most obvious corridors through which Communism could expand. In Korea, American troops intervened on the ground. But in Indochina, Washington relied on French Union Forces on the ground while agreeing to bankroll their war effort. In response, Chinese Communists promptly recognized the DRV, which in turn attracted the support of the Soviet Union. This was how the two antagonistic blocs of the Cold War collided, unexpectedly, in Vietnam.

Another drastic change compared to the first years came from the French decision in 1949 to create the Associated States of Vietnam, Laos, and Cambodia, which were set on a gradual path toward independence. Paris would keep firm control over diplomatic and military matters but accepted that any economic decision would be made jointly with these states. It also agreed to sign a series of treaties transferring authority over state matters—such as immigration, postal services, air space control, etc.—over the years.[6] Independence would eventually come at the end of this long process, Paris insisted.

Moreover, changes in the DRV also fanned the flames of civil war. Vietnamese Communists capitalized on this new momentum to redefine their war goals after 1949. Then, the war would serve not only to achieve independence from French colonial rule but also to introduce a Socialist revolution in Vietnam. As a result, Communist cadres took over all important positions within the DRV and its mobilization fronts, the Vietminh and the Liên Việt, as well as introduced land reforms in the areas of which they held a firm control.[7] Officially, the DRV never became a Socialist state, nor did it advertise to the rest of the world the results of the land reform and denunciation campaigns it had implemented in a few key areas. Still, this silent Communist takeover brought political purges, as well as desertions and defections to the French-backed Associated State of Vietnam (ASV). Truthfully, the armed conflict had been a civil war from the moment Nationalist leaders criticized Ho Chi Minh's leadership of the DRV in 1945. But it became a nationwide reality four years later, only because two states backed by two blocs tried to rule over the country. At this point, the war would decide who would rule over postcolonial Vietnam.

These intertwined struggles reflect how complex it was to negotiate, in Geneva, an end to the armed conflict. Still, after Joseph Stalin died in March 1953, both powers desired to de-escalate the Cold War in Asia, both in Korea and in Indochina. Even during other talks in Berlin taking place in February 1954—where superpowers discussed the situation of Germany and Austria, then also divided into military zones—the idea of a conference for Asia kept coming up. But all sides knew it was going to be a daunting task.

Although Vietnam had already been divided in the past, how to partition the country in 1954 was far from obvious. On the ground, there were no clear-cut military zones that had stabilized along a demarcation line by the time these conferences took place. Unlike Korea—for which the armistice had brought the belligerents to separate at the thirty-eighth parallel—French Union Forces and the People's Army held patches of territory scattered across the northern and southern halves of the country. Neither one could seamlessly exert its authority over a continuous territory; instead, they had to navigate across enemy-controlled and contested areas to reach other zones under their control.[8] On a map, Vietnam looked no different from a leopard skin.[9] Any division, especially one cutting Vietnam horizontally, meant ceding territory to the enemy. The DRV seemed to have a great command on land in the northern half. But accepting a partition meant losing control over the Central Highlands, which proved crucial to maintain a connection between the North and the South, as well as with Southeast Asian networks in Laos, Cambodia, and Thailand.[10] The ASV would face the same dilemma. Keeping control over the South exclusively would force the loss of important strongholds in the Red River Delta deep in the North.

Perhaps most importantly, however, any partition would fail to address the dispute actually dividing the Vietnamese. In the South, for example, many Vietnamese fighting alongside the French Union Forces or joining the ASV did not assemble into a single political party, like China's Guomindang. There were individual political parties, such as the Đại Việt and the Việt Nam Quốc Dân Đảng, which certainly shared a common opposition to the DRV and its mobilization front with religious groups like the Hòa Hảo and the Cao Đài. Yet they often called for a different vision of what postcolonial Vietnam should be in terms of its centralization of powers, the role of the military, and its alliances with foreign powers.[11] Assigning a single territory to these eclectic groups required some sort of consensus among them—or an internal strife to determine who could rule them all. For all these reasons, the organization of general elections seemed to people at the time the most sensible solution to achieve peace.

However, the 1954 Geneva conference did not even try to address all the issues raised by the war. Instead of a peace agreement, the negotiations tried to reach a ceasefire alone and, especially, allow the departure of the French from that armed conflict. The part of the Geneva conference dealing with Indochina opened on May 8, 1954—the day after the DRV defeated the French Union Forces at Điện Biên Phủ. Hence, at the conference, the French avoided any lengthy discussion on the political future of the country, because its only priority was to avert another humiliation and ensure the safe departure of the French Expeditionary Corps from zones held by the DRV.[12] Once again, colonial interests took precedence over Vietnamese politics. Worse yet, the talks only focused on a military settlement. Since the French were still heading the newly created Army of the Associated State of Vietnam, the Nationalist state could not even sit at the negotiation table, and France made decisions on its behalf.

The talks stalled until France made a decision, which pushed every party at the conference toward a partition. Without informing any of its allies and even while the negotiations were still underway, the French withdrew their troops from the southern part of the Red River Delta on June 29. Yet this Operation Auvergne was not designed to rush the negotiations. Faced by constant attacks from the People's Army of Vietnam, the French sought to protect the eastern axis connecting Hanoi, the ancient capital, to Haiphong, the largest northern port town.[13] Previously, the area protected by the French had been a triangle, covering most of the Red River Delta; yet this retreat shrank that area into a narrow yet strong corridor linking the two key cities in the North. Just days later, on July 1, the operation was completed, leaving Nationalist strongholds, such as the Catholic dioceses of Phát Diệm and Bùi Chu, to DRV rule and reducing by half the area controlled by the French Union Forces in the North.

This French fait accompli had immeasurable consequences. The French withdrawal significantly affected Vietnamese non-Communists in the North, their survival, and political options. With no protection from the French Union Forces, they had to either accept the idea of living under DRV rule or pack their bags to follow the departing army. This event strengthened the idea a partition could take place.

The withdrawal affected the negotiations just as much. Since the parties were still negotiating the ceasefire, this withdrawal also provided a miniature example of what Vietnam's partition could produce. The French had obviously reached a point where they prioritized the protection of their interests alone. In Paris, the nomination of Pierre Mendès France as the new prime minister of France—who swore he would resign if the parties could not agree—hastened the negotiation process and gave the last push to reach a consensus.

Ultimately, the partition mainly helped the French leave Indochina. Even once partitioned in the South, Paris realized that its actions in Indochina impacted whether it could protect its interests in North Africa.[14] Losing Vietnam was the price to pay to focus on other parts of the empire. Agreeing to its partition was simply a necessary evil to swiftly depart.

Seeing the Advantages of a Partition

The idea of a partition not only met the French needs to leave but also satisfied the demands of other states too. Partition allowed the DRV to gain strategic command over a densely populated and rice-rich area, whereas the non-Communist Vietnamese in the North, who did not have a say in the negotiations, could only watch the French withdrawal with horror. But regardless of the civilians, both political authorities started to contemplate the prospect of becoming sovereign over parts of the territory. The French withdrawal also brought the United States to the realization that there could be political gains in a partition: after all, the war could continue by other means at this point.

Ho Chi Minh, under pressure from his Communist allies, had to give in.[15] Despite a military victory over the French in Điện Biên Phủ, the DRV understood it could not keep an intransigent position at the talks forever.[16] Its representatives announced they were ready to accept ruling over parts and not Vietnam's entire territory provided that there were peaceful provisions to ensure a future unification. This cleared the path for a partition.[17]

Accepting the withdrawal from the North seemed a lot less appealing to the ASV. But its situation changed in the days following the French withdrawal from the Nationalist strongholds. On June 5, Paris officially recognized the independence of the State of Vietnam in the French Union, although, in practice, Saigon still had to become fully sovereign on economic and military matters. Ten days later, Chief of State Bảo Đại nominated a new prime minister, Ngô Đình Diệm, known for his long track record in opposing both French colonial rule and Communism. A strong-minded prime minister could, it was hoped, speed up Saigon's path toward independence, bring together all Nationalist groups, and stand strong in the face of the DRV. But even with those encouraging milestones, losing the northern dioceses of Bùi Chu and Phát Diệm to the DRV was a bitter pill to swallow.

Still, the prospect of becoming sovereign over the South alone became more interesting thanks to the growing interest of the United States. Suddenly, there was an opportunity in an unexpected theater—something that Washington understood when the news coverage of the French withdrawal of the Red River Delta conveyed the idea of a Vietnamese people desperately trying to escape from Communist tyranny. The withdrawal made it to the front page of the *New York Times* three days in a row. Together with the *Christian Science Monitor*, the general tone was alarmist. Articles did not refer to the withdrawal as a tactical or necessary move to better protect other parts of the delta. Instead, the newspapers insisted the French had abandoned Vietnam.[18] The media coverage mainly focused on the Catholics of the two dioceses. The sight of these "anti-Communist Roman Catholics" fleeing their homes "because they feared Communist vengeance" raised the question of what would happen to those who did not even have the means to leave.[19] Communists were making immense gains. "It was a far bigger victory for Ho Chi Minh's forces than their capture of Dien Bien Phu," the *New York Times* lamented.[20] The first page of the Sunday supplement published three maps summarizing the situation. Instead of patches of land scattered over Vietnam, the territory under Communist control kept growing from 1950 to July 1954.[21]

The narrative became significantly more streamlined. The French withdrawal was not a strategic initiative to make the defense of French interests more realistic; in the hands of American media, it was allowing Communist expansion to take over the delta and leaving the Vietnamese population at their mercy. As the newspapers painted a gloomy picture of the situation, the conclusion they implied was clear: the United States had to do something. Members of Congress disagreed over a direct involvement in Vietnam. But, as the *New York Times* and the *Christian Science Monitor* were strongly advocating, they refused to abandon "millions of souls to Red tyranny."[22] At least, it seemed, Congress could provide humanitarian support to these refugees and back this new Nationalist government against Communist expansion. While some works claim that the United States' efforts to build a new nation started after the ceasefire, it seems that the realization the United States could avoid a military intervention by backing a new Vietnamese political solution had actually begun weeks before.[23]

Thus, the US reaction to Operation Auvergne suggested that South Vietnam could emerge as a nation all on its own. The territorial division could be more than a temporary measure to regroup troops, pending a peaceful reunification. Instead, the 1954 ceasefire could establish a border between two nation-states adopting different models of democracy and competing against each other. On July 20, the parties to the ceasefire reached an agreement. It divided Vietnam at the seventeenth parallel and required all regular troops to regroup into their respective zones within a grace period of three hundred days.[24] None of the military zones could host new foreign troops or military bases. What ultimately proved most important, however, was that the United States insisted on the inclusion of provision 14(d)—that during the grace period, civilians were given the possibility to join the zone of their choice.[25] This, it was imagined by the United States, would generate massive displacement of civilians, and this, in turn, would open the door for a humanitarian rather than military intervention into Vietnam and give the impression that the Vietnamese people voted with their feet against Communism. However, all parties recognized this solution did not address the political strife that was actually dividing the Vietnamese. This was why the agreement mandated that the administrative authorities in the North and the South had to organize a popular referendum on the unification of Vietnam, which would happen in 1956.

This situation was entirely different from other Cold War partitions, like Germany and Korea. The Vietnamese population movement planned by the ceasefire had not been unfolding during the war, like in Korea, or secretly over the years, as in Germany. This time, the United States knew exactly when it would start and when it would end. It would take place over a limited time period, under the watch of international powers, and with the careful reporting of international news media outlets. At least partially, the United States could even shape the population movement, or its media representations, almost like a Hollywood production.

And so as soon as Ngô Đình Diệm called on "free nations" to help the country in this dark hour, the United States dispatched the navy to help transport civilians to the South in what it dubbed Operation Passage to Freedom. And indeed, this movement of civilians became a metaphor—by design—to show how eagerly the Vietnamese people fled Communist rule and chose the "Free World."[26] Nongovernmental organizations and religious charities rushed to the rescue of the SVN, which provided emergency relief and resettlement to the incoming population.[27] Western media reproduced the idea that Vietnamese did not want to live under Communist rule.[28] Over the following months, the news of the evacuation made it to the front page of all diocesan newspapers in the United States.[29] This narrative eventually turned into a book-length story when US Navy soldier Thomas A. Dooley wrote his recollection of the evacuation in *Deliver Us from Evil*. Through that novel, people in the United States could imagine what was going on at the edge of the "Free World." Soon, *Deliver Us from Evil* had made it into *Reader's Digest* and, by 1961, would be reprinted fifteen times.[30]

This broad mobilization and the favorable representations in the media gave the impression that the SVN had gained the support of the West such that it could become a nation-state on its own and, in the process, stand against Communism. This movement of civilians, in fact, appeared like a human referendum, taking place two years before the one planned by the Geneva conference. People, it seemed, had voted with their feet.

In this propaganda operation, the refugees were an abstraction meant to convey a political meaning. The urge to make this population movement larger than life became most apparent in the false claim that a million people had moved to the South—a symbolic figure that remained a long-standing feature of both official and romanticized accounts of the evacuation.[31] So, too, would be the distinction between military personnel and civilians. Soldiers, after all, were compelled by the agreements to regroup into their respective zones. But civilians made a deliberate choice to leave their homes and cross to the other side of the demilitarized zone, giving the impression that there was a political choice behind their movement. Hence, both Saigon's and Washington's accounts of the evacuation underscored the number of civilians leaving the North.

The unique media coverage and deliberate efforts to make it memorable explain the disproportionate significance placed on this population movement compared with other displacements at the time. In terms of number, the 800,000 people who left Northern Vietnam in 1954–1955 paled in comparison to the 1.4 million Koreans who escaped the North between 1945 and 1948 and the 2.75 million Germans who left the East by 1961.[32] But its psychological impact, amplified by the transportation involved and Western media coverage, gave a unique significance to this population movement. Unlike other population movements happening in the shadow of major offensives and lingering battlefronts, the Vietnamese evacuation to the South was *planned* to remain in the limelight and to capture everyone's attention.

Even if we focus on the 800,000 refugees, however, and not the inflated number of one million, still, the number of civilians might have been exaggerated. In particular, the French struggled to transport all the military personnel and material of the French Union Forces and the SVN's army (not to mention all the strategic infrastructure they systematically dismantled, such as railroad, telegraph, or hydro equipment they could take away from the DRV).[33] Since they could barely transport their own soldiers, France decided to restrict their servicemen's "families" to only their spouse and children. Other family members would be transported by the American navy. This might explain why many observers mentioned that a substantial part of the civilians transported were elderly people, women, and children.[34] Most men must have been already enrolled in the army, and some others, as reports have claimed, were retained by local authorities.[35] As a result, many extended members of these soldiers' families were counted as civilians of the evacuation when, in fact, they were French occupiers on their way to leaving Indochina.[36] In addition to these families, many people who left the North were civil servants whose job required them to go to the South. Also departing were a political, intellectual, and religious elite, which feared retribution and thereafter took a leading role in shaping the narrative of the evacuation.[37] While the French had departed on short notice, many Vietnamese Nationalists hoped that US support would stay and help them create a strong nation south of the seventeenth parallel.

Thus, the partition was not an obvious solution to the armed conflict. But it became a practical one because of the political gains imagined out of its media representations. Those victims of Communist persecution had become the human face of a new Vietnamese nation.

India's Chairmanship

This instrumentalization of migrants was not meant to happen. In fact, parties involved in the negotiations had actually taken steps to prevent the failure of the agreement and the consequent escalation of political tensions. The United States, or any other participant or foreign power, were not supposed to use the movement of civilians for their political interests. This is why the conference established the International Control Committee (ICC; formally created under the name the International Commission for Supervision and Control) composed of three countries. Canada represented the liberal world; Poland, the Socialist one. India was entrusted with the task of chairing the commission and serving as a third party, or as an intermediary, between these two antagonistic worlds.

However, India was not entirely neutral. It is true that the country did not align with either the liberal or the Socialist world and that it had emerged over the years as the champion of decolonization, nonviolence, and possibly an emerging Afro-

Asian world. But it had a firm position on the very purpose of a territorial division and its subsequent population movement. From New Delhi's perspective, the right given to individuals to join the zone of their choice should not become an open door for foreign interference.

The Third World was a project rather than a group of states created by default.[38] Its leaders sought not only to replace colonial rule but to bring about a new world.[39] To shape this emerging Third World order, India took the lead of two important projects. First, at the United Nations, it tried to form a bloc with other Asian and Arab countries. This blow would prove crucial to the Indonesian independence movement, and there was much hope it could support other independence movements. This bloc's first success was signaled by the election of Carlos Romulo, the representative of the Philippines, as the president of the UN General Assembly. Consequently—and partly thanks to India—anticolonialism would remain at the forefront of the United Nations' agenda.[40] Second, the country also explored the possibility of forming an Asian bloc through its 1947 inter-Asian conference and then expanding it to include Africa as well at the major conference planned in Bandung in 1955.[41] After concluding the Panchsheel Agreement on Tibet in April 1954, elevating the "five principles of peaceful coexistence" as foundational principles of relations with China, India hoped that more Afro-Asian countries could embrace the same spirit and form a bloc capable of pushing this agenda onto the international stage, such as at the United Nations. It was a very real possibility that the decolonized world could form a powerful bloc—an emerging development in which India was a key protagonist.

This is why, in the Cold War, India soon appeared as a possible Asian intermediary. New Delhi considered its leadership of the decolonized world to extend not only to the United Nations but also to local hot spots of the Cold War. Nonalignment was the corollary of nationalism in Jawaharlal Nehru's perspective, and this involved assuming, although reluctantly, the role of mediator among superpowers.[42]

India thus played a pivotal role in the Korean war as talks to sign an armistice stumbled upon the question of POWs. In situations where states were divided by the ideological divisions of capitalism and Communism, any prisoner choosing to join one zone over another—regardless of their actual reasons—could carry an outsized psychological impact on the broader Cold War. And so it was India that headed the Neutral Nations Repatriation Committee (NNRC), conducting interrogations with each prisoner to let them express their preference. It was also India that opened up the opportunity for POWs to repatriate to a neutral country. Eventually, over eighty POWs elected to move to India rather than being repatriated to North or South Korea.[43] As General K. S. Thimayya, the NNRC chair, put it, the choice of each POW carried a significance well beyond their own lives and weighed in a worldwide ideological struggle. India's arbitration, therefore, was a perilous "experiment in neutrality," showing that it was possible to defuse this competition with the intermediary of a third party.[44]

Despite this previous experience, India was not ready to incur the same risks in Vietnam. Besides, it clearly leaned toward the DRV. During the first years of the war, India ignored Ho Chi Minh's call to support the DRV's struggle for independence because New Delhi suspected the Vietnamese leader of hiding a Communist agenda.[45] But this reservation faded the longer the armed conflict dragged on. The most important influence on New Delhi's position regarding the evacuation came from its own experience of partition upon gaining independence. Back then, the June 1947 agreement created two states so as to allow the emergence of a mainly Hindu and a mainly Muslim state. But the agreement did not include a transfer of population. Even so, the attacks carried out by local militias or the anticipation of such violence eventually caused the forced displacement of fourteen million people. These local groups, on both sides of the partition lines, were convinced that nation-states aspired to achieve a certain cultural homogeneity and that leaving minorities outside of national borders carried the risk of them being taken as hostages by the majority.[46] While none of these thinkers ignored the disruption and suffering arising from the displacement of the population, they considered that democracies had little choice but to achieve homogeneity. The partition of the country and its inevitable displacement of the population, it was believed, were necessary conditions for India's recognition of self-determination.[47]

It was precisely with the purpose of sheltering India from unwanted influences that such population transfer never became a humanitarian crisis requiring foreign support. Both India and Pakistan refused international support to shelter or resettle the displaced population. The states' determination to undermine the situation contributed to a tragic consequence. Statistical data comparing the populations in Pakistan and India before and after the partition indicate that more than three million persons remained unaccounted for.[48] These people and their families paid the price for creating two sovereign nation-states.

Perhaps this is why, even if Indochina remained far from its own borders, New Delhi considered the neutralization of armed conflicts in Asia a key aspect of its anticolonial policy. Nehru formulated a six-point proposal to achieve peace in Indochina, which was based on promoting a climate of peace, imposing an immediate ceasefire, promoting independence, establishing direct talks, ensuring nonintervention from superpowers, and monitoring by the United Nations.[49] Thereafter, India drafted a six-point proposal appealing "to all concerned" to "promote a climate of peace and negotiation" and obtained the support of Indonesia, Burma, and Pakistan when the countries gathered in Colombo in April 1954.[50] Stability in the region would benefit everyone.

Just eleven days after the joint declaration in Colombo, the Geneva conference opened its discussion of the armed conflict in Indochina. Although New Delhi did not attend as one of the participants to the talks, it nonetheless "invited itself," believing it could sway London because of its importance to the Commonwealth.[51] Its most famous diplomat, V. K. Krishna Menon, stayed in Geneva for the first three weeks, meeting on a regular basis with all delegations to expedite the negotiations.[52] Menon wanted a ceasefire as soon as possible. One way to speed up the process was to acknowledge there could not be a one-size-fits-all solution for all countries affected by the war. Using cultural arguments, such as the difference between Vedic and Confucian culture, as an excuse, he insisted agreements on Vietnam, Laos, and Cambodia had to be treated separately. Each of these countries would have its own separate agreement, and Vietnam alone would have to face a possible partition.[53]

According to Menon, all postcolonial states competing in Vietnam did not enjoy the same prestige. The Associated States of Cambodia, Laos, and Vietnam were French creatures, and Menon only agreed to meet with their representatives after they complained to the press.[54] Moreover, he never disputed France's authority to negotiate on their behalf—a controversial interpretation with which, however, even Nehru agreed. Retrospectively, he replied to journalists asking whether it was fair that Paris signed a ceasefire deciding Vietnam's partition: "France was the power controlling that part of Vietnam and France signed them on behalf, not only of itself, but of its successor Governments."[55] In other words, France was entitled to make decisions for the SVN—a situation that Indian Nationalists would have likely disputed.

In New Delhi's view, the DRV was Vietnam's only legitimate political authority. When Nehru visited China a few weeks after the ceasefire and stopped on his way in Laos, Cambodia, and North and South Vietnam, he welcomed Hanoi's commitment to the five principles of coexistence. He even declared that Ho Chi Minh was the most likable head of state he had met. A referendum, Nehru had no doubt, would appoint the DRV to head Vietnam. This inclination to favor China and Hanoi not only came from their acceptance of the five principles of coexistence; it also stemmed from the perception that Western colonial powers' interference was more dangerous than Communism, which could be challenged, he believed, in the realm of ideas.[56]

India was striving for peace by bringing the two antagonistic blocs to accept they could only expand to a limited territory.[57] The Geneva ceasefire reflected this idea of a coexistence.[58] By 1954, India believed that China and the DRV were more attached to that principle than France, the United States, or the SVN.[59] Consequently, it was the DRV's independence that became India's priority, which meant that the partition and any other provision related to the territorial division should not become an excuse to interfere with its sovereignty.

A Technical Population Transfer

India could do little over media representations of the population movement happening in Vietnam. As the chair of the ICC, it could, however, influence the monitoring of the ceasefire. India made sure the population transfer remained a purely technical matter instead of a movement of people fleeing Communist persecution. It dismissed complaints that people experienced problems evacuating to the South. However, this approach generated unexpected results. The lack of protection provided to civilians not only drew widespread criticism of India but also created the impression that the evacuees were victims of an unfair agreement. It was this negative impression, accidently created by India, that allowed Ngô Đình Diệm to announce his refusal to organize the referendum planned by the Geneva ceasefire.

Originally, the agreements had planned a series of cut-off dates by which time areas and cities would be handed over to the new administrative authority. In these areas, people who wanted to leave only had to follow this general convoy to Haiphong, where ships would carry them south. Yet civilians in areas already controlled by the DRV at the time of the ceasefire experienced more problems. Individuals needed travel documents to journey across the DRV, but local authorities sometimes proved reluctant to provide them.

It did not take long for problems to arise. Catholics used their networks to inform the French authorities they were not free to reach the transportation points where they could be ferried south. The ICC received petitions claiming the population was not informed it could join the other zone and that, for those so informed, DRV authorities refused to deliver the authorizations to leave their villages. Parishioners barricaded themselves, complaining about the procedure for receiving travel permits and asking to be escorted by the ICC to the Nationalist zone. In one case, an investigation team recommended that the local authorities provide support to the local population desiring to leave. Barricading themselves in the seminary, 8,268 out of the 10,000 Catholics of the village awaited an escort to the other zone.[60] Confrontations were doomed to happen.

Despite this tense situation, India believed there was no danger for the population. It would not assume the role of umpire, nor would the ICC act as a supranational body by sheltering civilians trying to join the zone of their choice.[61] Unlike what happened in Korea, the ICC would not grant asylum to POWs.[62] When the Canadian representative suggested people could wait for their transportation in camps under the control of the ICC, the Indian chairman refused categorically.[63] "Any person who claimed asylum . . . should be kept in the temporary custody of the competent local authorities."[64] The ICC would not take any direct role in protecting civilians. Its sole responsibility was to monitor the ceasefire agreement's implementation. The duty to provide civilians with any assistance to join the zone of their choice fell on local authorities. Hence, the ICC's investigation teams only monitored the availability of and procedure for receiving travel permits.[65] Even when the investigation teams established that civilians asking for travel permits were subject to discrimination or reprisal, the committee only requested DRV offices delivering permits to refrain from asking why people wanted to go to the South and referred to this population movement as "people who chose to migrate."[66]

The ICC's intentions were clear. The reasons why people wanted to leave were irrelevant and did not need further investigation. This way, the Americans, the French, and Vietnamese Nationalists could not frame this displacement as the flight of refugees from Communist persecution. Population movement did not reflect a political choice. The DRV could not hope for better support than India's technical view of migration.[67]

At some point, the confrontation opposing civilians and local authorities turned violent. In the village of Lưu Mỹ, where 90 percent of the inhabitants were Catholic, people became impatient after the local authorities failed to deliver travel documents. After weeks, the same group of people feared mass arrests from the local police. The DRV sent a platoon of forty soldiers to explain their rights in the DRV. A few days later, on January 13, 1955, a delegation from local authorities came together with guerrilleros, the popular militia, and two armed platoons, which opened fire on the civilians, causing the death of fourteen of them.[68]

Even this incident would not sully the DRV's independence in the eyes of New

Delhi. India reassured the People's Army commander in chief that "there [had] been no proper execution by the parties of the provisions of the agreement due to ignorance, misunderstanding or narrow-mindedness of officials." The DRV had not violated the agreements, India maintained, because this was the result of misconduct at the local level. The Indian chairman commented that these "individual lapses [could] not be stopped altogether" and insisted that the ICC would "continue to exert [itself] to the utmost limit to discharge adequately [its] responsibility of supervision of the proper execution by the parties of the provisions of the Agreement."[69] Hanoi could be reassured that the population movement would not become an open door for foreign interference.

Predictably, what was experienced as a reassuring position for the DRV infuriated the United States, France, and the State of Vietnam even more. Civilians were still at the mercy of local authorities. The ICC did not settle the reported situation that people were placed under arrest to prevent them from leaving.[70] Nor did it address other violent confrontations between civilians and local authorities, causing, in one case, three casualties and several wounded.[71] The ICC only demanded that troops not carry automatic weapons when dealing with civilians choosing to move to the other administrative zone.[72] This lack of protection only reinforced the perception that civilians were innocent victims desperately trying to flee Communist rule.

India's obvious sympathy for the DRV cast a dark shadow on New Delhi's ambition to lead a new Third World united in the struggle against colonial rule. For example, at Bandung in April 1955, India wished to lead the countries gathered in a joint statement of support for the full execution of the Geneva ceasefire. But this initiative failed after the representative of the State of Vietnam reminded everyone that Saigon had never been party to the agreements.[73] The Third World, if it ever emerged as a coherent diplomatic force, would not back up the settlement reached in Geneva. Worse yet for India and its dreams of Third World solidarity, Saigon took advantage of this meeting to spread awareness about the unfairness of the partition and its human cost.

The delegates at Bandung regarded colonization as the main concern uniting them. Still, many countries wondered why India did not see Communism as another empire. The delegate of the State of Vietnam "injected a sharp dose of realism," according to Filipino president Carlos Romulo, by explaining that a million Vietnamese "had fled from a dictatorial regime" in North Vietnam, "which completely [disregarded] human values and personality and the basic rights of man."[74]

The same delegation from Saigon organized a reception at the Preanger Hotel, where two short movies were shown highlighting the plight of civilians leaving the North.[75] The movie showed scenes of the Geneva conference, but voices in the room commented on how India had allowed the partition to happen. The situation became so embarrassing that Menon had to leave the room. At the end of the film, representatives from Turkey and Iraq spoke up, congratulating the South Vietnamese delegation on how this discussion on "freedom" "had helped open the eyes of many delegates still believing in Communism."[76]

At Bandung, then, countries assessed the possibility of coming together in an Afro-Asian bloc. But they concluded that India, one of its leaders, was turning a blind eye to Communism. The infamous French intellectual Raymond Aron commented on the conference, declaring it was a pity India maintained a reductionist understanding of empire and failed to recognize Socialism as another form of imperialism.[77] And the press in Saigon reminded its readers why it was important to resist India's leadership at the Bandung Conference: "Nations of Asia and Africa recently liberated from an imperialist regime must not reproduce on each other the ideas and attitudes of their former masters. Peace and coexistence are possible only if nations respect each other on a perfectly equal basis."[78] Yet far from being the fair mediator between North and South Vietnam, India, it was understood, had a favorite.

The greatest and most violent critique came from within South Vietnam. In fact, India's handling of the evacuation and lack of protection provided to the evacuees suggested that no signatory power was ready to truly enforce the ceasefire agreement. This impression, in turn, made Ngô Đình Diệm come to believe Saigon would face no consequence if it refused to hold a referendum. The opportunity to abandon the referendum emerged in March 1955, after Ngô Đình Diệm used force to crush his domestic opposition. Even though the French Union Forces had already regrouped in the South, not once did they assist any of the Nationalist groups rebelling against Diệm's leadership. At this point, it was clear that France would not use its army to overthrow his cabinet. This allowed Diệm to make his move, declaring that there could not be "independence in shame," implying that the government refused to rule under limitations, such as the ceasefire agreement, imposed by the French.[79] Hanoi understood Saigon was trying to break free from its obligations, and it consequently intensified its mobilization campaign to denounce attempts to "divide the country forever."[80] Suddenly, the idea of canceling the referendum became a very real possibility.

When the first anniversary of the Geneva ceasefire approached, the evacuees' frustration reached its peak. So the SVN did its best to channel this energy and give the impression they enjoyed widespread support. The government organized an assembly of evacuees, gathering representatives of resettlement camps across the southeastern part of the country in early July. The meeting prepared the evacuees for the commemoration of a historic moment for the country and assigned them a new responsibility—they would lead South Vietnam's efforts to prevent Communism from creating trouble and dividing the population.[81] The evacuees became the popular support Diệm needed to oppose the ceasefire.

In the week preceding the anniversary, Ngô Đình Diệm officially announced his refusal to organize the referendum. Not only had Saigon never signed the agreements, but a vote could only take place in a democratic regime, he claimed.[82] Yet the North, he believed, "had allowed China to take over half of the country" and "enslaved the population."[83] The SVN did not oppose a peaceful reunification of the country but would only do so under four conditions, one of which was that there would be no Communist regime in the North.[84] Three times over the course of that one week, Saigon declared that it would not organize a referendum.

Both the prime minister and the evacuees converged in the same interpretation of the ceasefire. The evacuees felt they were paying the price of a partition they had not even wanted and that the DRV and France had sacrificed Vietnam's national unity. They also blamed India for its handling of the evacuation. French photographers captured evacuees protesting in the streets of Saigon in July 1955.[85] "Down with the ICC" painted one on a wall.[86]

The commission requested the protection of the police, but this did not prevent further hostile demonstrations. On the anniversary of the ceasefire on July 20, 1955, protests turned violent. A group separated from the main crowd, burst into the Majestic Hotel, where the ICC had established its headquarters, and ransacked the building.[87] The group of demonstrators destroyed all the ICC team's material and personal belongings; for this aggression, Nehru held Saigon responsible, because it had failed to provide adequate protection.[88] Clearly, both Saigon and some of the evacuees were lashing out at the ICC and its role in monitoring its provisions.

Despite this violence, the signatories of the ceasefire agreement—who were, after all, responsible for reacting against a breach—did not press Saigon or Hanoi to implement its provision. A ceasefire had been concluded. But no one would escalate the tensions over the violation of its provisions or the attacks against its monitoring commission. This lack of enforcement further confirmed that nothing would happen if the referendum was eternally deferred to a later date. Vietnam would remain separated, or it would reunite through violence.

Conclusion

Vietnam's territorial division, therefore, was not to protect civilians or ensure self-government. Instead, partition mainly served to accommodate the departure of the French Empire, the new role taken by the United States in Vietnam, and the interests of an emerging Third World. In this, then, it reflected features of both imperial and Cold War partitions. Like the ones arising with the fall of empires, the mass displacement was considered a necessary evil in order to create sovereign states capable of ruling over a population reflecting a certain homogeneity. And just like the partitions of Germany and Korea, these divisions were sustainable enough to de-escalate Cold War tensions and avoid a third world war.

The most immediate outcome was to grant territorial sovereignty to the DRV in the North and leave the fate of the South still undetermined. Most expected that the DRV would emerge as a credible contender to lead Vietnam as a whole since the ASV was handicapped by its French origins and because it was still lacking in democratic institutions. A referendum in 1956, should it occur, could very well confirm this significant head start and hand the country as a whole to the DRV. But an unexpected outcome emerged thanks to the provisions of the ceasefire, the mass displacement it caused, and the transnational support it generated. Rather than a solid DRV in the North and a leftover ASV in the South, the ceasefire created two proper nation-states. While the DRV enjoyed undisputed control over the North, nonetheless, the ASV emerged stronger than expected thanks to the international sympathy it gained from the evacuation and open rejection of the partition.

Putting Vietnam's partition and population displacement in perspective with previous territorial divisions also reveals several other conclusions. Though the partitions of Ireland, India, and Palestine were remarkably different from one another, still, all three divisions were influenced by common ideas, practices, and persons inherited from the British Empire. Similarly, the heritage of past territorial divisions affected decisions made in Vietnam. Even though Vietnam seemed a world away from the concerns of Ireland, India, and Palestine, still, there was, in fact, considerable continuity between the colonial and the Cold War partitions. Of particular importance was India's role as chairman of the ICC. Its experience in the repatriation of POWs during the Korean war suggested that there would be fair supervision of the ceasefire's provisions for Vietnam. But India's reluctance to protect civilians moving to the other side only fanned the flames of a precarious situation, especially since many Vietnamese already rejected the validity of the agreements. In fact, it employed its own interpretation of the evacuation as a counter to the moral argument made by the United States. India's anticolonialism has often been posited as the antithesis of the Cold War. Even so, its handling of the evacuation was an integral part of the disastrous partition and unwittingly contributed to the failure of the ceasefire agreement.

Another conclusion is that India's handling of the movement of civilians points to different perceptions of refugee protection. Western democracies, reeling from the aftermath of the Second World War, enshrined the protection of individuals from persecution by their state and expanded this trend to the first international conventions protecting individuals rather than states. Specialists note that the 1951 convention related to the status of refugees stands out in this matter, because it grants the right for states to extend protection, rather than guarantee shelter, to individuals.[89] This explains why the protection of refugees has been unequal and how that protection only expanded outside of Europe in a few select places, such as Hong Kong, because of the Cold War.[90]

However, these discrepancies came not only from Western countries' imperial and racial biases toward other populations. In fact, the inability to meaningfully extend refugee protections beyond Europe also reflected the priority of some Third World countries, such as India, which placed utmost importance on the protection of states' sovereignty at the expense of human rights. Thus, both the Cold War paralysis *and* the Third World's political agenda explain the lack of protection granted to many refugees and displaced populations.

Last, highlighting the role of an emerging Third World in this partition raises important questions on its internal divisions and the various strands of decolonization, which may have been included or rejected in this political project. While India tended to dismiss the State of Vietnam for being a creature of French colonial rule, a more accurate reading of the situation—considering how the colonial state was transforming itself to grant political autonomy while sheltering its own interests locally—allows us to consider a more nuanced situation. Not only was the decolonization of this state charting a different path, but it also relied on the protection of another imperial power to advance its political agenda. Decolonization, in this view, was not a unique end point but a constant process of balancing different kinds of foreign patronage.

Two

THE COLD WAR, ANTI-COMMUNIST PROPAGANDA, AND THE RESETTLEMENT OF DACHEN REFUGEES FROM COASTAL ZHEJIANG TO TAIWAN

DOMINIC MENG-HSUAN YANG

Introduction

On the morning of February 9, 1955, a fleet of American and Chinese Nationalist naval ships, churning out plumes of black smoke, sailed sluggishly into Keelung Harbor in northern Taiwan. Aboard the crowded vessels were eighteen thousand residents evacuated from the coastal region of China's central and southern Zhejiang Province, with the majority coming from the two larger Dachen Islands (Dachen dao 大陳島).[1] There, on the Taiwanese shore, the Nationalist (Kuomintang; hereafter, KMT) government organized a large welcoming party.[2] As the ships slowly began to dock, excited local well-wishers waved, cheered, and clapped their hands—all under the watchful eye of KMT party dignitaries, generals, and their American advisors.

The entire event was, in fact, a state-run photo shoot, staged for propaganda purposes.[3] Both the Nationalist authorities and their American friends wanted to present this instance of forced migration as a case of freedom-loving people escaping Communist tyranny. In a special radio broadcast, the KMT dictator Generalissimo Chiang Kai-shek lauded the Dachen evacuees as "righteous compatriots" (*yibao* 義胞): model anti-Communist citizens who voluntarily abandoned their homes and followed his withdrawing army to Taiwan.[4] According to the generalissimo, these common folks possessed extraordinary qualities of being righteous and selfless. They refused to stay behind and allow themselves to be "enslaved and persecuted" by the evil Chinese Communist Party (CCP).[5] As we will learn later on, however, despite Chiang's words, the migration itself involved much human misery and coercion.

For publicity, the KMT and the US officials made the refugees carry Nationalist flags, banners, and signboards with an image of Chiang Kai-shek for the cameramen and journalists waiting on shore. Amid the fanfare and flashing camera lights, the weary evacuees—who had, in prior weeks, experienced intensive aerial bombardment by the People's Liberation Army (PLA) Air Force and a grueling journey at sea—began to disembark. Many seemed overwhelmed, and even a little surprised, by the grand reception.

None of the Dachen Islanders had ever seen Taiwan. Most were illiterate island fishermen and seafood traders. These men and their families rarely ventured beyond the confines of their small islets and nearby coastal towns on mainland China. Holding on to one another, men, women, children, and the elderly observed their new surroundings vigilantly. They walked hesitantly and peeked sheepishly into the applauding crowd, not knowing how to react to the cheers and adulation. People clung on tightly to their personal belongings, ancestral tablets, and statues of their sea gods—things that offered them some degree of comfort in this dizzy pandemonium.[6] Some of the evacuees did seem happy and relieved that they were finally out of harm's way. Even so, their cautious smiles belied the profound trauma of living in the maritime front line of Cold War Asia—an active war zone—for years. There was also deep anxiety about the uncertain future in this unfamiliar place.

These events—the Nationalist withdrawal from the coastal Zhejiang islands and the relocation of the residents on these islands to Taiwan—were an integral part of the First Taiwan Strait Crisis (September 1954 to May 1955). The conflict was a major escalation in early Cold War Asia, which followed the Korean War (June 1950 to July 1953) and the First Indochina War (December 1946 to August 1954) yet occurred before the Bandung Conference (April 1955) eased the tension somewhat. There is a substantial body of work on the First Strait Crisis,[7] and, not surprisingly, such works have emphasized diplomatic history and nuclear brinkmanship. But little has been written about the eighteen thousand human beings who were displaced in the process.⁸

There are two other offshore island groups that have received some attention; there is one penetrating work of social history on Quemoy (Kinmen) and one remarkably detailed anthropological study of Matsu.⁹ Similar to Dachen, these island groups (which are still held by Taiwan today) were also the focal point of military conflict and atomic diplomacy during the First Strait Crisis. Yet compared to these experiences of Quemoy and Matsu residents, not much is known about the Dachen Islanders who were evacuated to Taiwan in early 1955. What happened to these people when they reached Taiwan? Were they successfully integrated into Taiwanese society? Did they encounter any difficulties? There is little information. It seems that because the number of these Zhejiang evacuees was small, no one really cares about them. In the standard narrative of the First Strait Crisis, then, these displaced people are brought up only as an afterthought, if they are mentioned at all.

Who were these Dachen refugees? How did they become Chiang Kai-shek's "righteous compatriots"? In what ways did the forced relocation to Taiwan affect their lives? What can this small and seemingly insignificant group—composed of evacuated fishermen, seaborne merchants, and their families—tell us about refugee relief and resettlement in Cold War East Asia? Unveiling this intricate story is the main focus of this chapter. I do so by examining a large amount of declassified official documents and utilizing some personal testimonies that have been made available in recent decades following Taiwan's democratization.

In *The Making of the Modern Refugee*, Peter Gatrell argues that "while refugees are the product of state-led practices, they also help to constitute the modern nation-state."¹⁰ In the present volume, the authors expand on Gatrell's thesis. They highlight the role played by refugees in demarcating political boundaries or urban spaces and in exerting various forms of political influence or leverage. Ijlal Muzaffar illuminates the ways in which different displaced groups from the Indian partition (and, later, from the wars in Afghanistan) altered the resettlement pattern and urban landscape in the city of Karachi—a pattern and landscape originally planned by Pakistan's US-backed military government. Sabauon Nassсri and Robert D. Crews show that Afghan exiles in neighboring host countries and in the West have been heterogenous political agents. They expressed diverse political views despite efforts by political forces in both Afghanistan and their asylum states to deny their agency. Phi-Vân Nguyen and Yumi Moon illustrate that forced migration from Communist-held territories to non-Communist territories combined with interventionist but self-serving international politics led to the division of both Vietnam and Korea. They also suggest that resentment and activism of radical displaced groups in both countries contributed to traumatic conflicts and paramilitary violence further down the road.

In this chapter, the reader will observe that although the number of the Dachen refugees was small, they constituted an important group of people rhetorically. And this status was employed not only on behalf of the KMT regime's anti-Communist crusade but also for state formation in Cold War Taiwan itself. The special status of the Dachen refugees—as the officially recognized "righteous compatriots" worthy of gaining entrance to Free China (Taiwan) and worthy of receiving state assistance—helped define the political boundary separating the KMT-ruled Republic of China (ROC) in Taiwan from the CCP-governed People's Republic of China (PRC) on the mainland. The Nationalist authorities touted the Dachen people as model citizens of the ROC. Their relocation and assistance by the KMT state were justified based on this fact.

The ability to govern the movements of people in and out of its border and the ability to define citizenship are manifestations of state sovereignty. The fact remains that permission to enter Taiwan was *not* granted to an overwhelming majority of the mainland Chinese who fled Chinese Communist rule during the Chinese Civil War (1945–1949) and the ensuing Cold War. Instead, this vast number of people were mostly stranded in Hong Kong.

The Dachen Islanders, by contrast, were among the few selected groups whose migration was directly facilitated by the Nationalist authorities. In a recent monograph that examines mainland refugees in Hong Kong and Macau after 1949, Angelina Y. Chin demonstrates that the political authorities in the "Free World"—that is, the governments of Hong Kong, Taiwan, and the United States—did not simply allow people to enter and leave freely. Instead, she maintains that "the immigration and refugee policies were never just about saving the victims and assisting them to build a new life in the host territories but were instruments for the states to socially engineer their citizenry during the Cold War."[11] Meanwhile, Hsiao-ting Lin contends that Chiang Kai-shek's regime in Taiwan was an "accidental state," forged by a complicated set of domestic and international factors as well as unintended actions taken by key historical figures, including the generalissimo and some of his American allies in Washington.[12] If Lin's argument is true, then the Nationalist regime's restrictive immigration policy and its political use of selected refugee groups—with the Dachen Islanders being a prominent example—had also unintentionally consolidated the political border dividing Taiwan and China.

Different from the North Korean and the North Vietnamese refugees described by Moon and Nguyen in their chapters, the Dachen Islanders did not flee separately and independently from the Communist territories. Instead, they were evacuated collectively from the KMT-controlled offshore islands, which were about to fall into the hands of the Chinese Communists. Prior to their evacuation, these Zhejiang islanders had lived under harsh war zone conditions and rigid military occupation from mid-1950 to early 1955. This made their experience not only different from the other refugee groups examined in this book but also different from a majority of other mainland Chinese that left home on account of the Chinese Communist Revolution.

The Nationalist and American Cold War propaganda claimed that the Dachen people did not want to live under Chinese Communist tyranny and that they voluntarily sought freedom in "Free China."[13] This chapter tells a different story. The deprivation and dispossession of the displaced Zhejiang islanders were, for the most part, *created* by the Nationalists and Americans, specifically, during the Korean War as both states worked together to conduct coastal raids and intelligence operations in the southeastern coast of China. It was these activities that threatened the people who would later become the Dachen migrants since the Nationalists and Americans transformed their home islands and fishing grounds into a dangerous war zone and a rigidly policed Cold War maritime border. Before this development, seafood trade with the coastal towns and cities on mainland China had been the mainstay of the local economy. The war prohibited fishing, commerce, and free movement at sea. It took the livelihoods of the island residents away. The decisions made by the political authorities in Taipei and Washington, therefore, resulted in the starvation and misery of these seafaring people and later facilitated their removal to Taiwan (when the Korean Armistice Agreement was signed).

By this time, however, staying home and living under CCP rule was simply not an option for the Dachen Islanders. This was because their existence as a people had been given a profound political meaning by an aging dictator bent on turning defeat into a prophecy for future victory. The generalissimo needed these freedom-seeking fishermen to demonstrate that his regime could return to the mainland one day. The idea was that the Chinese Communists could take more lands, but they would never win the hearts and minds of people living on these lands. This movement of people, then, came to define the legitimacy of the political authorities at war. They also came to delineate the divide between Free China, which was the generalissimo's ROC, and Red China, which was the PRC.

Rebecca Nedostup argues that ethnic Chinese refugees, despite their size and diversity, are underrepresented in modern world history. The omission is especially true for ordinary folks that were displaced by what she calls a "long war," which stretched from the late 1930s in China to the late 1950s in Taiwan. According to Nedostup, this omission is due to the absence of these uprooted people "from the records of the International Refugee Organization and the United Nations Relief and Rehabilitation Administration" outside of (Western) colonial settings.[14]

Nedostup is largely correct in the sense that in the research on Cold War Chinese refugees, much attention has been paid to Hong Kong.[15] The Hong Kong research is critical of the United Nations High Commissioner for Refugees (UNHCR), which was slow in recognizing the issue and also largely ineffective in providing the much-needed assistance. This body of work is also critical of the political calculus of white-settler nations, primarily English-speaking countries led by the United States and Great Britain. The selfish and sometimes conflicting interests of the Western Cold War allies contributed to their overall inaction in Hong Kong, which occurred alongside some limited and carefully orchestrated refugee-relief actions just for show. Furthermore, advanced Free World states implemented racist immigration policy that prohibited most Chinese and other Asian refugees in Hong Kong from entering their countries despite these states' anti-Communist stance or support for humanitarian principles.

This critique of racism and exclusionary border practices by white-settler states is certainly justified. And yet the current Hong Kong refugee scholarship unwittingly embodies another form of Euro-American centrism. It focuses mostly on issues and debates pertaining to the difficulty of Chinese or nonwhite refugees seeking asylum in Western countries. Instances of intra-Asian displacement during the Cold War remain largely neglected. This is a lacuna that contributors of this volume hope to fill collectively.

In filling this lacuna, this chapter makes two additional arguments on top of the state-formation thesis. First, the joint effort by the American and the Nationalist authorities to resettle the Dachen refugees failed miserably despite good intentions and millions of dollars spent. It failed mainly because both authorities prioritized politics over the actual relief work, strongly demonstrating both states' collective disregard for refugee petitions and voices. Specifically, both governments tried to promote the displaced Zhejiang islanders as people seeking freedom and prosperity in the "Free World." But even if that was a true assessment—which, as we've seen, isn't the case—both did a horrible job in assisting them.

The American aid program in Taiwan provided the bulk of the funding for the Dachen-resettlement scheme, which included the construction of thirty-five "Dachen new villages" (Dachen xincun 大陳新村), as well as the vocational-training projects within these villages. Yet the US officials managing the program in Taipei were largely detached from the local reality. Rather, the American officials were bent on cost saving and the refugees becoming economically independent sooner than later. Their funding structure and interference to improve the efficiency of the relief work did more harm than good. In the Americans' failed effort, we can observe two issues that Moon raises in the introduction. First, the Americans saw (nonwhite) refugees as a potential source of cheap labor. Second, they also held the mistaken view that all ethnic Chinese constituted a single nationality and, furthermore, ignored the specific linguistic and cultural diversity of Taiwan itself.

The Nationalists failed the Dachen refugees just as much as the Americans. It was Chiang Kai-shek's government that was responsible for carrying out the actual resettlement and the vocational-training work on the ground. Initially, the Nationalists had anticipated a limited, short-term endeavor; as such, their relief bureaucracy was both ad hoc and dysfunctional. Rushed by their American partners, the villages' vocational projects were hastily conceived and poorly executed. Worse still, the county-level KMT officials who engaged the Dachen migrants saw them as lazy country bumpkins who had developed an unhealthy appetite for government handouts. They did so without listening to the refugees and without considering the difficulties that the displaced Zhejiang evacuees faced in Taiwan, many of which were created by the ill-conceived resettlement scheme itself.

And yet the second argument advanced by this chapter is that the Dachen migrants were not mere victims or pawns of state authorities. Similar to what Muzaffar's and Nasseri and Crews's chapters illustrate, the Cold War refugees in this chapter were active agents in their own story. By protesting and petitioning repeatedly, the former fishermen from Zhejiang took advantage of their status as the "righteous compatriots," which was conferred, after all, by the generalissimo himself. The migrants voiced their discontent about ineffective government staff and poorly-conceived vocational projects that had reduced them to abject poverty. They demanded programs that could provide a decent living for their families. They did so until the Nationalist authorities finally started to listen when the US aid ran out.

This resulted in the Dachen-seamen training program for international shipping in the late 1960s. It was this program that finally lifted most of the refugee households out of dire economic circumstances. The seamen program also facilitated "jump ship" (*tiaochuan* 跳船), a form of illegal immigration by Dachen sailors abandoning their ships to find more lucrative employment upon reaching the United States. Once there, many were able to achieve great economic success. The development provides a strong counterargument to the idea that the Dachen refugees were lazy and only wanted to live on government aid and that they were hence largely responsible for their own misery. This idea, in fact, was simply invented by political authorities. A similar political fabrication was the myth that the Dachen people were the "righteous compatriots," which I will now analyze below.

Cold War Taiwan, Anti-Communist Propaganda, and the Myth of the Righteous Compatriots

In 1949, in mainland China, Chiang Kai-shek's KMT regime crumbled; in its place, the CCP established the People's Republic of China. Roughly one million mainland Chinese entered Hong Kong during the course of the KMT collapse and the CCP victory.[16] Another million were displaced with the remnants of Chiang Kai-shek's army and government to Taiwan in the process.[17] A majority of those involved in the mainland exodus in Hong Kong ended up staying in Hong Kong and later became Hong Kong citizens. Though these exiles initially saw their stay in the tiny British colony as temporary, ultimately, most could not return to Communist China, leave for Taiwan, or go elsewhere. Their plight and status have become the focal point of recent scholarship on the international politics behind Cold War Chinese refugees discussed earlier.

In contrast to the exiles in Hong Kong, the mass flight to Taiwan remains a poorly understood subject.[18] The mainland exodus to Taiwan during and following the Chinese Communist Revolution was a multifaceted and complicated migrant phenomenon. It involved different units, institutions, and groups from different parts of China, and these evacuees—including the Dachen Islanders discussed in this chapter—arrived at different times in Taiwan from the late 1940s to the mid-1950s. Contrary to popular belief, not all displaced mainlanders in Taiwan were government and military personnel or even diehard supporters of the generalissimo. There were war refugees from different walks of life: dispossessed landlords, business owners, migrant laborers, physicians, students, fishermen, and so on. This picture of diversity resembles the backgrounds of the North Korean refugees illustrated by Moon in her chapter.

There was, however, one more layer of complexity in the mainlander military population that reached Taiwan. During the course of the Chinese Civil War, a considerable number of male civilians, many of them teenage boys, were pressganged by the Nationalist army, often at gunpoint.[19] In this way, tens of thousands were abducted to Taiwan. Consequently, the morale and loyalty of the armed forces became a serious concern for Chiang Kai-shek and his generals who sought to reconquer the mainland militarily.

The army's loyalty was not the only problem. The relocated Nationalist authorities also had to face disgruntled and hostile Japanized native Taiwanese. Taiwan had been a colony of Japan until the end of World War II. Assisted by the American naval forces, Chiang's mainland officials and soldiers arrived in late 1945 to take over from the Japanese. At that time, the exiled mainland Chinese constituted only a minority (13 percent) ruling over a local majority, formed by Hoklo- and Hakka-speaking ethnic Chinese (85 percent) and a tiny minority of indigenous Austronesian peoples (2 percent).[20] Today, the Hoklos (70 percent) and Hakkas (15 percent) are often lumped together and called the "native Taiwanese."

For the native Taiwanese, the retrocession back to Nationalist China was a traumatic experience, an utter nightmare, despite their initial hope and enthusiasm for the "motherland." The KMT rule in early postwar Taiwan was plagued by rampant corruption and failed economic policy. When angry and disappointed Taiwanese rose up to protest in late February 1947, the generalissimo, who was directing civil war campaigns in China, mistakenly assumed that his CCP foes were behind the Taiwanese uprising. He responded with a bloody crackdown, known as the 228 Massacre.[21] This persecution of local civilians in the name of the anti-Communist crusade intensified after the Nationalist central government moved to Taipei in 1949. State suppression continued until Taiwan democratized in 1987. This multidecade KMT political persecution in Cold War Taiwan has been deemed by scholars as the "White Terror."[22]

While heavy-handed suppression was used to bring disgruntled Taiwanese and mainland draftees in line, an authoritarian state could not operate solely on violence and intimidation. The newly exiled KMT authorities had a pressing need to cultivate loyalty, cohesion, and a sense of purpose among its armed forces and citizenry. On the international front, the ROC—now deprived of all its territories on the mainland and confined to a small island—needed to compete with the PRC to win the support of millions of overseas Chinese living in Southeast Asia and North America. It was under these circumstances that the KMT conceptualized the notion of Taiwan as the anti-Communist bastion of "Free China." That people were escaping the PRC and seeking asylum in the ROC/Taiwan was touted as a clear sign that Free China was rising, while Red China was disintegrating.

Similarly, the term "righteous compatriots"—the honorary label that the KMT authorities used to describe the Dachen refugees—originated from a radio broadcast made by Chiang Kai-shek himself. This official broadcast was made on February 8, 1955—the day that the Nationalist military forces began their retreat from the coastal islands of Zhejiang with the assistance of the US Seventh Fleet. In his speech, the generalissimo praised the Dachen Islanders for their strong anti-Communist resolve. The exact words used were *buxi pojia dangchan er yixin baoguo yiwufangu zhi tongbao* (不惜破家蕩產而一心保國義無反顧之同胞), which roughly translates as "fellow compatriots who were so righteous and so single-minded in safeguarding the nation that they did not hesitate to wreck their homes and throw away their possessions."[23] Later on, the phrase *yiwufangu zhi tongbao* (義無反顧之同胞) was shortened to *yibao*—"righteous compatriots."[24] Thereafter, in all of Taiwan's publications, news reports, and even confidential documents, the Zhejiang evacuees were referred to as the "righteous compatriots" or the "Dachen righteous compatriots."

Still hoping to return to China, the sexagenarian Nationalist dictator was very reluctant to withdraw from the Zhejiang islands. He hated the idea. After all, Zhejiang was the generalissimo's home province, and any further loss of territories to the PRC was a blow to the ROC already in exile on Taiwan. Chiang was, however, pressured by the Eisenhower administration to do so. With the Korean War ended in the summer of 1953, there was no longer the need for coastal raids against the PRC. Furthermore, the Americans saw the presence of KMT forces on the offshore islands as a potential cause for CCP military actions, which finally came to pass in late 1954 with the First Strait Crisis. At this point, Washington used the ratification of the Sino-American Mutual Defense Treaty (and a somewhat vague promise to defend Quemoy and Matsu) as leverage to force Chiang to evacuate Dachen, offering US naval assistance to accomplish the task.[25] The generalissimo grudgingly agreed to the withdrawal. Even so, he told the secretary of state John Foster Dulles that the matter needed to be handled with care "to bolster morale and keep alive the hope that the Nationalists would one day return to the mainland."[26]

This was where the myth of the Dachen righteous compatriots was born. It also sealed the fate of the Zhejiang islanders living under the KMT military occupation. Staying behind and living under Mao Zedong's New China was not an option. All would be evacuated alongside the Nationalist military personnel because their migration as a people had now come to stand for a moral victory against the CCP in the face of actual defeat. There was, however, a catch. KMT Cold War propaganda may have publicly maintained that such movement was desirable and, indeed, honorable. But its immigration policy was actually very restrictive. Not everyone from the mainland who claimed to be loyal and anti-Communist could come to the land of Free China that was Taiwan. Despite claiming to be a safe haven for such people, the KMT government left hundreds of thousands stranded in Hong Kong and elsewhere. Only those that the state deemed righteous, self-sacrificing, and trustworthy could enter. Thus, the myth of the Dachen righteous compatriots embodied both model citizenry and political sovereignty of the ROC. It was an integral part of state making and state formation in Cold War Taiwan—one that exposed the lies at the heart of the state's project.

The Dachen migrants were among the few displaced mainlander groups that were "repatriated" to Taiwan by the Nationalist authorities in the first half of the 1950s. All were selected to do so for the same goals of ROC state making, including tens of thousands of former KMT military, government personnel, and their families who fled Vietnam and northern Burma and the fourteen thousand People's Volunteer Army (PVA) POWs captured by the UN forces during the Korean War.[27] These migrations were facilitated and controlled by the KMT authorities. They were different from the chaotic mass flight across the Taiwan Strait between late 1948 and early 1950, during which the Nationalist regime itself was on the run. Similar to the Dachen migrants, these groups were also lauded as model anti-Communist citizens. They were given the label of the "righteous people" (*yimin* 義民). The POWs from Korea were called "anti-Communist righteous warriors" (*fangong yishi* 反共義士) or "fourteen thousand witnesses" (*yi wan si qian ge zhengren* 一萬四千個證人)—that is, witnesses of the Chinese Communist destruction in China and of the Nationalist prosperity in Taiwan.[28] Of course, these state labels and narratives did not reflect the real lived experiences of these displaced peoples.

This is why, for the purpose of this chapter, it is important for us ask the following questions: Who were these Dachen refugees? How were their lives affected by the Cold War and the forced relocation to Taiwan?

Coastal Raids during the Korea War and the Making of the Dachen Refugees

The Dachen Islands are located about fifty kilometers (twenty-seven nautical miles) off the coast of central Zhejiang Province. The islands sit outside of Taizhou Bay (Taizhou wan 台州灣) and the port city of Taizhou at the river mouth of Jiaojiang (椒江). There are twenty-nine islands in the Dachen archipelago.[29] Of these, two larger islands—the Upper Dachen Island (roughly seven square kilometers) and the Lower Dachen Island (about five square kilometers)—were home to the majority of the population in the archipelago, numbering about 14,300 in 1951 with roughly two thousand families.[30] Still, even the smaller islands housed thousands of other fishing families.

During the Korean War, some of these islets also became the bases for guerrilla activities and coastal raids against the CCP on the mainland—operations sponsored by the KMT and the Central Intelligence Agency (CIA). From north to south, these included Yushan (漁山), Dongji/Tianao (東磯/田岙), Toumen (頭門), Yijiangshan (一江山), Pishan (披山), Dongtou (洞頭), and Nanji (南麂).[31] Together with the two bigger Dachen Islands in the center position, these littoral archipelagoes form a crescent that enfolds three main bay areas of central and southern Zhejiang: Sanmen Bay (Sanmen wan 三門灣), Taizhou Bay, and Wenzhou Bay (Wenzhou wan 溫州灣). By occupying these maritime choke points, the KMT guerrilla units—trained and equipped by the CIA—could collect intelligence and disrupt regular shipping in the southeastern coast of the PRC. More importantly for the Americans, they could tie down the PLA forces in south China so that more would not be sent north to fight in Korea.[32]

In the second half of 1949, Chiang Kai-shek's regime on the mainland collapsed. Consequently, in mid-May 1950, the Nationalists conducted a massive withdrawal operation from the Zhoushan Islands (Zhoushan qundao 舟山群島) in northern Zhejiang, near the thriving commercial hubs of Shanghai and Ningbo. More than 120,000 army personnel and 20,000 civilians were transported to Taiwan.[33]

Following this retreat from Zhoushan, roughly 10,000 pro-Nationalist paramilitary groups were left behind. Living on wooden junks and fishing boats, these were a motley crew comprised of local militia units, pirates, gangsters, dock workers, armed merchants, and war refugees from the mainland.[34] After the PLA occupied northern Zhejiang, these armed detachments moved south, establishing control over the Dachen Islands and a number of small but strategically important islets both north and south of the Dachen archipelago. These KMT paramilitaries survived on robbing ships, extracting tolls from local fishermen, and raiding coastal towns while also doing some fishing on the side.[35] There was no organized authority at this point. The guerrilla groups were run independently by self-appointed or elected commanders. They fought against one another constantly.[36]

Then, in late 1950, Mao sent the People's Volunteer Army over the Yalu River and entered the Korean War. At this point, the Americans saw the strategic value of the pro-Nationalist guerrilla bands on the offshore islands. And so, in the fall of 1951, Chiang Kai-shek sent one of his most senior and trusted aides, General Hu Tsung-nan (Hu Zongnan 胡宗南; 1896–1962),[37] from Taipei to reorganize the motley paramilitary groups, which were renamed the Zhejiang Anti-Communist National Salvation Army (Zhejiang fangong jiu guo jun 浙江反共救國軍; hereafter, ZANSA). American military operatives, under the guise of a private company called Western Enterprises Inc. (hereafter, WEI), were sent to the Dachen front line alongside Hu and his general staff.[38] The WEI was funded by the CIA. It was formed by World War II American veterans who had served in commando units and had carried out covert operations behind enemy lines. These WEI agents were charged with training, equipping, and supervising ZANSA units. They worked with Hu and his staff to conduct coastal raids and reconnaissance missions on Communist China.[39]

Under the patronage of the WEI and the KMT military high command, ZANSA became a destructive pirate force. The Chinese Communists did not have adequate naval and air forces during the early 1950s. Most of the available units were sent north during the Korea War. This left much of the PRC's southeastern coastline vulnerable to the American- and Nationalist-sponsored incursions. At this point, the ZANSA flotillas did not confine themselves to attacking mainland ships, fishing boats, and coastal towns. In addition, they robbed foreign vessels coming in and out of China's ports in an effort to enforce the economic sanctions on the PRC. This led to recurring protests and demands through diplomatic channels for the return of seized cargoes and crew members, especially those coming from the British colonial government in Hong Kong.[40] From 1951 to 1953, there were a total of 141 reported incidents involving British merchant ships off the coast of China. These included 61 attacks at sea, 14 on land, and 3 assaults from the air that contributed to four injuries and one death.[41] The PLA navy reported 137 incidents in the first half of 1951 alone.[42] These figures demonstrate the extent of the disruption caused by ZANSA piracy. Still, these coastal raids and piracy backed by the Nationalists and the Americans had limited effect on the outcome of the Korean War. They also contributed little to the generalissimo's dream of returning to the mainland.

Yet what these frontline operations did was devastate the livelihoods of the local island residents. The offshore islands were too small and too rugged to sustain agriculture. Over 80 percent of the islanders were fishermen; the rest all engaged in seafood production and trade.[43] Merchants and wholesalers provided credit to the fishermen and transported their catches to business partners in Taizhou, Wenzhou, Ningbo, and Shanghai. The proceeds were then used to bring back rice, flour, oil, salt, household items, and other daily provisions that the islanders could not produce locally.[44] The ability to navigate the sea freely and to freely exchange goods with the mainland was thus vital for the offshore islands' economy. This is why most island residents had family or business ties with coastal communities on the mainland. These ties were severed—and this mobility destroyed—by the CIA-sponsored ZANSA operations and the KMT war zone policy. The result was deprivation and hardship: a widespread shortage of food and other daily necessities.

Moreover, the Nationalist military authorities feared that the Dachen seafarers would come in contact with the CCP patrols at sea and divulge sensitive information (such as troop deployment, mission preparations, and warehouse locations) or, worse still, accept bribes to work as moles for the enemy. And so the KMT took strict measures to govern the movement of civilian junks.[45] Officials compiled a registry of all the fishing boats, as well as the names of every fisherman working on each boat. They also set strict guidelines on where and when to fish, which was based on strategic concerns and the counterintelligence effort. Indigenous fishing knowledge—such as seasons, tide schedules, and suitable locations—was largely ignored. Predictably, the policy led to the collapse of the local fishing industry.

To exercise effective control, the KMT military authorities also implemented a "collective punishment scheme" (*lian zuo fa* 連坐法). If one member of the boat crew was found guilty of infringing the rules, all others would be punished, including the boat owner.[46] When patrolling the sea, the Nationalist ships kept the civilian junks under watch, making sure that they operated only in the designated waters and did not come into contact with boats from the mainland side.[47] Fishing vessels returning to port were subjected to a mandatory inspection by the port authorities. The boat owner and the captain faced imprisonment if their crew failed to answer questions by the inspectors in a satisfactory manner.[48]

According to oral history testimonies, those Dachen residents that dared to make clandestine trips to China to purchase food and supplies—even just to feed their starving families—were treated as CCP agents and thrown into jail upon return.⁴⁹ Traders and fishermen from the PRC side who happened to land on the Nationalist-controlled islands for whatever reason came under immediate suspicion as spies and saboteurs, regardless of their intentions and circumstances.⁵⁰ Then, to counter the US-KMT infiltration and raids, the Chinese Communist side also instituted tight measures. It thus became increasingly difficult and dangerous for the local seafaring communities from both sides to operate at sea. The deprivation produced by these conditions compelled many local islanders on the KMT side to join ZANSA and participate in dangerous frontline missions. A former Dachen resident, who enlisted when he was only a young teenage boy, recalls that many of his peers did not return from these missions.⁵¹

In short, during the Korea War, the American and Nationalist military operations in the central and southern coasts of Zhejiang turned the entire region into a hazardous war zone and a strictly policed maritime border of the Cold War. The development was catastrophic for the local residents.

When the Korean Armistice Agreement was signed on July 27, 1953, the WEI and ZANSA operations were gradually phased out. Washington no longer needed to tie down the Chinese Communist forces on the southern flank. As the Americans pulled back their resources, however, the Nationalists remaining in Zhejiang faced increasing pressure from the PLA in 1954. With the war in Korea ended, Beijing could now shift its focus south to Taiwan and the offshore islands still held by the KMT. The ensuing conflict in late 1954 and the first half of 1955 was the First Taiwan Strait Crisis. The war resulted in the signing of the 1954 Sino-American Mutual Defense Treaty to deter further CCP aggression. In addition, Washington also promised to assist in the relocation of eighteen thousand Dachen Islanders and other Zhejiang residents to Taiwan.

By the time of their involuntary displacement to Taiwan in early 1955, the islanders living under the Nationalist military occupation had been reduced to a wretched state. With their mobility at sea and their livelihoods taken away, most of the Dachen families were starving. Many had become completely dependent on the meager government rations for survival. Toward the end of the battle for the Zhejiang offshore islands, family members huddled together in the cold and trembled in makeshift air-raid shelters. The Chinese Communist air force had achieved absolute air superiority in the Dachen region by late 1954. They pounded the KMT-held islands relentlessly for days on end. People watched in horror as swarms of PLA warplanes descended upon their little islands and turned everything in their paths into a sea of fire.[52] Many refugees heaved a sigh of relief after boarding the American and Nationalist naval transport ships to Taiwan since they had been living in a state of shell shock.

Sadly, leaving a dangerous war zone for resettlement in Taiwan did not spell the end of their misery. The displaced Dachen Islanders would soon find out that they faced a new set of challenges due to the failed relief effort by their "saviors."

Failed Nationalist and American Resettlement Effort

When eighteen thousand Dachen refugees arrived in Keelung Harbor in early February 1955 (alongside roughly fifteen thousand military personnel and guerrilla forces), the refugees had certain expectations.[53] Contrary to the glorified image of the noble and self-sacrificing "righteous compatriots," the refugees were, in fact, quite reluctant to leave home. Even with all the destruction around them, the Zhejiang islands were their native land—a place where they prayed to their sea gods for favorable winds and good catches, a place where their ancestors were buried.

Instructed by the military to take only what they could carry, the refugees had to abandon most of their possessions. Consequently, the relocated Dachen Islanders had expected some compensation and some form of government assistance to help them reestablish in Taiwan. The ways in which the refugees were received when they first landed in Keelung also deepened their anticipation. These humble seafarers were treated as celebrities. They were greeted by applauding crowds who lined the docks, the streets, and the train stations to welcome them. As previously stated, these lively events were photo sessions staged by the Nationalist and American officials for propaganda purposes.[54] The same goes for the intensive media coverage for the first couple of months, an audience with the generalissimo at the presidential residence, and visitations from Madame Chiang and other prominent KMT and American dignitaries.[55]

The migrants would be sorely disappointed. Notwithstanding the festivity and public attention and despite the rhetorical elevation of their status as the "righteous compatriots" by the state media, the evacuees soon faced the grim realities of their new life in the desolate rural backwaters of Taiwan. The Nationalist and American joint resettlement scheme consisted of building thirty-five Dachen new villages in twelve remote and sparsely populated counties.[56] In each of the new villages, a designated vocational-training program was established.[57] The American aid office in Taipei provided most of the funding while the actual relief work in the countryside was carried out, first, by a Nationalist-government-sponsored ad hoc relief committee and, later (from the second half of 1956 onward), by its county-level civil servants.[58]

The KMT-US joint relief effort would fail spectacularly. None of the vocational projects designed to make the Dachen new villages economically self-sufficient—farming, fishing, business cooperatives, and handicraft workshops—could achieve desirable results.[59] And then, when the US money ran out, the village residents found themselves in dire economic circumstances. Once again, the Dachen Islanders were starving and struggling to support their families. Consequently, another form of involuntary displacement and dispersion occurred. Able-bodied men and also some women left home to find work in big cities and towns. This meant that many of the thirty-five newly constructed villages were quickly emptied out.[60] For many of the relocated Dachen households, this also meant family separation. It was, in short, a disaster.

With the failure of the state-sponsored resettlement scheme, the deprivation of the Dachen migrant families in the late 1950s and early 1960s contrasted starkly with the media limelight that they had once enjoyed. This became somewhat of an embarrassment for the authorities in Taipei and Washington. Obviously, both the Americans and the Nationalists wanted these displaced people to achieve some success in Taiwan. Their prosperity in Free China would constitute an important symbolic victory for the Free World. In March 1956, the information-service section of the US aid office in Taipei made plans for a motion picture about the Dachen migrants living happily in their newly constructed villages. The American officials in Taiwan saw the Zhejiang evacuees as prime materials for "an excellent moving picture." The film, they thought, if made properly, could inspire overseas Chinese communities in Southeast Asia and elsewhere in the Free World. It could serve as "a blow at communism and a boost for Taiwan."[61] No records in the same file collection indicate if the film was ever made. It probably was made given the enthusiasm of the US staff who wrote the proposed plan.

What one can clearly discern from reading these declassified documents is that both the American and the Nationalist authorities in Taipei had devoted considerable financial and human resources to the Dachen-relief work. This then begs the question, What went wrong? Why did the joint effort fail so miserably? The answer is a little complicated, though it is fair to say that both governments were responsible for the fiasco. The American aid officers sitting in their comfy office building in Taipei can be faulted for their general detachment from the local reality, bent on cost saving, and ill-advised interference. The Nationalists can be condemned for their short-term outlook, hasty planning, poor execution, and an ad hoc dysfunctional relief bureaucracy. All these failings, however, share one cause, which both American and Nationalist officials involved admitted in a confidential report filed in early 1958: they started off seeing the Dachen-resettlement work as "primarily a political issue," whereas the "economic considerations were less important."[62] It was thought that the refugees could be on their feet soon with only moderate government assistance. The most conspicuous mistake made by both authorities was thus their detachment from the true economic plight of the Zhejiang evacuees, in conjunction with disregarding their needs, circumstances, protests, and petitions.

In retrospect, American financial assistance was indispensable for the Dachen resettlement. On paper, close to 60 percent of the Dachen-relief funds in the second half of the 1950s came directly from the US aid programs in Taiwan.[63] In real terms, however, the American contribution was much greater because many of the Taiwan provincial government (TPG) bureaus that participated in the Dachen-assistance work were also partially funded by the Council of US Aid in Taipei during this time. Nearly half of the American funding was used for the construction of the thirty-five Dachen new villages. The rest was applied toward the vocational-training projects in these villages that were designed to help the migrants become economically independent.[64] In total, more than 3 million US dollars were invested by the American and the Nationalist authorities on the Dachen-relief effort from 1955 to 1959. This really was a significant amount given the small size of the population, the strong US dollar, and the impoverished socioeconomic conditions in Taiwan's countryside.[65]

But despite America's pivotal role in providing the bulk of financial support for the Dachen resettlement, its officials in Taiwan were mostly detached from the local reality. The US fund managers sitting in their comfy Taipei office could not speak Mandarin (which was spoken by most mainlander officials), not to mention Hoklo and Hakka, the two main dialects spoken by the native Taiwanese, or the Taizhou dialect, used by a majority of the Dachen migrants.[66] The responsibility for carrying out the actual relief was delegated to the Nationalist authorities. Moreover, examining the contemporaneous American involvement in the Hong Kong–refugee relief (via the CIA-funded Aid Refugee Chinese Intellectuals Inc., or ARCI), one can discern that the US officials focused narrowly on assisting a small number of intellectuals that were politically and strategically valuable. In Hong Kong, the Americans were only interested in individuals who could speak English, who were employable, and who could contribute to the economy of the Free World, not the masses of uneducated peasants, fishermen, and workers.[67] It is thus not surprising that, in Taiwan, they quickly lost the appetite for the Dachen relief and refrained from further investment upon seeing the poor results.

By examining the correspondence between the US aid officials and the Nationalist bureaucrats and also among the Americans themselves, one can identify the overarching American concern: how to save money and make the refugees economically self-sufficient as soon as possible.[68] Ironically, there was a fundamental problem in the Nationalist resettlement scheme, which made the failure of the Dachen new village projects almost inevitable. The Americans' inability to comprehend or anticipate this problem reflects the extent to which they were detached from the perspectives of the foreign officials that they worked closely with, not to mention the displaced people that they had intended to assist or administer.

The problem has to do with the questionable economic logic of the Dachen new villages scheme itself. The Nationalist authorities sent the Dachen families away from the major cities and towns to the remote countryside, where thirty-five isolated village settlements were built for them in twelve different counties. They then expected these communities to develop independently into self-sustaining economic units, each specializing in one particular type of occupation or industry. There were villages for farming, fishing, handicraft manufacturing, and business cooperatives in sauce making, construction, street vending, dry-fish production, and ship repair.[69] The plan looked good on paper, but it did not work in real life. In another paper, I analyze and trace the origin of the thinking behind the failed Nationalist resettlement scheme, which I term "wartime developmentalist logic." The logic considered lower-class war refugees as merely human resources, which the state could utilize to open up underdeveloped territories.[70]

Thus, the main issue with the Dachen new villages is that most of these new settlements were erected in remote and sparsely populated places. The villages were founded far from markets and infrastructure, such as roads, railways, and port facilities, to transport the products. It is hardly surprising, then, that these village settlements could not become economically self-sufficient and that the residents had to leave to find employment elsewhere to sustain their families.[71]

In the hundreds of pages of declassified official documents that I examined, the US officials in Taipei never raised any doubts about the Dachen new village scheme proposed by their Chinese partners. It might seem that the Americans agreed with the KMT authorities that displaced people would be a good source of manual labor to develop marginal lands. But, in fact, the Americans were mainly just concerned with efficiency and cost saving. Since they were suspicious of the Nationalist bureaucracy—which had previously been accused of corruption and incompetence during the Chinese Civil War—the US officials rushed the KMT civil servants on the ground to get things done quickly and effectively. But their advice and interference did more harm than good. The mid- and low-ranking county TPG officials who managed individual vocational programs in the Dachen new villages found that they had to design their programs in accordance with the funding structure and the terms set by the US administrators in Taipei. The latter usually had little understanding of the local conditions. The proposed plans then became impractical and unfeasible—a complete waste of the resources invested.[72]

The ill-fated Dachen-handicraft manufacturing is a case in point. The handicraft program was, from its very inception, hamstrung by the limited funding and unrealistic timetable for completion set by the US funding managers. As a result, when put into actual practice, it had little chance to succeed. The pilot project focusing on training the refugees to produce bamboo screens and rattan chairs proved to be a nonstarter and was terminated after only a three-month trial.[73] Trying to salvage the situation, the TPG officials solicited the investment and expertise of an overseas Chinese entrepreneur from Thailand who already had factories in Taiwan that made these products and could export them abroad. The entrepreneur was able to train the Dachen workers and get the production started. However, the effort was stalled by suspicious US administrators, who saw the entrepreneur's involvement as a deviation from the proposed plan—a possible sign of foul play.[74] This was a bad decision.

The stoppage disrupted the ongoing training and production already underway. It greatly upset the Dachen migrants, who had been living in a state of anxiety since the failure of the initial pilot project. Many feared that they would not be able to feed their families when the government subsidies ran out. Representatives of the Dachen-handicraft villagers submitted a petition letter stating that they wanted to work with the Chinese entrepreneur and the TPG staff conveyed this message to the American aid office in Taipei.[75] Still, the US office disapproved of this change from the original project proposal.

While the refugees stayed idle and waited anxiously, some of them started working for the entrepreneur privately to produce firecrackers in one of the villages. This led to infighting among the refugees since not everyone benefited. Depressed and feeling desperate, disgruntled villagers rose up to protest violently. They occupied the factories, beat up assistance staff, and sabotaged the finished products. Nationalist security forces had to be called in to restore order in the villages. Those who started the riot were arrested and punished.⁷⁶ The Dachen-handicraft-industry program was brought to a standstill by this unhappy incident; in fact, it would never recover. The outcome was devastating for the hundreds of Dachen-refugee families that resided in the villages designated to produce handicrafts. From this point onward, they were mostly left to fend for themselves.

The Nationalist regime was, of course, not free from blame. The generalissimo's government in Taiwan was, without doubt, the main culprit of Dachen people's dislocation and misery, first, on the Zhejiang front line and, later, in Taiwan. The Americans were bent on efficiency and cost saving but got the opposite results because of their detachment from the refugees and the local reality. For their part, the Nationalist relief bureaucracy was ad hoc, dysfunctional, and, like that of their American counterpart, deaf to refugee voices. It wasn't until a decade later that the situation began to change.

In late January 1955, the KMT authorities formed a temporary administrative body to manage and coordinate the Dachen-resettlement work, called the Committee for Assisting Anti-Communist Righteous Compatriots Coming to Taiwan from the Dachen Region (Dachen diqu fangong yibao lai tai fudao wei hui 大陳地區反共義胞來台輔導委員會; CAARC[CTDR]).⁷⁷ The ad hoc nature of the CAARC demonstrates that the Nationalists had initially anticipated a short-term assistance program limited in scale, with the Americans picking up most of the bills. Thus, instead of hiring additional personnel for the Dachen work, the KMT leaders decided that the best option was secondment: pulling state employees out of existing government agencies to, for a limited time, perform different tasks and run different programs. It was mainly this makeshift arrangement that caused the Nationalist relief bureaucracy to become dysfunctional and ineffective, not the corruption that the Americans had anticipated.

Though the CAARC drew its working staff from a number of central government institutions and representative offices, many of the prominent KMT party officials participated only in name.⁷⁸ The resettlement of the Dachen refugees in Taiwan's distant countryside required cooperation and participation of local county authorities in these areas. Therefore, the TPG bureaus and their local branches, staffed by mid- and low-ranking civil servants, emerged as the principal agencies and agents. Both the Nationalist central government and the American aid office in Taipei relied on the provincial- and county-level officials to carry out the relief work on the ground. This arrangement was in place before the CAARC was disbanded in September 1956, after which the TPG formally assumed the responsibility for managing all the Dachen vocational programs in the villages.[79]

The vocational programs were hastily planned and poorly executed not just because of American pressure and demands. It was also because the TPG officials who were put in charge of these programs were not released from their original positions and responsibilities. As it turned out, the "seconded" local civil servants were expected to multitask, without getting extra pay or benefit. Most of the TPG bureau heads were too busy to supervise effectively. The Dachen-resettlement work was often far down the list of their pressing concerns. Some bureau heads even held back their best personnel from the Dachen projects. The ad hoc and disorganized nature of the relief bureaucracy contributed to its dysfunction. An internal investigation report produced in early 1958, following a joint meeting between US and KMT officials, noted that for the mid- and low-ranking civil servants who were assigned to work face-to-face with the refugees, "it was hard psychologically for them to take full responsibility for the relief work."[80]

The refugees, in turn, noticed the lack of professionalism that some of the government-assistance staff exhibited. A prominent example was the fishing program. Dachen folks settled in one of the fishing villages in the remote Taitung (Taidong 台東) County recalled that the fishing instructors sent by the TPG were themselves unfamiliar with the maritime conditions in eastern Taiwan. As a result, their instructions were useless.[81] One-third of the thirty-five Dachen new villages were established as fishing settlements on the eastern and southwestern coast of Taiwan.[82] This was a fairly reasonable development given that most of the Zhejiang evacuees were former fishermen. In these settlements, the government not only bought new boats for the residents but also provided them with loans for purchasing fishing equipment using the US money. And the American and Nationalist authorities, in their joint assessment report filed in August 1959, deemed the final outcome of the Dachen fishing program "satisfactory."[83]

Oral testimonies offered by former village residents tell another story. Most of the transplanted Dachen fishing families were struggling. Many barely survived during this time. Several families had to share one single boat. The catch was not enough to feed everyone, and there were inadequate funds for boat repair and maintenance.[84] Moreover, the fact remains that the terrain and marine ecosystems were completely different from that of their previous home. The Dachen migrants were ignorant of the local fishing techniques, and their previous skills developed in the shallow waters of coastal Zhejiang were of little use in Taiwan's deep-sea waters. Despite the shinning new boats and tools provided by the government, no one trained the refugees how to fish properly along the local shores. Consequently, Dachen fishing boats went out and returned to port empty-handed. This caused great economic difficulty and anxiety for the families.[85] The situation improved only after the refugees learned longline and trolling-line fishing methods and only by observing and inquiring local fishermen operating nearby.[86] The inability of the TPG staff to identify and address this rather simple and fundamental issue demonstrates the incompetence and inattentiveness of the Nationalist relief effort.

There is another fundamental issue that the KMT-US resettlement scheme also ignored. A majority of the Dachen migrants lacked formal education. Many were illiterate and could not speak fluent Mandarin or the Hoklo and Hakka dialects used by the local majority population, the native Taiwanese. The language barrier made it difficult for them to interact with the local population or obtain official employment. As the transplanted Dachen migrants left the new villages to find work in the cities and towns, they were perpetually condemned to unstable, low-paid menial labor—and hence their continued impoverishment, depression, and misery. The state-sponsored resettlement scheme did little to address this language barrier—a challenge that could have been overcome with adequate lessons, which were fairly cheap to provide. Later, in the late 1990s, one Dachen community leader reflected that the government had made two big initial mistakes in the 1950s: sending everyone to the barren countryside and not teaching the migrants how to speak Mandarin.[87]

Apparently, the Dachen migrants knew their situation; they knew exactly what they needed. The problem was neither of the authorities involved took the refugees seriously. This was even acknowledged by both the KMT and the American officials involved in the process. The same 1954 report mentioned earlier indicated that not involving refugee representatives in the decision-making process was one of the main reasons that the Dachen-resettlement work had abjectly failed.[88]

Refugee Petitions and the Dachen-Seamen Training Program

The Dachen migrants were vocal about their difficulties. Similar to the partition refugees in Karachi described by Muzaffar, the Zhejiang migrants organized and made demands the moment that they were placed in the state-designated settlements. From reading the declassified official documents and the petition letters submitted by the migrants, we can observe that these evacuees from Zhejiang were not just wretched victims or mindless pawns of the two powerful nation-states. Fighting to end their own misery and build a better future for their families, they petitioned the authorities relentlessly for more assistance. They exposed inept TPG officials and rose up to protest when their pleas fell on deaf ears. And yet the mid- and low-ranking KMT officials who received their "complaints"—namely, the overworked TPG civil servants—came to see the Dachen migrants not as legitimate petitioners but rather as troublemakers who possessed what they described as a "dependent mentality" (*yilai xinli* 依賴心理).[89] They came to see the righteous compatriots as country bumpkins who had developed an unwarranted sense of entitlement and an unhealthy appetite for government handouts.

But this was only the opinion held by frustrated officials. It is not how the story should be told. From the same archival documents and letters, we can see that the Dachen refugees were, in fact, quite adept in turning the KMT Cold War propaganda to their advantage. Keenly aware of their special status as the "righteous compatriots"—a status that allowed them to exercise limited power in a place where all the odds were stacked against them—the refugees appealed repeatedly to the higher authorities and clamored boisterously for what they needed and deserved. They did it until the Nationalist power holders came to appreciate the gravity of their situation and start to listen more attentively to their requests. And only then did things begin to change. The Dachen migrants were the unsung heroes in their own story.

The residents of the aforementioned handicraft villages were a good case in point. Following the collapse of the US-funded project, a portion of the tenants left the villages to find jobs in the cities to support their families. Those who stayed in the villages continued to petition the government for monetary assistance and sustainable employment while also trying to safeguard their communal interests. For example, in March 1958, an empty factory building located in a Pingtung (Pingdong 屏東) County handicraft village was forcibly occupied by a nearby public middle school. This started with one greedy villager conniving with the school authorities to appropriate the property, with the apparent consent of the TPG aid officer supervising the handicraft village.[90] The middle school administration turned the building into a dormitory for their teachers and staff. The villagers reported this development to the Pingtung County government. The school, probably backed by some of the public servants in the county government's office, refused to clear out and return the building.

Seeing the move as an illegal seizure of their communal property by unscrupulous local officials, the residents protested vehemently. They wrote petition letters to the TPG, the American aid office, and a number of government institutions in Taipei. In the end, the villagers were able to force the school to return the building. Even then, they had to send another petition letter to the US aid office to regain the use of the property.⁹¹ The empty factory building was later rented out to a group of discharged KMT veterans; the proceeds were shared by the village households.⁹²

In 1960, in response to repeated requests for employment by the residents of a handicraft village in Kaohsiung (Gaoxiong 高雄), the TPG agreed to set up a new trial project for the residents to produce straw bags.⁹³ By this time, the American money had stopped, so this was a TPG-only endeavor. But despite requesting employment, when local TPG personnel and workers transported the bag-production machines to the village and began to install the equipment to the empty factory floor, the residents rebelled. They not only halted the installation but also held several TPG agents hostage for hours before the police arrived on scene to rescue the agents and disperse the crowd.⁹⁴ The entire project was then canceled. The official report did not specify what caused the village residents to rebel all of a sudden. But it is reasonable to assume that distrust and poor communication between the TPG staff working on setting up the straw-bag production and the village residents were the reasons.

After this ugly confrontation, whatever trust that had previously existed between the TPG relief instructors and the residents of the Kaohsiung handicraft village was gone. Any further suggestions from the government for the refugees to resume handicraft production were simply ignored by the latter. Instead, the residents of this handicraft village sought to become state employees. They knew that government jobs, even at the lowest levels, meant stable income and long-term security. They resorted to what perturbed TPG officials termed "petition and snitch" (*chenqing gaozhuang* 陳情告狀) to achieve their goals. This was done by writing letters to high-ranking party officials and TPG bureau heads, putting pressure on the lower-level county officials to solve their employment problem.

The tactic was effective in prompting the relief staff into action but ineffective in securing the actual positions. A situational report in 1964 shows that the TPG bureau responsible for assisting the Kaohsiung handicraft village had tried to get the Kaohsiung port administration to hire fifty of the villagers as longshoremen and the Kaohsiung city and county police departments to hire another thirty as janitors and street sweepers. The effort was not very successful. The report states, "Most of the [official] institutions that we contacted have been reluctant to accept the placement of Dachen righteous compatriots. The compatriots have a strong dependent mentality. They make it known that it was the [central] government that asked them to come to Taiwan. They petition and snitch all over the place, and they do not listen to advice. As a result, getting jobs for them has been a very difficult and complicated task. Our bureau has been giving our best effort over the years. Our misery is hard to describe in words."[95] Here, we can see the amount of pressure that these uneducated and supposedly unsophisticated fishermen could exert on the public servants responsible for their welfare. This was due to their status as the state-sanctioned "righteous compatriots," as well as their tenacity and self-reliance.

Similar assertiveness was on display in March 1958 when the TPG head official responsible for overseeing the Dachen farming villages in southwestern Taiwan found himself in the hot seat. This was because the residents of these villages complained to the investigators from Taipei about the poor performance of his office.[96] In the parlance of the Nationalist officialdom, they had "snitched" on him. Then, on April 25, 1958, the head official submitted a full report to his superiors in the TPG, with copies also sent to several US aid institutions in Taipei involved in the Dachen relief.[97] In the report, the official tried to answer serious allegations made by the refugees with regard to the corruption and mismanagement of his office.

The refugees claimed that a portion of their monthly rations had been appropriated by the staff members supervising the program. The cows, seeds, and farming tools provided by the TPG were of very low quality.[98] Among the accusations was that the agricultural instructors that the head official sent to the villages had little experience in farming. They lived a comfy life in the villages, enjoyed bossing people around, and were completely detached from the refugees. In response to these allegations, the head official dismissed all the wrongdoings as hearsay. He even suggested that there were "bad elements" (*buliang fenzi* 不良分子) in the villages who constantly spread rumors and encouraged families to just pack up and leave. There were also people who tried to damage the irrigation system.[99] The head officials did admit that two of the instructors that he had sent to the villages were problematic, but these individuals had already been removed from their posts. He defended the rest of his choices.[100] This exchange once again demonstrates the Dachen refugees were vocal about their plight. And it also shows that they did not shy away from pointing the finger at the officials whom they thought were responsible for their deprivation and suffering.

By the first half of the 1960s, the failure of the Dachen-resettlement scheme had become apparent to most high-ranking KMT party officials in Taipei despite repeated efforts by the county-level civil servants to revive the Dachen new village programs or to provide short-term employment for the refugees. Things got so bad for the Dachen people that their poverty and struggle for survival had become somewhat of an embarrassment for the Nationalist leadership. If the vaunted "righteous compatriots" escaping Communist China assisted by two "free" governments and funded by millions of US dollars could not make a respectable living in Taiwan, what did it say about the conditions in "Free China"? What did it say about the "Free World"?

In early 1964, the Nationalist Party Central Committee initiated a fact-finding mission formed by three different groups of senior officials to visit righteous compatriots living in different parts of Taiwan. The officials went into the homes of the Dachen refugees. They knocked on the doors to offer greetings from President Chiang and to deliver some compensation money on behalf of the government. As it turned out, things were a lot worse than what these prominent party officials had anticipated. The Nationalist authorities thus launched the second effort to assist the Dachen migrants in late 1964.[101] At this point, the officials recognized the ad hoc and disorganized nature of their previous effort. Without the latitude of American financial support, the relief work needed to become more precise and more practical. The officials started to listen more carefully to the refugees. They became more attentive to the welfare of the righteous compatriots.[102]

In early 1967, a closed-door meeting was held to assess the progress of the second relief attempt. The meeting was attended by many TPG bureau heads and senior party officials. The TPG secretary, General Hsu Nai (Xu Nai 徐鼐; 1910–1992), chaired the discussion. He admitted that even with the government's best effort, many of the Dachen families remained destitute. In Hsu's opinion, these poor folks were still in need of assistance.[103] Even so, Hsu continued to make disparaging comments about the dubious characters and dependent mentality of the righteous compatriots—an indication that old prejudices did not go away completely.

Yet, at this particular juncture, there was indeed something different about the KMT approach and mentality. This change in attitude is clearly demonstrated by Hsu's concluding remarks to his TPG bureau heads. The secretary general reiterated the importance of the Dachen-assistance program to the power holders in the party, including to him. He also pointed to the inattentiveness of past relief work that had led to the current predicament. Hsu said, "I hope all responsible agencies can carry out your assigned work seriously and in a realistic manner. If certain things cannot be accomplished, I want you to explain (to me) in all honesty, the reasons why they cannot be done."[104] Hsu stressed that the goal was to find practical solutions. This emphasis on practicality made the officials more receptive to refugee petitions instead of seeing these as unwarranted demands.

And, in the end, it was the refugees themselves who knew how to improve their lots. In the late 1960s, the villagers asked the government to provide the special seamen training for international shipping. It was this particular program that vastly improved their economic conditions and solved the Dachen employment issue once and for all.

By the early 1960s, many transplanted Zhejiang islanders who left their depressed new villages found employment as ship-repair workers, longshoremen, or fishing-vessel deckhands.[105] They knew about the development in the major seaports. In the second half of the 1960s, as Taiwan's export-oriented industrialization began to take off, a large number of professional sailors on foreign-bound vessels were needed, and these jobs paid handsomely. Dachen men had seafaring skills and many favored a life at sea. The problem was that they needed some formal training and a professional license to work on transnational liners. Unfortunately, almost all were excluded from the state maritime academies that provided the special training and the licensing due to their low education and older age.[106] Many aspiring Dachen seamen were in their middle ages or even older. Most did not even finish elementary school.

In June 1966, twenty-eight Dachen workers appealed to the KMT authorities. They were accepted into a temporary sailor-training program, but a vast majority of the migrants were still being excluded. Thus, in late 1967, representatives from the Dachen communities petitioned the government to lift the education and age requirements for the Dachen people to pursue professional careers at sea. Different from their previous attitude, the officials took the petition seriously. After some deliberation, the Nationalist authorities responded positively to the petition. All male righteous compatriots under the age of forty were exempted from the minimum-education requirement (middle school). They were also exempted from taking the entrance exam to the maritime academies. Instead, the Dachen candidates were placed in a special expedited training program, tailored to their needs.[107]

In the next couple of years, more than three thousand Dachen men were trained and licensed as professional seamen. These individuals found steady and rewarding employment aboard international commercial-shipping vessels.[108] Over the next two decades, in fact, Dachen sailors came to represent 10 percent of all registered professional seamen in Taiwan.[109] This was a conspicuous overrepresentation given their tiny population in relation to the rest of Taiwan at the time. The figure speaks to the preferential treatment by the government and the effectiveness of the policy. On average, deckhands on transnational cargo ships earned 100 to 300 US dollars per month in the late 1960s and early 1970s, depending on their positions and experiences. This was a small fortune for the impoverished migrant households. And the Dachen sailors regularly sent half or even two-thirds of their income home.[110] The effect of this remittance was immediate. With a large amount of capital now injected into their communities, life improved tremendously for average Dachen families and did so in a very short span of time.

Working in transnational commercial shipping also gave rise to a form of illegal immigration to the United States. The Dachen people called it "jump ship." Starting in the mid-1970s, an increasing number of Dachen seamen abandoned their ships and work contracts upon reaching the United States. They found far more lucrative employment as dishwaters and cooks in the thriving Chinatown restaurants. The Dachen immigrants worked hard, continued to send money home, and saved enough to start their own restaurants and other businesses. Then, they began to facilitate a chain migration of their children and immediate family members to America.[111]

The Dachen success stories in the United States are fascinating, but they are beyond the scope of this study. What these success stories do indicate, in a clear manner, is that the Dachen migrants were hardworking and enterprising people. They could accomplish amazing things if they were not held back by the circumstantial and structural limitations imposed upon them by the nation-states at war. The Dachen righteous compatriots did not possess an unhealthy appetite for government handouts; they did not have a "dependent mentality." These were excuses that the political authorities concocted in order to shift the blame on the refugees for their own failure.

Epilogue

Notwithstanding the migration to the United States, the Dachen people remain a distinctive and tightly knit community in contemporary Taiwan. Nowadays, most of the original thirty-five villages have either been hollowed out or abandoned altogether. The elder Dachen folks who retired from their businesses and careers in the United States and those who still prefer to live among fellow natives have recongregated in two larger communities established in New Taipei City and Kaohsiung

City.[112] Many former refugees and their Taiwan-born children have visited their home islands after Taiwan and China resumed trade and cross-strait contact in the late 1980s. Not many have returned to live there since all the evacuated Zhejiang offshore islands are now fully occupied by strangers: mainland settlers and their descendants sent to repopulate the islands by the CCP in the late 1950s and early 1960s.[113]

The Dachen story constitutes just one of many lesser-known instances of intra-Asia forced migrations produced by the Cold War. The intricacies, dynamics, and interconnections of these cases remain to be explored by future scholarship.

Figure 2.1. Mural portraying the evacuation from Dachen to Taiwan in early 1955 in Shijian Dachen New Village, Cijin District, Kaohsiung City. Photo by author.

Figure 2.2. A Chiang Kai-shek temple built by the Dachen refugees in Shijian Dachen New Village. Photo by author.

Figure 2.3. A Chiang figure inside a Chiang Kai-shek temple in Shijian Dachen New Village. Photo by author.

Three

NORTHERN REFUGEES AND THE RISE OF COLD WAR NATIONALISM IN SOUTH KOREA, 1945–1950

YUMI MOON

Introduction

When Korea was liberated from Japanese occupation by Allied forces in August 1945, Yu In-bŏm was a student at the Kwangsŏng Middle School, run by Christian missionaries, in P'yŏngyang, southern P'yŏngan Province, north of the thirty-eighth parallel.[1] After the parallel became the dividing line between Soviet- and US-occupied Korea, he crossed into the South in 1946. Later, he became the chair of the Northwestern Student Association (Sŏbuk Haksaeng Yŏnmaeng).[2] Between 1946 and 1949, he crossed the parallel several times and contacted an underground youth group in the North. He proudly engaged in espionage to disrupt the North Korean leadership and was even captured and interrogated by Russians, whom he believed to be the KGB (Soviet State Security Committee).[3] He participated in subduing the 1948 Cheju Island uprising, an armed protest of leftists rejecting the separate election in South Korea; the quelling of the uprising is known for the South Korean government's massacre of civilians. When I asked what had motivated him to go to Cheju, Yu answered, "We lost our home and suffered from living as the thirty-eighth parallel's leftovers [samp'al ttaraji]. We wanted to create a new land for settlement on that island to replace our loss."⁴

Yu was one of more than a million northerners who left Soviet-occupied Korea between 1945 and 1949. In ending the war with Japan, the United States and the Soviet Union occupied Korea but divided their individual military occupations along the thirty-eighth parallel. Though divided, this joint occupation was originally intended to lead to the establishment of an independent, unified Korea. However, the partition of Korea rapidly transformed into a proper border, dramatically affecting the lives of Koreans and triggering their migrations across the parallel.

Despite the large number of northern migrants during this period, their history has been relatively unknown. The mainstream historians of postcolonial Korea argue that a left-leaning revolution was taking place in Korea, which the US occupation deliberately interrupted to protect American interests in Asia. In this framework, the northern youth groups are depicted as reactionary as well as instrumental to the US counterinsurgency scheme. Only in the past decade have some South Korean scholars started compiling oral interviews of northern refugees⁵ and several important works on them have since been published.⁶

Yu In-bŏm's desire to make up for his loss poses a critical question about what prompted the rightist militancy in postcolonial Korea. Many northern refugees intensely criticized the changes in the Soviet zone, while their youth groups in the South used terror against leftists and assisted the counterintelligence agency of the US military. Sources reveal that the violence committed by northern youth was not entirely disconnected from the sentiments of northerners in South Korea. When I interviewed northerners who moved to the South between 1945 and 1949, I was struck by their positive memories of the infamous rightist organization called the Northwestern Youth Association (Sŏbuk Ch'ŏngnyŏndan). For example, Yun Il-yŏng crossed the parallel in the spring of 1947 after his mother was arrested by the North Korean police, who interrogated her about Il-yŏng's brothers who had left for the South. Il-yŏng's brothers had entered the South in 1946, and one of them joined the Northwestern Youth Association. Il-yŏng stated that the members of this association were "the educated and politically awakened [mŏri ka kkaein saram]" in their twenties and thirties.⁷ Dr. Ch'oe Ŭn-bŏm, my interviewee from Hamgyŏng Province, concurred. He said that the members of the association had been victimized in the northern system and their organizational power was "indispensable in countering the violence of the leftists."⁸

Once in the South, northerners took various life trajectories as they sought to survive and resettle. Nevertheless, they shared a sense of loss as "a people deprived of their homes," maintaining their networks and identity as northerners in the South. Such discourse and activism of northerners were critical in reshaping Korean Nationalism against the backdrop of the ideological conflicts of the Cold War. In this chapter, I will discuss this dynamic by investigating the following subjects: the origins of the term "refugees" in postcolonial Korea; the transformation of the thirty-eighth parallel into a border, as well as refugees' experiences of crossing it; the motivations and social characteristics of northern refugees; and the discourse and activism of northerners in the South between 1945 and 1950. In examining these subjects, I use a variety of sources, such as US documents, oral interviews with refugees, North Korean sources seized by the US Army during the Korean War, and *Ibuk T'ongsin* (Correspondence from the North), the magazine published by northern refugees in South Korea during this time.

Definitions: Displaced Persons and Refugees in Postcolonial Korea

The US military applied the term "refugees" to northern Koreans who entered the South from the Soviet-occupied zone after August 15, 1945, but their use of the term originated earlier in wartime discussions by the Allied forces about occupying areas under Axis domination. In October 1944, the US Department of State's Special Committee on Migration and Resettlement drafted a secret report entitled *Displaced Populations and Groups in Korea*.[9] The report investigated different ethnicities and nationalities in Korea, estimated the potential dislocation they would experience if the Allied forces started fighting there, and made provisional recommendations for how the military commanders should administer displaced persons. In deciding how to regulate the movements of displaced persons, the special committee (as discussed in this volume's introduction) employed the principle of nationality. And, in so doing, it devoted particular attention to how to evacuate Japanese civilians from regions occupied by Japan.

In a future occupation, the United States would classify displaced persons into several categories, to which different rules would apply. This was stated in a document from October 26, 1944, titled "Recommendations to Military Authorities with Respect to Displaced Groups in Korea," which identified groups like Allied prisoners of war, Allied civilian internees, other Allied nationals (primarily Chinese), displaced Koreans, stateless people, and displaced Japanese and other nationals from Axis states. As for these respective categories of the displaced, the State

Department proposed different procedures, which involved their registration, screening of their allegiance to the Allied cause, and either repatriation or organization into labor units by the occupation forces.[10]

With Japan's surrender after the atomic bombs in Hiroshima and Nagasaki, the actual fighting between Japanese and US forces did not end up occurring in southern Korea as expected. These 1944 guidelines, which had been meant for during and after combat, then instead informed how the US military managed population movements in South Korea after the fighting was over.

At war's end, the US military in Korea estimated that they would be handling a total of 6.2 million displaced persons, comprising diverse nationalities and ethnicities.[11] By September 15, 1945, the Bureau of Planning in the US military government in Korea drafted a plan entitled "The Relief Organization for Refugees and Laborers." According to this plan, the headquarters of the relief organization would be established in the former colonial government building in Seoul, with branches or control-point offices in Seoul, Taejŏn, Taegu, and Pusan. Representatives from that military government would also be stationed in Japan so as to oversee the repatriation of Koreans there. The plan designated local control offices to provide housing, food, and transportation provisions. The headquarters in Seoul would maintain regular communication with the local offices and coordinate local transportation requests with the Transportation Bureau of the US military government.[12]

However, this initial plan was discarded due to its lack of "central control and coordination." Ultimately, it was determined that the enormous task of repatriation required the full involvement of the US military government instead of being entrusted to an organization outside the command chain of the occupation forces. Archibold V. Arnold, military governor of Korea (1945–1946), and Major Gordon B. Enders, chief of the Foreign Affairs Section, directed Lieutenant William J. Gane to conduct a study on the repatriation problem. Based on Gane's study, the US military developed a program capable of repatriating approximately five million displaced persons. This program ensured the organized control of repatriation by the military government, along with a system of coordination among the Transportation Bureau, the Bureau of Health, and the Foreign Affairs Bureau. Additionally, the program enhanced the roles of Japanese-settler organizations and involved fostering unified assistance from numerous Korean societies to aid in repatriating Koreans.[13]

On September 23, 1945, the Foreign Affairs Section of the military government began its work on repatriation.[14] The Displaced Persons Bureau, created within the

Foreign Affairs Section, started recording the nationality and *original departure points of people* who entered the South. In these records, the US military did not differentiate displaced persons from refugees. Instead, everyone who entered the South was called a refugee, including the Japanese in Korea and China; Korean repatriates from Manchuria, China, and Japan; and northern Koreans who crossed the thirty-eighth parallel.

At first, when an increasing number of people crossed the thirty-eighth parallel southward, the US military ascribed this mass migration to Korean repatriation from Manchuria. Quoting the Displaced Persons Bureau, it insisted, "A large portion of the 461,497 Koreans entering Korea from the Russian-occupied zone during the period 15 August–13 December 1945 are refugees from Manchuria or China. The remainder is believed to be composed of persons dissatisfied with conditions in North Korea and persons habitually travelling back and forth for reasons of business and politics."[15] The US military, however, acknowledged that they lacked accurate records on the origins of refugees from North Korea and the underlying reasons for leaving their previous homes.[16] This means that the US military had hitherto treated northern refugees as displaced persons without explicitly linking their entry to the South with the issue of Soviet occupation.

Soon, though, the US military began to recognize the need to differentiate northerners from the original broader category of all persons displaced by the war. In early December 1945, the US occupation forces in Korea initiated the publication of a weekly intelligence report on the Soviet zone, known as *Intelligence Summary North Korea*, which was distributed among US officials.[17] The inaugural edition of this report conveyed a sense of suspicion regarding the intentions of the Soviet occupation, writing, "The division of Korea at the 38th parallel of North latitude was a matter of military expediency.... Subsequent events, however, have demonstrated that the Russians have either changed their mind concerning the future of northern Korea, or had designs on that area which were not made public at the time of the surrender of the Japanese."[18]

With such commentary, the US military began collecting information on the Soviet zone from northern refugees, using transcriptions and translations of their interviews with northerners. In an issue of *Intelligence Summary*, for instance, a letter from a Korean Communist who had arrived in Seoul from Hamgyŏng Province was quoted. The letter—addressed to Pak Hŏn-yŏng, the leader of the Korean Communist Party—criticized party activities in the North, arguing, "In some parts our policy was oppressive so that many of the influential persons fled to southern Korea.... Some of our policemen interfered with ... freedom of speech and activities and devoted themselves to obtaining money. This caused public opinion to turn against us."[19] Another example is the story of a northerner named Kim Pyung Yuh. He was arrested in November 1945 in North Korea on charges of being a "national traitor" for having asked, "Why does the present administration take away all the rice from the farmers and oppress the upper class?" Kim also mentioned, "*In order to establish a nation there should be some individual enterprises.*"[20]

Based on the information from northerners, *Intelligence Summary* stated in March 1946 that "increasing Communist control of every phase of life in North Korea is reflected in all reports received. Suppression of civil liberties, freedom of assembly, speech; government by minorities; arbitrary and unreasonable methods of taxation; disposal of private property at the whim of the People's Committees, and stripping of the country is meeting with some semblance of organized resistance from church and student organizations."[21] Soon, northern refugees were subjected to a propaganda competition between the United States and the Union of Soviet Socialist Republics (USSR). According to *Intelligence Summary*, US radios and newspapers in early July 1947 gave broad coverage to the number of refugees crossing the thirty-eighth parallel from the Soviet zone. Within a week, the Russian news agency Tass called this US report "unfounded and completely lacking in truth." Simultaneously, the Soviets increased border control, which reduced the stream of refugees. US intelligence estimated that the Soviets, not completely insensitive to world opinions, knew that the "dissidents from North Korea" might eventually constitute an opposition to their "police state" regime.[22]

At this point, the United States had clearly differentiated northern refugees from the wartime conception of refugees—that is, the displaced groups of Koreans, Japanese, Chinese, and other foreign nationals—whom the US military were compelled to relocate after the war. By July 1947, the US military defined northern refugees as *dissidents from North Korea*, who could challenge the "police state" formed under the Soviet occupation. Meanwhile, South Koreans used two terms for refugees: (1) *chŏnjaemin* (war refugees) and (2) *wŏlnamja* (person who crossed the parallel to the South) or *wŏlnam tongp'o* (fellow Koreans who came to the South across the parallel). *Chŏnjaemin* corresponds to the early US use of "refugees"—a broader category for all those who had lost or left their homes due to the war. But *wŏlnamja* specifically refers to the Koreans who had crossed the parallel from the Soviet zone. The term *wŏlnamja* has no pejorative connotations, and the term *wŏlnam tongp'o* conveys the imperative for southerners to embrace the northern refugees with national solidarity. The North Korean government, meanwhile, criminalized the refugees by categorizing them in the police records as *samp'al tojuja*: "runaways to the South who have crossed the thirty-eighth parallel."[23] Northerners in the South called themselves *samp'al ttaraji*: "the leftovers [or losers] of the thirty-eighth parallel." With this self-deprecating term, they deplored or satirized their social stigmatization and the sense of deprivation they experienced in the South.

Later, in the 1970s or 1980s, northerners in the South would adopt the terms "separated families" (*isan kajok*) and "the people who lost homes" (*silhyangmin*). Specifically, they employed these new terms when they asked the Korean governments and the United Nations to help them reunite with their family members or visit their hometowns in North Korea.[24] These new terms were invented by northerners in order to clarify the humanitarian nature of their requests for family reunion.

The Occupying Forces and the Transformation of the Parallel into a Border

Wŏlnamja, the Korean term for a person who crossed the border to the South, was the neologism of the period. And, in defining the identity of northerners in South Korea, it pointed to the significance of crossing the parallel. Thomas Nail argues that a border is a "process of social division" and becomes a "social condition necessary for the emergence of certain dominant social formations, not the other way around."[25]

The transformation of the thirty-eighth parallel into a border was a process that materialized Korea's partition. It intensified new activities in the societies adjacent to the parallel and gave new identities to the people migrating from one side of the border to the other. The experiences of northern refugees varied according to when, during this border-making process, they entered the South. The annual size of the refugee population from the North also fluctuated depending on how the US and Soviet occupation forces controlled the traffic of people across the thirty-eighth parallel. When and how, then, did the occupying forces transform the parallel into a border?

In the early days of the divided occupation, the US and Soviet troops exchanged officers to patrol the thirty-eighth parallel. On September 25, 1945, Soviets sent a liaison team to US-occupied Seoul, while American officers arrived in Soviet P'yŏngyang.[26] These liaisons hardly went smoothly, and each side began installing outposts along the parallel. The US Army reported violations of the "border" by Russian soldiers, accusing them of committing theft, violence, and rape south of the parallel. Reportedly, such crimes declined after the United States installed its outposts along the parallel.[27] Meanwhile, some of the US Army's supply roads passed through Soviet-occupied areas. The Soviets reduced US access to these roads from three days a week to once a week and required a Russian armed escort.[28] As *Intelligence Summary* reported in mid-December 1945, "Border outposts are heavily manned and traffic in both directions across the border is strictly controlled. The Soviets treat the 38th parallel as a barrier between the occupation forces."[29]

Ordinary Koreans first recognized the division when railway transportation across the parallel ceased. The line between Seoul and Wŏnsan stopped on August 24, 1945—the day the Soviet Army entered P'yŏngyang.[30] On the ground, however, the exact dividing line was unclear to Koreans and occupation forces alike. When US forces discovered areas south of the parallel occupied by Russian troops or vice versa, the lack of surveying and the differences in their maps made it difficult to properly enforce the border.[31] But the need to locate the parallel on the ground became pressing as refugees entered the US zone in large numbers. In mid-November 1945, the US Army observed that the Russians were building more roadblocks along the parallel and had even erected a thirty-foot-tall observation tower. When an American officer asked about the tower and posts, the Russians answered that they were taking "additional precautions in an attempt to apprehend Koreans who were taking large sums of money across the border to southern Korea." The Russians also mentioned a security threat from Japanese soldiers, insisting that a substantial number of them had not surrendered.[32]

In principle, the occupying powers did not allow movements of people and goods between the two zones. According to a US document, troops of the Thirty-Second Infantry Regiment stationed along the thirty-eighth parallel had received orders to prevent anyone from crossing the line in either direction.[33] However, despite patrols, trade and economic activities continued between the two zones. Various trade and smuggling activities were detected by the US Army—activities that sometimes involved the government in northern Korea. On December 15, 1945, for instance, ten ships from northern Korea arrived in P'ohangdong Harbor in southeast Korea with a cargo of fish and vegetables, trying to sell these goods and buy rice. These ships, the US military found, were owned by the People's Committee of a town in northern Korea. Similarly, it received reports that merchants from the South entered the Soviet zone "by the hundreds" each day (though they estimated that this might be an exaggeration), carrying stocks of everyday necessities, such as piece goods, shoes, and leather, and making good profits on the items they sold. A Korean police chief near the border claimed the merchants bribed the Red Army guards to proceed north with their goods.[34]

In early 1946, US and Soviet forces made a new push to reach an agreement in controlling the border and refugees. Ultimately, though, they failed in softening the border and normalizing movements across it. Instead, their urgent agenda at the time was the repatriation of Japanese settlers.[35] In January, the Russians proposed that approximately one hundred thousand Japanese be categorized as displaced persons and moved from North Korea to Japan. The two sides discussed the installation of joint US and Soviet control posts along the boundary and negotiated over transactions across the parallel.

A main subject of the negotiation was the freer movement of Koreans across the parallel, listing the following items for agreement: (1) permit return of Korean civilians to their former place of residence under control of Soviet and US commands; (2) permit movement, through an application process, of Koreans between zones provided transportation capacities allow for it; (3) transfer food items for the relocated persons based on existing rations, period of time between the persons' movement and August 1, 1946, and the number of people relocated; (4) permit movement between zones by Koreans engaged in trade and commercial activities and the goods that are the object of this business; and (5) permit movement between zones by students of universities, middle schools, and elementary schools in the vicinity of the boundary and also of Koreans whose trips are necessary for pressing personal and family needs.[36] During negotiations, the USSR relaxed its control of refugee movements by withdrawing some roadblocks and outposts and reducing the number of guards at certain posts.[37] This negotiation was intended for the occupying forces to normalize transportation, trade, and movements of people across the parallel, even rearranging food rations for those relocated from one zone to the other. Notably, this negotiation occurred in early 1946—a time when Koreans, especially in urban areas, were beginning to suffer from a severe famine.[38]

Another point of the negotiations was the reconfiguration of the boundary between the US and USSR zones. The parallel artificially divided Hwanghae, Kyŏnggi, and Kangwŏn Provinces in two, creating administrative problems, as well as difficulties in people's daily lives. The Americans proposed returning all of Hwanghae Province to the Soviet zone, bringing all of Kyŏnggi Province into the US zone, and readjusting the border in Kangwŏn Province to include the entirety of Hwach'ŏn and Hongch'ŏn Prefectures in the US zone. The Russians agreed to consider this adjustment and study the details, and the Americans expected that the Russians would accept it.[39]

But the negotiation in early 1946 resulted neither in the exchange of Hwanghae and Kyŏnggi between the two zones nor in granting freer movements across the parallel. On the contrary, by May 1946, the two forces began to demarcate the border on the ground and made it compulsory for local people to observe that new border. The US military unit in P'och'ŏn reported, "American and Russian Officers met and established the exact position of the 38th degree line on 8 May 1946. They marked the location with poles. In Yong Moon Ri (Yangmun-ri), the changing of the line to its present location placed 112 houses in Russian occupied territory that were formerly classified as in the American zone."[40] In early August 1947, the US military reported that the Soviets and the North Korean guards had increased the number of constabulary posts and troops and tightened the checking of passes and transient personnel between the thirty-eighth and thirty-ninth parallels.[41] The US Seventh Division reported a total of 411 North Korean constabulary units on outpost duty along the thirty-eighth parallel as of August 1, 1947.[42]

The enforcement of the border and the relocation of an area from one zone to the other might look easy on paper, but it violently disrupted the lives of local residents. This is attested by events that occurred in Changdan Prefecture in Kyŏnggi Province. At that time, the thirty-eighth parallel divided Changdan in half, with five of its counties in the North and five in the South.[43] The Soviet Army entered the prefecture but did not strictly enforce the border until mid-1946. Chinsŏ Elementary School was located five hundred meters south of the parallel, but the boundary between the occupation zones was unclear to the residents. Students and teachers on both sides commuted to the school without restrictions. Residents would see soldiers and guards from both sides mingling on the school grounds, talking to each other or sharing food.

Then, in July 1946, on the school's graduation day, the Russians changed the situation, claiming that the school lied within the Soviet zone. For that day's graduation ceremony, all the parents, students, and teachers from the northern and southern sides came to the school. When the ceremony was over, Soviet soldiers arrived and arrested the adult participants from the South. They released the school's director of academic affairs four days later and the principal, almost at death's door, after a week. The school was then closed.[44]

After this, Soviet soldiers mobilized Korean farmers to dig military trenches in Changdan along the thirty-eighth parallel. They frequented the southern zone and took watches, fountain pens, and other useful things from residents. Amid such continuous conflicts, the southern police killed two Soviet soldiers in March 1947.[45] The two soldiers had robbed some Korean peasants of grain rations received from the US military government by forcing the peasants to deliver the grain to the Soviet zone.[46] When this was reported, the South Korean police chased the Soviet soldiers and killed them in the ensuing gunfight near the border. After their deaths, several thousand North Korean guards and Soviet soldiers invaded Changdan to capture the South Korean policemen. The US Army dispatched American soldiers to the district. Finally, the two occupying forces held a court trial to judge the case, and the verdict was declared in favor of the South Korean policemen. Witnesses affirmed that the shooting occurred in the southern zone, meaning that the Russians had crossed the border. The US Army installed a station in Chinsŏ Elementary School, and local residents moved farther to the South.[47] Thereafter, the routes across the thirty-eighth parallel in Changdan were entirely shut down.

The Changdan case demonstrates how the occupying powers' relative leniency toward traffic across the parallel shifted to a hardening of the border in mid-1946, which became even stricter after spring 1947. On April 18, 1947, the Ministry of Police Affairs in South Korea announced the order given by John Hodge, the commander of the US forces in Korea, that the military government arrest anyone who crossed the thirty-eighth parallel to the South and place them in a quarantine camp (these camps will be discussed later in this chapter).[48] Then, in November 1947, the South Korean interim government reported that the Soviet Army and North Korean administration had prohibited all Koreans in the North from crossing the parallel to enter the South. Monitoring the militarization of the border and the strength of the Soviet and North Korean military, the US intelligence reported between April 1947 and May 1948 that North Korea's armed forces rapidly grew from a "hastily organized constabulary" to a well-trained force, much better equipped than its counterpart in South Korea.[49]

The Number of Northern Refugees and Their Routes to the South

The US military created charts of the number of people crossing the thirty-eighth parallel to South Korea by weeks. The highest volume entered between March to May. In April 1946, approximately 50,540 entered the South; in April 1947, the volume was 40,164.[50] In 1948, the number declined to 20,000 to 30,000 refugees a month, but by the autumn of 1948, the Korean newspapers reported that the total number of *wŏlnamja* had reached 1.4 million.⁵¹ Due to the lack of an accurate census, it is difficult to determine the exact number of northerners who entered South Korea before the Korean War.

The number of northern refugees during this period has been a political issue in South Korea. The chief of the South Korean police, Cho Pyŏng-ok, and the Chosŏn Democratic Party founded in northern Korea insisted in 1948 that a total of 4.5 million northerners had come south. This exaggerated number was proposed in the interest of demanding special-election districts to represent northern provinces in the general election of South Korea.⁵² Sociologist Kang Chŏng-gu insists that a total of 850,000 crossed from 1945 to 1953. Among them, he speculates, only 350,000 had been born in the northern provinces, and the rest were southerners who had migrated to the North during the colonial period and subsequently returned to their homes.⁵³ In comparison, the demographer Kwŏn T'ae-hwan suggests that 740,000 northerners crossed between 1945 and 1949.⁵⁴ Kwŏn used the refugee-registration statistics compiled by the Ministry of Foreign Affairs of the South Korean government and adjusted the figures using additional data, including birth rates and select census records.

According to my research, the base number suggested by Kwŏn must derive from the US Army records, which added up the daily number of refugees who arrived at US checkpoints near the thirty-eighth parallel. This total of those originating from North Korea was close to 655,678 through the end of 1948.⁵⁵ As the US Army acknowledged, though, that many refugees crossed the parallel by "stealth" without passing the US checkpoints. In fact, of the dozen refugee survivors whom I interviewed, only one said that he had passed through US inspection.⁵⁶ Newspapers of the time stated that the total number of Korean refugees in the South was more than 2.12 million in September 1948, of whom 1.4 million were northern refugees (*wŏlnamja*). This figure exceeds the total recorded at the US checkpoints, and these newspaper articles identified the source of their data as the South Korean interim government.⁵⁷ Finally, in 1961, after the Korean War, the South Korean government investigated the number of North Korean refugees and counted 2,451,000, although the actual total was higher, because this figure excluded about 500,000 refugees from north of the parallel in Kyŏnggi and Kangwŏn Provinces.⁵⁸ Other surveys say that 40.46 percent of northern refugees entered South Korea between 1945 and 1949, while 55.34 percent came south during the Korean War (1950–1953).⁵⁹ Kim Kûi-ok argues that according to the 1955 census, the ratio was 38.5 to 61.5.⁶⁰

If we apply this 38.5 percent to 2,951,000 (2,451,000 plus 500,000 from Kyŏnggi and Kangwŏn), the refugee population from North Korea between 1945 and 1949 would be at least 1.1 million, if not over 1.4 million.[61]

The North Korean refugee organization Ibuk Odominhoe (Association of the People from Five Northern Provinces) summarized annual trends of refugee migration in its official history (and, though it does not indicate its sources, it likely used interviews with refugee survivors). According to that history, in 1946, many refugees traveling by land used the railroads. They descended from trains at the stations near the thirty-eighth parallel and then crossed the border itself on foot. By 1947, when North Korea increased searches of trains, many refugees got off at stations farther from the parallel and took longer pathways on foot to the South. Between the fall of 1948 and the summer of 1950, after the inauguration of the Democratic People's Republic of Korea (DPRK), North Korea fiercely guarded the border. This made it difficult for refugees to cross the parallel by land.[62] The arrival of northern refugees continued in 1948 but decreased toward year's end. Civilian migration from the North dropped in 1949 as military conflicts along the parallel halted them. Instead, the North and South Korean governments advertised the defection of soldiers from the other side.[63] Still, that the South Korean government reported that 6,390 northerners (mostly from Hwanghae or P'yŏngan Provinces)[64] arrived at the Ongjin Relief Camp between December 1948 and October 1949 shows that even then the movement of civilian refugees had not entirely stopped.

To gain a full picture of refugee movements, it is important to understand how the Soviet occupation administered the movements of displaced persons, especially Koreans from Manchuria. According to the US military, the Soviet occupation installed a Bureau of Emigrant Assistance in the Department of Agriculture and Forestry to administer migration from Manchuria, with offices in all the major cities on the Korean-Manchurian frontier. Its officers questioned migrants and segregated them into three categories. The first category, those with relatives in Korea, either North or South, required no government assistance. The second category, skilled workers or technicians, were employed in the government-owned factories. Finally, landless peasants were placed in transient camps until land was made available for them. The Bureau of Emigrant Assistance planned to offer aid to all these refugees from Manchuria in the form of food, clothing, money, etc. until they could settle themselves in North Korea. Manchurian peasants received land appropriated from landlords who owned more than five *chŏngbo* (one *chŏngbo* equals 2.451 acres). In spite of such promises, US intelligence believed that the Soviets were not committed to accommodating Manchurian immigrants in North Korea.[65]

According to US interviews of northern refugees, many of them crossed the parallel by stealth, usually at night, and avoided Russian outposts. Others passed the Russian outposts with Russian knowledge. Some Japanese and Korean refugees carried passes for travel within northern Korea.[66] These passes did not explicitly permit travel from the Soviet zone to South Korea, but the US Army guessed that the Russians were tacitly construing them as permission to cross the border or were "turning their backs on this traffic."[67] This assumption is confirmed by an article published by a refugee in June 1946 in *Ibuk T'ongsin*—the publication whose history I will look at more closely near the end of this chapter—about his "escape" from the North. Its author, Kim T'aenam, originally returned from Manchuria to his home in northern Korea. But with unwanted attention from the security office in his hometown, Kim decided to leave for Seoul and then asked a friend in the security office for a travel pass so that he could bring back the remainder of his belongings from Manchuria. With this pass, Kim was able to take trains to Haeju, Hwanghae Province. In Haeju, the security guards inspected all train passengers, but Kim was able to avoid detention by claiming his status as a repatriate from Manchuria. He then crossed the parallel on foot.[68]

Motivations and Social Characteristics of Refugees: The Case of Anju, North P'yŏngan

Refugee migration to the South was fueled by dissatisfaction with the political conditions in North Korea and by the economic chaos and food shortages there. The people in the first category had various individual motives: they included landlords who had lost their properties during North Korea's land reform; people who had dubious records during the colonial period; Christians; Nationalists, such as members of the Chosŏn Democratic Party; and people who suffered from police surveillance, the conduct of Soviet soldiers, or oppression against non-Communists. The people in the second category—those who were affected by hunger and economic concerns—also made up a considerable part of northern refugees. I want to note, though, that it is difficult to separate economic factors from political motivations because economic issues were often the result of policies made by the North Korean regime. In this section, I will discuss the complex motivations and social composition of northern refugees using various sources, including North Korean records captured by the US Army during the Korean War.

In 1992, a South Korean research center surveyed 1,030 refugee survivors, asking when they had moved to the South and what had motivated this choice. This survey applied to all northerners who crossed the parallel before and after the Korean War. The percentage of respondents that had moved to the South after the liberation but before the outbreak of the Korean War was 40.46. The majority of the interviewees (50.83 percent) answered that they had disliked the rule of the North Korean government. The next largest group (16.09 percent) said that they had escaped the North after being involved in anti-Communist protests. The third-largest group (15.7 percent) had been designated "reactionaries" by the Communist Party and were thereafter expelled from their homes. According to the survey, around 80 percent of the survivors made the active choice to leave the Communist regime. Other answers included that they stayed in the South for study, business, or other reasons but could not return home due to the division (4.08 percent); that they left home to avoid the war (3.44 percent); that, as children, they had followed the adults (3.19 percent); that after being conscripted into the People's Army (DPRK), they had escaped it or defected to the South (1.02 percent); and that they had been released as anti-Communist prisoners of war (1.91 percent). A small fraction of the participants (0.76 percent) answered that they had been former officials of the colonial government and had left the North to avoid being purged as pro-Japanese collaborators.[69]

However, this 1992 survey showcases the views of the survivors several decades after their flight rather than capturing their original mindsets when leaving the North. Multiple contemporary sources mention the importance of economic factors in leaving the North. *Ibuk T'ongsin* reported food shortages in the Soviet zone, especially in its August to September 1947 issue.[70] Several *Ibuk T'ongsin* articles reported severe cases and rumors of deaths and crimes because of lack of food.[71] Such *Ibuk T'ongsin* reports were perhaps exaggerated, but they were not groundless. A secret Soviet document dated January 11, 1946, written by a Lieutenant Colonel Fedorove to his commander, criticized the Soviet collection of grain because of an emerging famine in North Korea. According to Fedorove, the planned Soviet purchase of grain in Haksan, North P'yŏngan Province, was 133,000 bags, while the total gross harvest of rice was 142,000 bags. With only 9,000 bags left over, the district was facing famine.[72] The US military also reported Korean resentment toward the Red Army's food-procurement practices.[73]

North Korea's currency reform in December 1947 triggered another wave of refugees in 1948. Through Ordinance 30, the North Korean People's Committee authorized the Central Bank of North Korea to issue its own banknotes. The ordinance nullified all Bank of Chosŏn notes issued prior to August 15, 1945, as well as the military currency issued by the Soviet forces in Korea. The old notes could be exchanged only during the week of December 6–12, 1947. The exchange rate between the old and new notes was one-to-one; however, the amount that people were allowed to exchange and the conditions under which they could do so differed depending on circumstances related to property ownership, organizations, and social classes. For example, the currency law privileged state enterprises, consumer cooperatives, political parties, and social organizations over private companies, small businesses, and religious organizations. For the families outside the entities and groups designated by law, householders were allowed to exchange at most 500 won, and all members of families over eighteen years of age could exchange up to 200 won.[74] US intelligence estimated that this currency reform would decimate the savings of economic actors who had been surviving outside the North Korean regime. Nevertheless, the US military said the law's main objective was to combat inflation.[75]

By contrast, *Ibuk T'ongsin* suspected that the goal of the currency law was to let the USSR avoid paying the tremendous number of military notes that had been issued by the Red Army.[76] At the beginning of the occupation, the Soviets had paid for their expenses with rubles, but they soon changed the means of payment to military notes. The volume of military notes increased rapidly, and the ratio of these notes to the total currency circulating in North Korea reached 92.3 percent in September 1947.[77] The Red Army's purchasing power had brought a commercial boom to North Korea, according to *Ibuk T'ongsin*. Merchants trading with Russians or Chinese made money and could buy food in the market, even though they were discriminated against in the government's ration system. But the new currency law made these merchants' savings useless. Because the law undermined commerce and businesses, many northerners in these sectors wanted to go to the South.[78]

Interviews with refugee survivors and other sources suggest that the backgrounds of northern refugees were diverse, ranging from landlords to peasants, Christians to members of the South Korean Workers' Party. To identify the social characteristics of northern refugees, I analyzed a document from Anju County, North P'yŏngan Province, seized by the US Army during the Korean War.[79] The title of the document is *Ilban Pumun T'ujaeng Taesangja Myŏngbu* (hereafter, *Myŏngbu*), meaning the "list of target people to be struggled against in the general sector." *Myŏngbu* was compiled between January and June 1950 by the Anju branch of the Political Security Bureau (Chŏngch'i Powibu), the powerful surveillance agency of North Korea. I suspect that the Security Bureau compiled this list in order to monitor people whom they considered threats to the regime.

The bureau classified individuals according to several political categories, including "suspicious people who newly moved to the region" (*yo ijuja*), "landlords who lost lands during the land reform" (*t'oji molsu chiju*), "malicious petite bourgeoisie and delinquent youth" (*akchil sosimin pullyang ch'ŏngnyŏn*), "those who voted no in the elections" (*pandae t'up'yoja*), "families and relatives of runaways to south of the thirty-eighth parallel" (*samp'al inam tojuja kajok ch'inch'ŏk*), and more. Then, the Political Security Bureau assigned agents to monitor the individuals on the list. For example, *Myŏngbu* contains several reports on the families and relatives of runaways to the South in various villages of Anju. Forty-nine names appear under this category. The bureau investigated each family member's name, gender, social class status, occupations before and after Korea's liberation on August 15, 1945, membership in political parties, and religious affiliations. It also reported the names of the runaways and their relationship to the family members on the list. The education levels of family members of runaways appear in two reports within *Myŏngbu* but not in others. The bureau also investigated people who came from the South. Two names appear under this category: one was a thirty-eight-year-old man (a merchant) who returned to his hometown in Anju, and the other was a thirty-nine-year-old man (an office worker) with an elementary school education. The bureau added a note to the latter man's file that he had been a member of the Northwestern Youth Association in South Korea. The records in *Myŏngbu* primarily contain information on the refugees' close family members who remained in the North. They were fathers, sons, brothers, cousins, uncles, or brothers-in-law of the refugees to the South.

Myŏngbu is far from offering a complete picture of refugees in Anju. Except for a few cases, most names of runaways and their family members were men: it seems that the Political Security Bureau listed the names of women only when they did not find close male family members of the runaways. Still, *Myŏngbu* provides a critical snapshot of the backgrounds of northern refugees before the Korean War. According to *Myŏngbu*, more than 20 percent of the families of runaways were affiliated with the South Korean Workers' Party, the ruling party of North Korea. Out of forty-nine individuals in the category, ten were members of the South Korean Workers' Party, eleven were members of the Chosŏn Democratic Party (the Nationalist party founded in the North), and two were affiliated with the Friends of the Youth Party (the party of the Ch'ŏndogyo religion). The rest had no party membership. Christianity was a significant factor. Sixteen percent of the families were Christians. Beyond the Christians and two Ch'ŏndogyo believers, the refugee families had no religious affiliations. Most likely the bureau did not count believers in Buddhism or Confucianism.

Myŏngbu identifies the class status of a person in the list by reporting both his or her class origins (*ch'ulsin*) and social class (*sŏngbun*). A person's occupations before and after the liberation is also reported. One report on *samp'al inam tojuja* in *Myŏngbu* does not include the section on class origins and social class and records only occupations (this omission is reflected in table 3.1).

In terms of class origins, we see that the majority of these refugee families were from the middle class, neither landlords nor peasants: middle-sized farmers (48 percent), merchants (21 percent), and wealthy farmers (15 percent). Landlords (9 percent) and poor farmers (6 percent) were a minority. As far as the government's designation of a person's social class at the time, the major groups the refugee families belonged to were merchants (36 percent), middle-sized farmers (27 percent), and office workers (15 percent). These numbers challenge the mythology presented by the North Korean government or by revisionist interpretations of Korean history, which have portrayed northern refugees as a minority group composed primar-

Table 3.1. Class composition of northern refugees to the South from Anju County, Northern P'yŏngan Province.

	Class origins	Social class	Occupation after liberation
Poor farmers	2	3	6
Middle farmers	16	8	2
Wealthy farmers	5	2	1
Landlords	3	1	1
Business	0	2	7
Merchants (petite bourgeoisie)	7	12	17
Office workers and students	0	5	11
Workers	0	0	2
Unemployed	—	—	2
Total	33	33	49

Source: Anju Chŏngch'i Powibu, *Ilban pumun t'ujaeng taesangja myŏngbu*, comp. North Korean Political Security Bureau (January–June 1950), RG 242, container 873, SA2010, box 3, item 105, National Archives and Records Administration, College Park, MD.

ily of families from the landlord class or reactionaries expelled during the North Korean Revolution.

Comparing the class origins and social class figures, we can also observe social changes among the families of refugees in North Korea. The families in agriculture (farmers and landlords) declined by 46 percent. Those in commerce and business increased by 100 percent. The refugee families in agriculture declined in status as well, with the number of wealthy farmers and landlords declining from eight to three. These numbers indicate that refugee families in the agrarian sector experienced downward mobility. While some landlords or wealthy farmers potentially did migrate to South Korea, many of them instead made lateral transitions to the commercial sector within North Korea. Turning to people's occupations after the liberation, 57 percent of the refugee families were in commercial or urban sectors; 34.5 percent were merchants, 22 percent were office workers, and 14 percent were in business (entrepreneurs). Twenty percent of the refugee families belonged to the categories of poor farmers, workers, and the unemployed. These groups were privileged in North Korea's new class system; even so, a portion of them still opted to leave for the South.

Considering the small sample of refugee families in *Myŏngbu*, it should be compared with other sources to gain a better understanding of the social composition of northern refugees. A survey conducted by the US military in 1947 provides insights into the backgrounds of northerners who entered the South between May and December 1947. According to the survey, the total number of northern refugees recorded during the period was 103,628,[80] 13.46 percent (13,948) of them came from agriculture, while 9.98 percent (10,348) were in commerce. Surprisingly, 7.78 percent (8,065) were factory workers, and 8.99 percent (9,320) were laborers in mining. The cumulative figure for these workers (17,385) exceeds the percentage of northerners from agriculture (16.77 percent). In the category of office workers, constituting 9.52 percent (9,871) of the total, I include teachers (1,954), students (5,348), clerks (1,557), and government officials (1,012). Professionals and businesspeople were grouped together since the US survey recorded specific numbers within certain sectors but still differentiated them from workers. This category comprised 2.2 percent (2,310) of the northern refugees, with representation from various fields, such as medicine (309), fishery (670), mining (639), printing (508), forestry (6), ironwork (158), inn managers (2), and preachers (18).[81]

The category of skilled workers combined carpenters (1,439), public workers (2,009), drivers (415), tailors (274), barbers (678), and cameramen (17). These skilled workers accounted for 4.66 percent of the total (4,832), and it is possible that some of them ran small businesses, such as barbershops or photo studios. The US survey does not offer specific details regarding public-work positions, but they were differentiated from office clerks and likely included engineers, plumbers, and other technicians. The survey categorizes the remaining portion as having miscellaneous jobs (710) or being unemployed (44,224).The high number of unemployed people (42.68 percent) can be attributed to the inclusion of many women and children in the refugee population.[82] If the unemployed were considered a distinct class, their migration to the South would raise important questions about the nature of the North Korean Revolution.

Setting these questions aside for now, I recalibrate the distribution of the occupation groups, subtracting the unemployed figure from the total. After this adjustment, the new sum is 59,404, with 23.47 percent involved in agriculture, 17.4 percent in commerce, 29.27 percent as factory workers and miners, and 16.6 percent as office workers. Professionals, businesspeople, and skilled workers together comprised 12 percent; in this group, some individuals likely owned businesses, large or small. Given that middle-class or wealthy farmers probably made up more than 50 percent of the northerners from the agricultural sector,[83] we can argue that, in this recalibrated breakdown, the majority of the northern refugees belonged to middle and propertied classes, if not capitalist, and likely favored property ownership. However, this suggestion is almost meaningless because the unemployed, factory workers, and miners comprised approximately 60 percent of the original survey numbers.

In summary, the refugee families from Anju belonged to the midsized propertied class and were engaged in commercial and business sectors during the ongoing revolution in North Korea. However, the 1947 US survey suggests a broader and more diverse social background of northern refugees. The largest class group among them consisted of workers and the unemployed. When we combine together the numbers from commerce, office workers, professionals, businesses, and skilled workers, over 46 percent of them were from commercial and urban sectors. The significant number of factory workers, miners, and the unemployed suggests that laborers also faced hardship in North Korea and chose to move to the South when they suffered from famine or other troubles.

Refugee Experiences of Crossing the Parallel and the US Quarantine Centers

Many refugees experienced violence and other hardships before, during, and after crossing the parallel. Kang In-suk, a professor of literature, wrote a memoir of her long journey from her home in Kapsan, Hamgyŏng Province, to Seoul. In November 1945, when she was thirteen, she and her family left for Seoul with the early groups of refugees. They traveled by train—not inside but on top. At that time, North Korea ran only cargo trains due to the energy shortage; as such, the space for passengers was on the roof, where they hung on to some type of wooden holders. To protect the children, Kang's mom wrapped all the family in a blanket and tied them together. Kang remembers the cold weather in early winter, the danger of sleeping together on the fast-running train, and the pains of hunger and of holding her pee. The final station was Yŏnch'ŏn, north of the thirty-eighth parallel. There, she met a large crowd of refugees that spread into the nearby fields and villages, waiting to cross the bridge over the Hant'an River and enter the South. Soviet soldiers guarded the bridge's northern side, and Americans were on the other end. At the time, only repatriates from Manchuria could pass. And so Kang's father spoke with some Manchurian repatriates in the crowd, joined them, and bribed the Russian soldiers to let them cross the bridge at the front of the group. The Hant'an railway bridge was not for pedestrians but had a narrow space for one person to cross at a time. Kang recalls the fear of that night: crawling on the high bridge alone, watching the dark river rumbling beneath her, and hearing loud gunshots from the Russian soldiers behind her.[84]

Kang's family was lucky because the border patrol was flexible in 1945. Refugees who traveled later had more trouble. According to *Ibuk T'ongsin*, the shortest path in the northwestern region to the thirty-eighth parallel was via Sinmak and Kŭmgyo in Hwanghae Province. When passengers arrived in Sinmak Station, the security guards lined them up and arrested them if they were suspicious of their destinations. During the inspection process, the guards "plundered" the possessions of the people. Hearing of this, many refugees avoided this route.[85]

In February 1946, a northerner called Kim T'aenam traveled from Haeju to the South and faced multiple police inspections, as he later wrote in an article in *Ibuk T'ongsin*. He had obtained a travel pass to Manchuria, which allowed him to move freely within North Korea. After passing a security check at the final station on his way south, he joined a group of people walking to the South. On the road, five armed guards stopped Kim's group and checked whether anyone in the group had guns or money. One refugee was carrying 1,000 yen in cash—his entire fortune after working for decades in Manchuria. The guards seized all the money except for 300 yen—the limit the government allowed each refugee to carry. The Manchurian man wept in despair. Kim's group moved on, but soon they were chased by Soviet soldiers and Korean guards. Hearing gunshots, the refugees started running in fear. About ten women in the group were easily caught by the soldiers. Husbands returned for their wives but were tied up. The Russian soldiers made the Korean guards watch over the arrested men and raped the women. Mr. Kim finished the story in resentment asking, "Did we miss our home country so much just to see this happen?"[86]

The editor of *Ibuk T'ongsin* organized a campaign against plunder at the border. He asked readers to send in reports if their cash or belongings had been confiscated or stolen while crossing the thirty-eighth parallel, indicating the date, the location, and the amount of money or valuables that had been seized.[87] *Ibuk T'ongsin* also acted as an information center for the families victimized by border violence.[88] It is difficult to verify whether episodes like this published in *Ibuk T'ongsin* actually occurred. But other sources corroborated similar Russian violence toward women and civilians in North Korea. Several interviews with refugees confirm that many neighborhoods in P'yŏngyang developed an alarm system to protect their people. Kang In-dŏk, the former minister of unification under the Kim Dae-jung government (1998–2003), witnessed such a system in P'yŏngyang. Kang's second brother had a traditional house (*hanok*) in the city. He and his neighbors connected their houses with a rope, hanging empty cans on it. When Russians entered the area, the neighbors pulled the rope and alerted the entire neighborhood.[89]

Because of the heightened border surveillance, brokering guides for refugees to the South became a booming trade in the North. Dr. Ch'oe Ŭn-bŏm, whom I interviewed, remembers how his family hired a secret guide when they crossed the parallel in December 1948. Ch'oe was born in 1934; his father was a landlord who taught Confucian classics in a village school (*sŏdang*) in Myŏngch'ŏn, North Hamgyŏng Province. The family lost their land in the spring of 1946 during the land reform. That summer, Ch'oe's grandmother passed away. After her funeral, the family moved to Kilchu and then settled in Sŏngjin, where a relative (Ch'oe Sŭngjong) was the head of the People's Committee. After moving to Sŏngjin, the family lived hand to mouth. Ch'oe's mother carried fruits in baskets to sell downtown. Ch'oe's eldest brother, who faced discrimination given the family's landlord background, packed dried squids and traveled around to sell them. One day, the brother left for P'yŏngyang to sell squids and never returned. The family discovered later that he had left for the South with his wife and child. Thereafter, the parents decided to join their eldest son.

Ch'oe's family hired a guide and took the route from Sŏngjin to Wŏnsan, then to Yŏnch'ŏn in Hwanghae Province. The guide gathered a group, about ten people, in Wŏnsan. It took four to five days to get from Sŏngjin to Yŏnch'ŏn. The group left the train at a station before Yŏnch'ŏn, where security inspection was intense. They walked westward for two hours and arrived at a farmhouse. At midnight, the guide woke up the group to cross the border. Everyone carried their packs and quietly followed the road under the dim moonlight. They arrived at the river's narrowest point and crossed it. Ch'oe's sister-in-law carried her baby on her back while holding a Singer sewing machine on her head, the water up to her waistline. Luckily the baby stayed asleep. When the group passed the river and then a hill, the guide said, "We are in the South." They were led to a farmhouse and spent the night there.

The next day, Ch'oe's group was taken by the farmhouse owner to a US Army inspection center. The US Army dusted Ch'oe's group with DDT and transferred them to a government office near Munsan, where their backgrounds were checked and their names were registered. The government gave the group a ride, free of charge, by truck from Munsan to Seoul.[90]

By early November 1945, the US occupation forces in Korea had developed the standard procedures for processing repatriation and refugees. The Displaced Persons Office of the US miliary government coordinated the multiple agencies involved in administering repatriation. Local units of the US military government were responsible for controlling the movements of refugees within their jurisdictions. The Transportation Bureau of the military government was responsible for routing and supplying trains for transportation. Local Korean government agencies assisted in facilitating the movements of refugees and providing protection to them. The Health and Welfare Section of the US military government supplied medical provisions. For controlling the movements of refugees by sea, the US occupation forces relied on navy port control, navy patrol, and other port authorities.[91] However, it became apparent that establishing such standard procedures was not as straightforward as originally planned and took time in local areas.

There were five stations for refugees operated by US occupation forces near the thirty-eighth parallel, overseen by the local US Army bases. Weekly reports from US Army bases reveal the daily administration of the US military of receiving refugees across the parallel. The US military at the time worried about the spread of epidemics, potentially through refugees crossing the parallel, and they prioritized vaccinating both refugees and local residents. The troops in Hongch'ŏn received "dusters, DDT, and typhus vaccine to dust and inoculate refugees and the local area."[92]

It was in this context that the US military opened a "Welfare Quarantine Camp" for refugees in Ch'unch'ŏn, which began operating in early May 1946. They built an oven and began serving hot meals to refugees on April 5. The first group of refugees in the camp, composed of fourteen Koreans and nine Japanese, stayed for ten days of quarantine before being released.[93] The US military investigated the number of refugees entering the region and their destinations after quarantine. For the final week of June 1946 in Hongch'ŏn, for example, a total of thirty-three Korean refugee households (139 people) entered the South. Among them, thirteen households (57 people) moved to Seoul and the rest wanted to stay in nearby counties.[94]

The reports from the US military in Kyŏnggi Province reveal the coordination in refugee administration between different US military units and select Korean agencies. In Kap'yŏng, P'och'ŏn, and Yangju Districts, the Korean police assisted US troops to apprehend all refugees crossing the thirty-eighth parallel so that they could be placed in a refugee camp for quarantine.[95] The US inspection here involved cruelty toward refugees.

In P'och'ŏn, the refugee-DDT-dusting stations were placed near the P'och'ŏn Police Station and operated by the K Company, Thirty-Second Infantry of the US Army. A US military report from P'och'ŏn noted that "the US soldiers were occasionally forcing women to take off their clothing and stand absolutely nude while the soldiers dusted them with DDT." Inspector Ahn of the P'och'ŏn Police Station complained about this action to a sergeant identified only as Ellison, who oversaw the troops. Ellison replied, "You keep your nose out of my business." The US military also prohibited refugees from keeping cash beyond a permitted amount. The same report noted that P'och'ŏn District "received 60,313 Japanese yen and 24,080 Korean yen from 'K' Company, 32nd Infantry Regiment. This money was confiscated at the 38 degree line in Pochon District."[96]

Two months after the report on the abuse of refugee women, in July 1946, Charles A. Anderson, military governor of Kyŏnggi Province, G. A. Berry, commanding officer of the Sixty-Eighth Military Government, and an individual identified only as Staff Sergeant Krammin, military governor of the districts in Yangju and P'och'ŏn, visited the district, conducting an inspection trip to the refugee camp at Ŭijŏngbu. In the camp, Koreans and Japanese were separated by a fence and safeguarded by tactical troops and civilian police.[97]

Tonga Ilbo published many articles on refugee administration in the South. There were sixteen inspection posts (*kŏmyŏkso*) along the parallel to process refugees entering the South.[98] In April 1947, the Ministry of Health and Welfare of the Korean interim government opened government relief and inspection centers in five areas near the parallel. These centers had the capacity to accommodate 2,750 people a day: 500 people in Ch'ŏngdan, 750 in T'osŏng, 1,000 in Tongduch'ŏn, 250 in Ch'unch'ŏn, and 250 in Chumunjin. These centers provided refugees with food, urgent medical treatment, lodging, free transportation, and maps to their next destinations. The government also ran temporary relief and inspection centers in Kangwŏn and Kyŏnggi Provinces.[99] Because these centers housed far more refugees than they had the capacity for, the task of supplying food to them was a major issue.[100] In May 1947, the South Korean government sent the standing officers of the Foreign Ministry to several entry points, such as Chumunjin, Ŭijŏngbu, and Kaesŏng, to issue refugee identification cards (*ijuminchŭng*) and free transportation cards (*muim sŭngch'achŭng*).[101]

Once the refugees passed the initial relief centers near the parallel, they had to find stable shelter within South Korea. Seoul was where many refugees aimed to settle, and the city's Welfare Bureau (Husaengguk) was hard pressed to offer them relief. *Tonga Ilbo* reported that over 3,700 people were sheltered on May 15, 1947, in Changch'ungdan Relief Center in Seoul. Due to the fair weather, the city offered the refugees tents as temporary shelter. But the city officials screamed that they could not accept more people without serious support measures.[102] Elsewhere, the Ministry of Health and Welfare decided to build relief centers run directly by the provincial governments (*chigyŏng suyongso*) in Ch'ŏngju, Ch'ungju, Taejŏn, Chinju, Taegu, Yŏngju, Ŭisŏng, Masan, Kwangju, Chŏnju, Ch'unch'ŏn, Wŏnju, Kich'ŏn, and Osan.[103]

This daily entry of several thousand refugees strained the US military government's food distribution in South Korea. By May 1947, the government had to change the daily ration of grain. First, the Bureau of Food Administration (Singnyang Haengjŏngch'ŏ) slightly changed the daily grain ration from one *hop*, five *chak* (270 mg) of rice and one *hop* (180 mg) of multigrain blend (total 450 mg) to one *hop*, four *chak* (252 mg) of rice and one *hop*, one *chak* (198 mg) of multigrain. This means that one *chak* of rice (18 mg equals one-tenth of one *hop*) was substituted with one *chak* of multigrain.[104] When the number of northerners in the South increased from approximately 450,000 at the end of April 1947 to one million by October 1947, the government had to reduce the grain distribution again: from three *chak* (54 mg) per person in June to, at this point, just one *hop* of rice (180 mg) and one *hop*, two *chak* (216 mg) of multigrain (total 396 mg).[105]

This reduction of the grain ration in the middle of a food shortage caused tension between southerners and northerners. In one neighborhood of Seoul, some people cursed northerners, blaming them for the reduced food ration and causing a big fight between southerners and northerners. *Ibuk T'ongsin*'s editor reported this fight, pleading, "Our fellow southerners, please do not despise and mistreat our northern compatriots [*ibuk tongp'o*], who were [already] in misery. They were harshly harassed and abused in the North before they came down to the South, with the appearance of beggars after losing all but their naked bodies."[106]

The Growth of Northerners' Organizations and Activism

In the shockwave that emerged from the sudden division of the new border, among the first people to be hit were students from the northern provinces that had been studying in the South at the time of the liberation. Abruptly unable to receive money from home for tuition and lodging, they struggled with hunger and the danger of dropping out.[107] The Friendly Society of Northern Students (Sŏbuk Haksaeng Ch'inhwahoe), organized in December 1945, launched activities, such as a publishing business and musical concerts, to raise funds for students from the northern provinces. During that winter's vacation, they also decided to send fellow students to northern areas and teach people about "true democracy."[108] Northerner youth groups expanded their membership bases by volunteering to support northern refugees and holding cultural events to console them.[109] The Northern Student Self-Help Organization (Sŏbuk Haksaeng Wŏnhohoe) promoted sponsorships from various social agencies to assist refugee students in the South.[110]

And, as soon as they arrived in the South, northern refugees also organized themselves. A renowned refugee pastor of Korean Protestantism, Han Kyŏngjik, founded the Yŏngnak Presbyterian Church and expanded the size of its congregation. Pastor Han compared the escape of northerners from the Soviet zone to the biblical exodus of the Israelites and called his congregation a church of northern refugees. Staying together in churches or relief centers may have helped expand refugees' networks. They first looked for people from their hometowns, and such gatherings turned into formal associations of northerners according to their provincial, prefectural, or county origins. Famous leaders originally from Hwanghae Province announced the creation of the Hwanghae Association (Hwanghaehoe). Approximately eight hundred people of Hwanghae origin joined its opening ceremony in June 1946. Following this event, northerners in the South organized city- or prefectural-level associations based on their hometowns in the North: Haeju, Anak, Sŏhŭng, Sunch'ŏn, and Maengsan in 1946; Songnim, Kimch'ŏn, Sŏnch'ŏn, P'yŏngsan, Chaeryŏng, Yangdŏk, and Sŏngch'ŏn in 1947; Sariwŏn, Pongsan, Pyŏksŏng, Sin'gye, Changyŏn, Songhwa, Sinch'ŏn, and Suan in 1948; Ŭnyul and P'yŏngyang in 1949; and more.[111]

Further study is required to know how the leaders of northerner organizations interacted with ordinary refugees. On the one hand, these northern leaders claimed to represent the interests of *all* northerners in the South. For instance, the leaders of the Northern Academic Society (Sŏbuk Hakhoe) negotiated with the government to alleviate the difficulties that children faced in entering schools in the South without access to documents proving their prior education. The association's committee gave endorsements to help northern students transfer schools.[112] On the other hand, the organizations of northerner youth were quickly politicized. This politicization was triggered by the anti-Communist student protests in Sinŭiju and Hamhŭng in North Korea and the massacre of protesters in late November 1945. The association of northern students in the South called a national student conference on December 17, 1945, at Hwimun Elementary School in Seoul. At this conference, presidents of student associations discussed actions to protest the massacre and prepared a memorial service for the "martyred" students.[113] The massacre in Sinŭiju continued to be a focal issue among northern leaders in the South.[114]

The movement of northerners introduced complex new dynamics into the broader politics of Korean Nationalism. At the Moscow conference in December 1945, the foreign ministers of the United States, USSR, and United Kingdom agreed to have the United States and the USSR organize a joint commission to establish an independent Korean government; this government would remain under the trusteeship of four powers for up to five years. Most Korean Nationalists considered this trusteeship a denial of Korean independence. Soon, though, the leftists changed their policy and supported the trusteeship following Russia's recommendation. At this juncture, the leaders of the Northern Association (Sŏbuk Hyŏphoe) opposed the trusteeship, supporting the position of the Chosŏn Democratic Party, which was organized by a Christian Nationalist in the North, Cho Mansik.[115] Once the US-USSR Joint Commission began its activities, as mentioned earlier, Koreans hoped that the occupying powers could alleviate the problems of partition by reopening railways between Seoul and both P'yŏngyang and Wŏnsan and also by resuming communication and postal services across the parallel.[116]

But when the US-USSR Joint Commission failed to agree on enabling free movement across the parallel, northerners in the South became extremely frustrated and angry. Recognizing the prospect of an extended division, they organized a meeting in Seoul on May 21, 1946, to discuss the reasons behind the halted negotiations of the US-USSR Joint Commission.[117] The northerners saw all their ills emanating from the border itself, which severed their ties from their families. A speaker at this meeting, Kim Chihwan, said that "the 38th parallel is now choking our necks and cutting off our breath." Another speaker, Kim T'aesŏng, had arrived from P'yŏngyang about ten days before the assembly and reported on the northern situation. His body trembling in fury and distress, he said,

> Many tragedies, such as the student massacre, took place. I do not want to recount them all. I can vividly recall the national student demonstration on May Day as if it were now occurring in front of my eyes. When the May Day ceremony started in downtown P'yŏngyang, many students were silent, not responding to the slogans of "Long live the people's revolution of North Korea" or "Long live Comrade Kim Il Sung" shouted by the organizers of the ceremony in front. Later, when someone in the assembly cried out, "Long live Korean independence" [*Taehan tongnip manse*], the students followed the call with thunderous roars, waving the Korean flag. The ceremony was then overwhelmed by angry student cries, such as "That is true" and "Nobody can sell our beautiful country to others."[118]

Speeches and articles by northerners in the South during this period identified the situation of the Soviet zone not as a class struggle within the nation but rather as a crisis in which Korea was losing its independence—again. They did not criticize Communism in itself, but they did fault its instrumental role in the Soviet occupation and in the Russians' violation of Korea's interests, customs, and morality.

Korean right-wing leaders quickly embraced the prevalence of such narratives among northerners. An antitrusteeship assembly held in May 1946 included a program for reporting the "true condition of the Northern region."[119] Paek Namhong of the Chosŏn Democratic Party and Ryu Ch'ŏl, a former executive of Hŭngnam Nitrogen Company, gave speeches on the anti-Soviet student protests, material shortages, and dire living conditions in the North. Their speeches, according to the newspaper *Tonga Ilbo*, deeply stirred the emotions of the people in the assembly and made them weep in sympathy with their "northern brethren who had fallen in the horrible trap and were living in a 'foreign country that is not foreign' [*iguk anin iguk*]."[120]

Tonga Ilbo supported the northerners' movements.[121] Run by Kim Sŏng-su, the leader of the Korean Democratic Party, *Tonga Ilbo* published a column the day after the northerners' assembly described above, stating that the assembly was not focused on local concerns but addressed the agony of the whole nation. The column noted that the thirty-eighth parallel forced Koreans to accept the condition of North Korea, where "the nation's autonomy was being entirely violated with the pretext of liberating the weak nation and defending the welfare of the working class." It praised the pledge the northerners made during the assembly to sacrifice their lives to end the division. *Tonga Ilbo* demanded urgent actions from northerners, arguing, "We are interested in the northerners' assembly not because of their brave statement but in *our anticipation of their fearless practice.*" *Tonga Ilbo* continued, "Some propaganda says that the northerners in Seoul were pro-Japanese traitors and escaped North Korea. . . . If such [pro-Japanese] people exist among northerners, they should repent their misdeeds and restrain their behavior. But the northerners who were not [such traitors] must fight courageously to reject such blackmail."[122]

To understand this column, it must be noted that, at the time, Korean leftists were advertising that the North Korean Revolution had eliminated social evils and thoroughly punished pro-Japanese collaborators. And this propaganda, in turn, cast a negative light on the northerners who had fled to the South. Amid ongoing popular discontent over the survival of pro-Japanese collaborators in the US zone, this disturbing *Tonga Ilbo* column picked up on this stigma, calling on northern refugees to fight to nullify such a label and reverse what was happening in North Korea. Such rightist provocation may not have been what initiated northerners' activism but instead embraced it after the fact: northerner youth groups were already engaged in anti-Soviet protests constituting the most violent elements within Korean Nationalist politics. In June 1946, the Northwestern Student Association (Sŏbuk Haksaeng Yŏnmaeng) held its inaugural ceremony in Sich'ŏngyo Building in Kyŏnjidong, Seoul.[123] The association's statement in August 1947 declared, "We, the students from the northwestern region, will fight with all our passion and spirit for the students in the North and for the liberation of our country [*choguk kwangbok*] even though we are now in the South."[124]

In 1946, a new formidable organization was formed after uniting various organizations of northerner youth (including the aforementioned Northwestern Youth Association, the Great Korean Progress Youth Association [Taehan Hyŏksin Ch'ŏngnyŏnhoe], the North Korean Youth Association [Puksŏn Ch'ŏngnyŏnhoe], the North Hamgyŏng Youth Association [Hambuk Ch'ŏngnyŏnhoe], the P'yŏngan Youth Association [P'yŏngan Ch'ŏngnyŏnhoe], the Hwanghae Youth Association [Hwanghae Ch'ŏngnyŏnhoe], and the Yangho League [Yanghodan]). This merger became official on November 30, 1946, at the YMCA in Chongno, Seoul,[125] where the birth of the infamous Northwestern Youth Association (hereafter, NYA) was announced. By 1947, the NYA had expanded its local branches and, at one point, claimed one hundred thousand members.[126]

Starting in June 1947, the NYA built temporary housing for northern refugees, with tents donated by Seoul City. The organization also opened an information center for refugees, which received a thousand people a day, many of whom had no money or were accompanied by old parents or young children.[127] The NYA expanded its membership by recruiting young men at this center. Such voluntary work for refugees involved policing activity by the NYA branches, which checked on the background of northerners before their settlement in the South. According to Kang Ch'ang-jin, the NYA investigated him when he entered the South and stayed in a relative's house. Kang later joined the NYA.[128] My interviewee Kim Chin-sŏp, who crossed the parallel in 1947, called the NYA a civilian agency (*sasŏl kiwan*) but one that was more intimidating than the South Korean police. Kim said that the NYA had threatened refugees who had any leftist connection and called them "Commies."[129]

The NYA branches were paramilitaristic and waged armed conflicts with the North Korean security forces. While the NYA continued assaulting protesters under the influence of the South Korean Workers' Party, the North Korean police attacked the NYA branches near the thirty-eighth parallel. On August 25, 1947, the NYA headquarters announced that at dawn on August 7, about two hundred North Korean security guards (*ibuk kyŏngbidae*) had illegally crossed the border and attacked the dormitory of the NYA branch located in Pyŏksŏng Prefecture, Hwanghae Province. Three members were kidnapped by the security police of Haeju (Haeju Poansŏ), and one was tortured to death.[130] On September 6, 1947, the NYA also reported that 111 North Korean security guards armed with Soviet-style weapons had crossed the border, attacked the P'och'ŏn branch of the NYA, and arrested its twenty members.[131] And on January 8, 1948, Ch'oe Kit'ae, a NYA guard at the thirty-eighth parallel, was assaulted by about fifty North Korean security guards and shot to death.[132]

Why did some young men from the North, both educated and uneducated, turn to such violent activism and join together to terrorize their political opponents? Some of the reasons derived from the youth culture of refugees, who were destitute and accustomed to obtaining resources (money, houses, or jobs) with their fists and organizational power. Yet such behavior was not limited to refugees but was widespread in postcolonial Korea among youth groups of various political affiliations, including leftists. The youth groups grew up with a wartime culture that glorified militarism and violence as viable means of achieving one's goals. The aforementioned Yu In-bŏm recommended that I watch *Yainsidae* (*Rustic Period*, 2002) because it accurately portrayed the way things were at the time. This popular South Korean TV drama is set in the liberation era and centers on politicized gangsters.[133]

A deeper reason for the violence of the northern youth can be seen in the narratives of refugees who recast their ordeal in the Soviet zone as a *colonial experience*. Using the analogy of a liberation war, northern activists justified bloodshed to gain independence back home. Over time, they constructed the images of Soviet soldiers, male and female, as bestial and of Korean Communists, including Kim Il Sung, as fake and traitorous.

Ibuk T'ongsin and the Narratives of the Northern Refugees

Inaugurated in June 1946, *Ibuk T'ongsin* is a magazine that reveals the development of northerners' narratives as they integrated the ideological conflicts of the period in their own terms. Its editor in chief was Yi Puk, a man whose background is difficult to trace. His name literally means "North of the parallel." Whether his original name or a pen name, Yi Puk was known by this moniker until he died in 1954.[134] After naming the magazine's publishing company Samp'al (Thirty-Eight), Yi Puk, in the first issue of *Ibuk T'ongsin*, wrote that he had planned the magazine right after escaping from the North.

The magazine had correspondents in the North, whose articles it published under their initials in English or their surnames only. The original price of a copy was twenty won, though it increased over time with inflation. *Ibuk T'ongsin* collected regular subscribers by mail and opened local branches for sales.[135] Yi Puk insisted that the magazine was very successful and that at one point it had more subscribers and monthly copies than South Korea's top newspapers.[136] In January 1948, the magazine celebrated two of its local branches, Taejŏn and South Kyŏngnam, reaching more than ten thousand readers.[137] *Ibuk T'ongsin* was circulated in North Korea, according to an interview with Kang Ch'ang-jin, who had crossed the parallel in 1947 from Pyŏksŏng, Hwanghae Province. Before coming to the South, Kang had joined a secret organization called Southern Wind (Namp'unghoe) and had read a South Korean magazine called *Ibuk*.[138]

An editorial in that same first issue of *Ibuk T'ongsin* in 1946 announced the magazine's objective and dubbed the thirty-eighth parallel "the Nation's Gallows."[139] A year after the liberation, the editor wrote in the editorial that Korean independence seemed to be an empty dream. At first, the thirty-eighth parallel had been a line of liberation to expel the Japanese, but then it became the "murderous gallows" dividing the nation, the "suicide border" separating families and couples from each other. The editorial insisted that the magazine did not belong to any political party but sought to enhance the nation's awareness of North Korea's "dark condition" and the goal of national unity.[140]

In some *Ibuk T'ongsin* articles on crimes committed by soldiers, the words "USSR" and "Soviet" were not used; still, readers could recognize when writers were referring to Russians. *Ibuk T'ongsin* published many articles on the transfer of Korea's resources to the USSR. A correspondent in Ch'ŏngjin, North Hamgyŏng Province, reported that the Russians moved the machinery and equipment out of the Nippon Steel Company by twenty-car-long trains daily and loaded them onto a Soviet battleship to Vladivostok.[141] In addition, *Ibuk T'ongsin* frequently reported disturbing rape cases by Soviet soldiers. These stories were misogynous or written in a sensational style meant to entertain readers. For instance, Ch'oe Sŭng-hŭi, a legendary female dancer who left Seoul for the North, was the subject of such unverified gossip, including claims that she opened a ballet institute in P'yŏngyang, where her ballet students, and possibly Ch'oe herself, were allegedly raped by drunken Soviet soldiers who broke into the school.[142]

Ibuk T'ongsin's growth, I suspect, occurred partly because it adopted some features of an activist group in the way it organized its correspondents and distributors. The editorial office called their correspondents "comrades" and occasionally reported on their imprisonment or even death in North Korea. A column entitled "Notice for Comrades" included advertisements of meetings and events, brief reports of past meetings, and occasionally a welcome party to celebrate the return from "Siberia" of someone who had lost communication with the magazine for a time. On the anniversary of its founding, the magazine acknowledged deceased comrades and asked readers to remember their heroic acts for the "liberation" of the country.[143] In later issues, the magazine solicited readers' contributions of poems and short essays. With titles such as "Mother," "The Thirty-Eighth Parallel," "Phoenix," and "To My Teacher," the poems expressed, in raw and rough language, feelings of loss, the humiliating conditions in the South, anger, and the determination to fight and recover one's home.

Ibuk T'ongsin is a complicated source. Its articles and reports vary from sophisticated intellectual essays to unverified news and rumors. Some of its authors and correspondents, if not the editor himself, may have communicated with the US military at the time.[144] Regardless of any possible connection, *Ibuk T'ongsin* has had its own voice and changed its political position over time. Some articles give updates on North Korea, analyzing its land reform, currency conversion, and other changes. Such analyses inform readers on what has been occurring in their hometowns while also conveying the magazine's criticism.

The magazine is a complex medium, meant to allow northerners to transcend the partition and their distance from home, as well as to discursively reclaim the unity of Korea in their own terms.[145] This complexity can be seen in the magazine's stance on South Korea, especially from mid-1948 on, when it proposed ways to recover the nation's unity with North Korea and criticized the role of South Korea's establishment, including Syngman Rhee, in alienating northerners and North Korea from the nation. Indeed, *Ibuk T'ongsin* warned of southerners' indifference to what was happening in Korea, both North and South. My interviewees said that they had experienced the systematic control of society in the North but had also seen the naivete of southerners with respect to the detrimental effects of Communism on the nation. They had seriously worried about where they would go if South Korea, too, fell into the hands of the Communists.

Ibuk T'ongsin has echoed similar sentiments in its publication. An article written by a refugee stated that, after coming to Seoul, the author was surprised that the offices of leftist organizations, like the South Korean Workers' Party or the Democratic United Front, stood in the city's downtown. He had heard of arrests of leftists and the censorship of newspapers in the South, but, in his view, such oppression in the South was weak compared to the control of thoughts in the North. The author warned that southerners' ignorance of the North would eventually undermine the stability of the southern system.[146]

Ibuk T'ongsin has also advocated for the precarious lives of northern refugees in the South. When a group of northerners paid to build shacks on empty land near the Southern Gate (Namdaemun) in Seoul, the government destroyed them, arguing that the shacks were unlicensed and degraded the city's landscape. In response, *Ibuk T'ongsin* demanded that the southern government develop a plan to rescue refugees in distress. Yi Puk himself diagnosed that the condition his refugee brethren found themselves in had reached an extremely dangerous and emotional point.[147]

Despite all the difficulties, Yi Puk claimed, *Ibuk T'ongsin* was at the "vanguard" of Korean journalism, surpassing other top media outlets in circulation. Yi attributed this success to the "comrades" in local branches who carried copies of the magazine on their backs, delivering them to readers in the nooks and crannies of South Korea. The magazine's special notice to comrades in March 1947 announced a plan to visit Cheju Island, calling the region "the stronghold of Communists." The notice asked those interested in joining to inform the company office, adding that they might not be able to accept everyone if demand outstripped the number of tickets.[148] Yi Puk bragged that "there is little concern of revolt where many read *Ibuk T'ongsin*." But he doubted whether the established southern leaders in power appreciated that his comrades were fighting against the "Reds," shedding their own blood in local areas.[149]

Such overt provocation of anti-Communist activism in *Ibuk T'ongsin* coexisted with its more nuanced political columns. The articles published after South Korea's election in 1948 were intelligent in proposing a new direction for Korean Nationalism. The authors included reputable leaders, such as An Chae-hong, a moderate Nationalist, and Kim Kwang-sŏp, the famous poet of "The Doves of Sŏngbuk-dong Village." In his article, An Chae-hong, who was in conflict with Syngman Rhee at the time, urged citizens to support the Republic of Korea, even while acknowledging its shortcomings. He called democracy in the South a prerequisite for Korea's transition from US military rule *and* for achieving unification with the North.[150] Kim Sam-gyu, the editor of *Tonga Ilbo*, criticized the US occupation for its arbitrary use of power and its lack of a plan for Korea. He argued that such abuse of power was only possible because Korea was in a "warlike" situation. Kim urged Koreans to normalize the government by curbing the use of power that was not supported by law.[151] Ko Chae-uk, meanwhile, advocated for the merits of the parliamentary system as a way to compete effectively with North Korea. While expressing his conviction in the southern system of capitalistic ownership, Ko criticized the presidential system and Syngman Rhee's use of it, arguing that it would diminish the role of political parties and leave South Koreans unprepared to counterbalance the organizational power of the Communists.[152]

Finally, the columns of accomplished writers emphasized the value of individuality in building a new Korean culture. Kim Tong-ni, the author of "Munyŏdo" (The shaman sorcerer), argued that Korean Nationalists were losing the "cultural warfare" against Communists. To create this new culture required to combat the North, he urged South Korea to establish a comprehensive policy that relied on individual initiatives of writers and artists.[153] Kim Kwang-sŏp called for advancing Korean Nationalism from a primitive stage—defined by biological traits, customs, or languages—to an advanced stage in which a nation emerges as a "historically developed community of culture." For this advancement, Kim asked Nationalists to move beyond a mere pursuit of self-determination and to embrace individual freedom (*kaesŏng ŭi chayu*) and national solidarity with humanity. Kim warned that any revolution that destroys humanity is anachronistic, rejecting a Soviet-style revolution if it meant subordinating Koreans to the values and lifestyles of Russian peasants and workers or to an ideology serving Russian culture.[154]

Considering *Ibuk T'ongsin*'s promotion of militant activism, it is unexpected that the magazine's political essays sought to anchor democracy, individuality, and humanity as foundations for revitalizing the Korean nation and its culture after colonialism. Further investigation is needed to determine whether such criticism of US occupation and Rhee's presidency represented the collective alienation of northerners from the southern regime or simply reflected the editor Yi Puk's growing alignment with Rhee's opponents. Nonetheless, it is significant that certain discourses of *Ibuk T'ongsin* supported a political trajectory that emphasized individual freedom and democratic processes as a means to counter Communism.[155]

Conclusion

Bruce Cumings, in his influential book *The Origins of the Korean War*, argues that the outbreak of the Korean War originated in the decisions of the US occupation in Korea in 1945 and 1946. According to Cumings, Korea was on the verge of revolution after colonialism. Throughout the country, Koreans under leftist leadership organized people's committees and thereby established the People's Republic of Korea. But this people-led revolution in Korea was rejected by the US occupation, which restored the colonial-state apparatus by recruiting pro-Japanese collaborators.[156]

However, the stories of northern refugees compel me to think that Cumings's narrative—of an "indigenous revolution" and US intervention to reverse it—makes for a limited way to explain Korea's postcolonial history. The initial partition and the violent measures to impose the border between the two zones played a more critical role in creating peril for Koreans than the exact moment the United States or USSR began envisioning their expansive empires and the Cold War in Asia. Focusing predominantly on the decisions of local elite leaders, such as Kim Il Sung or Syngman Rhee, is inadequate to understand the experiences of northerners explored in this chapter. It does not account for the violence that displaced these refugees and their struggles to find breathing space for survival.

Regardless of the original intentions of the United States and the USSR, the partition of Korea was a violent act that uprooted many Koreans, northerners and southerners alike, and triggered aggressive behaviors among northerner youth and gave rise to a combative conservatism in South Korea. Simultaneously, the history of northern refugees mirrors the violence and militancy of the North Korean Revolution. It would be unfair to attribute all the violence and armed conflicts in postcolonial Korea to the actions of the United States and USSR. In that sense, it is important to reconsider the history of the Cold War in Korea from a longer perspective of the imperial shift, which transformed Korea from Japan's wartime colony into a peripheral region of the two Cold War empires.

I suspect that both the terrorism of the northern youth and the militarism of the North Korean Revolution were overdetermined by this imperial shift. In explaining "the overdetermination of any contradiction and of any constitutive element of a society," the French philosopher Louis Althusser argues that "the new society produced by the Revolution may itself *ensure the survival, that is, the reactivation of older elements* through both the forms of its new superstructures and specific (national and international) 'circumstances.'"[157]

Therefore, it is overly simplistic to call the fierce and terrifying activism of the northern youth merely an instrument of the US counterinsurgency. In fact, such activism was a complex amalgamation of factors: the culture of colonial war and mobilization, the displacement of refugee lives, the revolution carried out by means of the military and other forms of violence, and the strategies employed by the US military in mobilizing northern youth during its occupation of Korea and beyond.

Four

RETHINKING SPATIAL POLITICS AND THE LEGACY OF THE COLD WAR IN KARACHI

IJLAL MUZAFFAR

In 1959, Greek architect and planner Constantinos Doxiadis was invited by the military government of Field Marshal and President Ayub Khan to design a housing project in Karachi, Pakistan. The project was to be in the Karachi neighborhood of Korangi and intended for "settling" refugees (now, actually, citizens of Pakistan) who had arrived from India after the partition of the subcontinent in 1947.[1] Doxiadis's proposal for Korangi was a curious design that grew linearly out of the city like a marching army—settling the refugees even as it simultaneously claimed to prepare Karachi for a modern future (fig. 4.1). This promise of continuous growth was highly valuable for Pakistan's military regime, which had invited Doxiadis on the recommendation of the Ford Foundation. As long as the project was incomplete, it allowed the regime to frame itself as a perpetual custodian of settling the nation into modernity itself.

Yet there is something more in Doxiadis's approach to design as incompleteness. It is incompleteness as a theater of perpetual war. In a letter to Colonel Nasser Humayune, the military director of the National Housing and Settlement Agency, and Harry Case, the Ford Foundation representative in Karachi, Doxiadis makes this undertone explicit: "In the four and a half years of my acquaintance with the

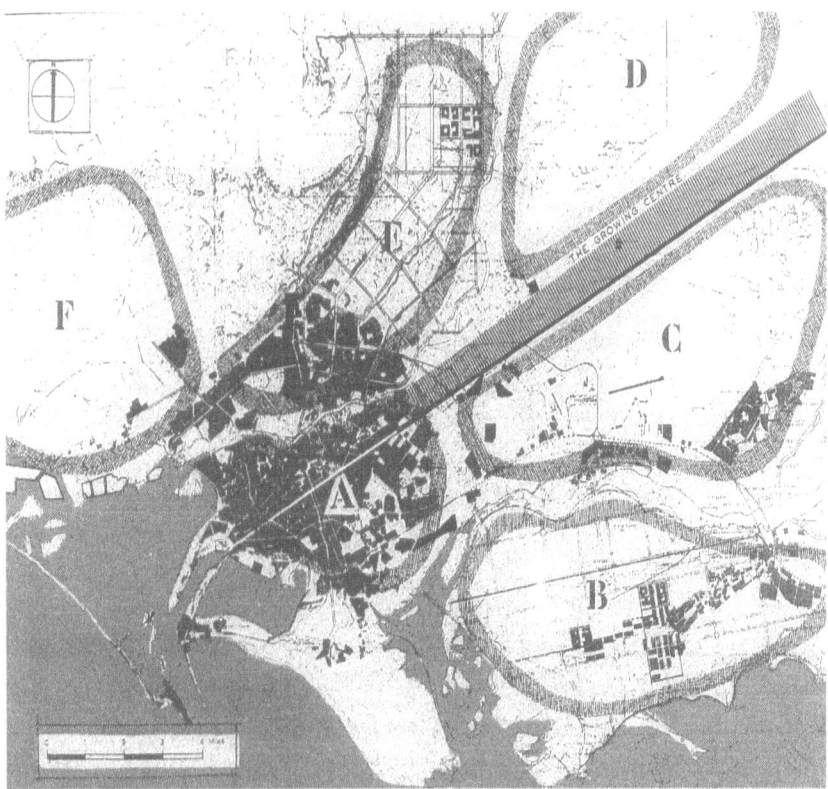

Figure 4.1. Doxiadis Associates' map of presumed direction of growth (from left to right) of Korangi, Karachi, connecting to other future outposts of the city, 1959. Source: *The Development of Korangi Area*, 1962, periodical report 2, E. Vassiliadis Files, Korangi-Karachi (1959–1962), ref. code 36395, Doxiadis Associates, C. A. Doxiadis Archives, Benaki Museum, Athens.

urban problems of Pakistan," Doxiadis asserted, "it is the first time that I have seen such an enthusiasm, inspiration and coordination of effort under a unique command for the achievement of a natural goal in this field. The 'Operation Korangi' as I think it should be called has all the characteristics of a beachhead started by commandos in hostile territory—by commandos who have the desire to achieve a national goal even by deciding to have greater sacrifices and casualties than normally.... Even more: it should be turned into the beachhead that is going to open the enemy land for conquest."[2] Certainly, this statement reflects the authoritarianism that would overcast Pakistan for decades; moreover, it is self-aggrandizing and steeped in aggressive military metaphors. Yet even coming from an architect seeking favor from his military interlocutors during the Cold War, the quote points to a broader question: Why turn these refugees—who, after all, were being hailed as representatives of a national future, their settlement framed as the settlement of the nation itself—into a specter of an enemy that the project needed to fight?

Seeing the project as a beachhead, as Doxiadis did, turns the nation into a realm at war with itself. Rather than promising to stabilize the future, then, the architect's rhetoric of secret invasion actually promises perpetual instability. Doxiadis's rhetoric shifts our understanding of the term "Cold War" in fundamental ways. It shows that open-ended, perpetually incomplete urban-planning schemes—like Doxiadis's plan for Korangi, Karachi—actually open and maintain theaters of the Cold War. For Anna Lowenhaupt Tsing, all plans, all planning, have to encounter the unpredictability of the physical world, the point "where the rubber has to meet the road."[3] That's why, Tsing famously argues in *Friction*, no modeling of globalization has ever proven true. But in theaters of cold wars, like Karachi, this unpredictability doesn't figure only as friction but also as a necessary lubricant, a desired quality. Institutions of managing globalization might shun unpredictability, but, I argue, that same unpredictability is relished and promoted in Cold War planning. Maintaining unpredictability surely introduces risk in any outcome, but in contexts like Pakistan—where the military maintained contested borders to stay in power—a Cold War–nurtured unpredictability also formed the very premise of the nation.

Doxiadis's statement also shows how physical planning shaped Cold War political theaters. This is because the Cold War can be understood as a war over space, not territory. This distinction is important to consider: space and territory are not opposing spheres, but they do function as different ways of defining and controlling the physical world. Even though space is imbedded in the physical world, it is also an abstraction drawn on it, and yet it defines the way the physical world is recognized and governed. Controlling space doesn't so much require changing the physical world as having the ability to change its meaning—turning the stable into the unstable, the visible into the invisible, and vice versa. In this realm, physical planning is akin to a clandestine operation that is meant to continuously change the meaning of the terrain it acts upon. Doxiadis's statement shows that the Cold War is as much about gaining territory as about destabilizing space.

Here, within the Cold War, planning must be put on its head. Military planning and city planning must intersect. The enemy must be seen to be never far from home. It could be the neighbor, the friend, the refugee. It must be possible, at any moment, to recast the very public—which is invoked to claim legitimacy—as an enemy so as to justify exercise of power. Thus, suspicion and surveillance go hand in hand with promise and planning.

Thanks to Doxiadis's proposal, the contours of city planning in Karachi were set for years to come—not because it presented some overarching masterplan but because its indeterminacy gave it a certain resiliency. There had been other proposals before Doxiadis's to settle the refugees in Karachi, but they all had failed to materialize.[4] Doxiadis's scheme took root because it spoke to the covert and unpredictable model of governance through which the military regime in Pakistan enabled the extension of the Cold War into the region. For this reason, Doxiadis's planning model would continue to cast a long shadow on Karachi's development far beyond its author's intentions.

Ultimately, the Cold War folded into other forms of warfare, including a proxy war against the Soviet invasion of Afghanistan in 1977 and the continuous war against "terrorism" after 9/11. Throughout these changes, Karachi became a city with elastic, covert spatiality, claimed by both governing and countervailing forces—including competing Taliban groups, contesting national political parties, government departments, and military agencies—each opening new beachheads into their shifting enemy territories. These beachheads took various forms from cutting highway passes through mountains to interrupting perceived enemies' movements to letting mountains of garbage emerge in the middle of the city to consolidate new economic and political "beachheads."

This expanding and contracting logic—which claims, defends, and usurps the meaning of the physical environment—challenges how we think about the very category of the city and planning itself. I would argue that for environments like Karachi, which have been mired in the long Cold War, the idea of the "city" has never been an adequate epistemological category to explain change. To understand how the physical environment is thought of, controlled, and governed in such theaters, we have to shift instead to the militarist and covert logic of spatial planning that was inaugurated with the onset of the Cold War.

Covert Planning

By the late 1950s, Constantinos Doxiadis was running perhaps one of the largest planning firms in the world, with offices in the United States, Athens, and the Middle East. This rise to fame was due, in part, to Doxiadis cloaking his ideas of planning within a language of both science and "human rights"—reflected in terms like "shelter" and "settlement"—which were increasingly being adopted by UN development programs.[5] With frequent appearances on US television, Doxiadis touted his projects as a revolutionary approach to planning.[6] Yet Doxiadis was far from revolutionary. Indeed, the backbone of his practice was designing the housing and planning schemes of countries like Iraq, Nigeria, Ghana, and Pakistan—Cold War military regimes favored by the United States. The projects that his firm orchestrated were actually part of the concerted US effort to mobilize UN development "missions" and private American foundations to counter the perceived threat of Soviet influence and propaganda in key theaters of the Cold War, like Karachi.

Doxiadis arrived in Karachi in 1959, when Pakistan was already steeped deep in Cold War politics. In the early years of independence, American influence in Pakistan was asserted quietly through a US-leaning bureaucracy. But this was outright replaced in 1958 by the Allied military dictatorship of General Ayub Khan, which would outlast all democratic challenges for more than a decade to come.

The Korangi proposal appealed to Ayub Khan's military government far more than Doxiadis probably realized. The casting of refugees as enemies was already a strategy of control pursued by the government. For the Pakistan military, the logic of opening "beachheads" in enemy territory was tied to the strategy of the "stay-behind forces"—the next stage of the beachhead. Having already fought one war with India in 1948 (with two more to follow in the coming years), the invocation of conflict had become central to the sustenance and legitimacy of military governance. Pakistan under Ayub Khan was, as one Pakistani diplomat is said to have put it, not a country seeking an army to protect itself but an army looking for a country to defend.[7]

This inversion, however, was not just a product of authoritarianism imposed from above. It had only been effective because it emerged from a certain crisis of boundaries that defined the new nation itself. As Vazira Zamindar explores in detail, the ambivalence around boundaries had formed the very condition of independence.[8] The uncertainty of the boundary between India and Pakistan was betrayed by the very thickness of the line of partition on the maps announcing the birth of the two nations—so wide at certain points that it consumed entire villages in its breadth.

But this was not just a mere accident of inadequate printing technology. The ambivalence stemmed from the logic followed to draw the partition itself. The British government, in its panic to leave the subcontinent without accruing additional political and economic costs after World War II, had made an ad hoc commission, headed by a London lawyer, Cyril Radcliffe, to determine how an indivisibly heterogenous countryside could be expediently partitioned.[9] Radcliff had never been to India before and knew little of its administrative complexity. Upon landing, he summoned all the municipal maps he could get access to and started allocating municipalities to one side or the other depending upon whether they had a majority Hindu or Muslim recorded population. When such a majority couldn't be convincingly determined, a municipality was simply divided on the map, cutting villages, towns, and streets into two countries. The result was a meandering line, pushing and pulling on a shifting criterion, if not whim alone, often generating a unique boundary phenomenon called "*chhits*," forming not only enclaves of one country in another but enclaves of one country within enclaves of the other within enclaves of the first (fig. 4.2).

Quickly, the militaries on both sides realized the impossibility of maintaining stability of these conditions. And so they both started developing strategies, which

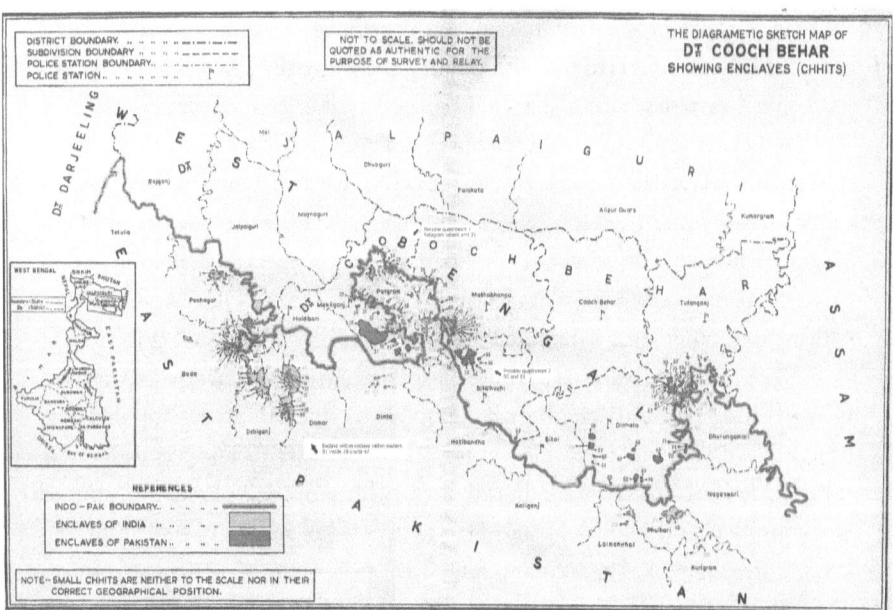

Figure 4.2. "Diagrametic Sketch Map" of Cooch Behar District showing enclaves, district map of Cooch Behar, government of India. Source: © 2001 by Brendan R. Whyte.

thought of the border as a series of beachheads, opened and closed as opportunities emerged and receded. A "diagrametic sketch map" of the district Cooch Behar, marking the boundary between East Pakistan (Bangladesh after independence in 1971) and India, apologetically notes that "small chhits are neither to the scale nor in their correct geographical position" (see fig. 4.2). This ambiguity was less a result of a lack of information than its contested nature, with both countries touting their own "correct location and scale" of *chhits*.[10] In their ambiguity, such diagrammatic sketch maps served as diplomatic means of representation, conveying a general condition without rousing contestation. But they also betrayed the very limits of mapping an ad hoc partition.

It was precisely to exploit this necessary ambivalence that Aboobaker Osman Mitha (then, colonel; later, major general of the Pakistan Army) formed the Special Services Group (SSG) in 1956.[11] Mitha soon acquired legendary status in army lore, credited with forming the strategy of "stay-behind forces," in which the army, instead of confronting an overwhelming enemy, retreated, but they would leave behind certain forces, who would stay to counter the advancing foe from behind at a convenient time. At its founding in 1956, the SSG was formed with the help of the Americans, who were interested in preparing a "stay-behind force" of their own in Pakistan in case of a Russian invasion. But the strategy's leading specialist would become Mitha, who is credited with training the US Army officials themselves in stay-behind warfare strategies that could be employed Eastern Europe.

When the Ford Foundation introduced him to the Pakistani government, Doxiadis quickly learned how deeply this was entwined with Pakistan's military. For example, all his counterparts for refugee planning on the Pakistani side were military personnel. Even so, Doxiadis's use of militaristic language was more than an opportunistic attempt to earn the confidence of his interlocutors. The plan for refugee settlement he proposed also reflected the covert spatiality of the stay-behind forces.

This dimension is betrayed by the design of the scheme itself. Doxiadis proposed a nested model of social organization controlled by a disseminated administrative structure, without an identifiable locus of authority (fig. 4.3). The population was to be divided into different "community sectors," beginning with the basic unit of "community Class I," which included ten to twenty households of similar income levels. Three to seven of such communities were grouped together to form the next administrative level of "Class II"; when an elementary school was added to a grouping, it formed a community level of "Class III." The residents of each Class III community were supposed to share the same income and class, but the Class III

Figure 4.3. Doxiadis Associates' Korangi master plan, 1959. Source: *The Development of Korangi Area*, 1962, periodical report 2, E. Vassiliadis Files, Korangi-Karachi (1959–1962), ref. code 36395, Doxiadis Associates, C. A. Doxiadis Archives, Benaki Museum, Athens.

communities themselves could differ in their economic level relative to each other. Thus, when *different* income-level Class III communities were grouped together—and a mosque, a teahouse, a market, and a cinema were included—a Class IV community was formed. These Class IV communities were, in turn, combined to form Class V, which formed the basic "community sector" of the Korangi plan.[12] These community sectors were then multiplied to form the initial scheme and were then supposed to grow on a linear path over time.

Clearly, Doxiadis's structure was hierarchically organized. Still, he argued that the purpose of this arrangement was "consolidating" the structure of public administration rather than "centralizing" it. Korangi was to be built through the cooperation of both public and private enterprises.[13] Various private industries were to pool together their resources and form cooperative bodies. These cooperatives were to be part of the Korangi's board of management and were to fund Korangi's housing sectors according to the needs of their surrounding industries. As a 1959 Doxiadis Associates' "progress report" on Korangi shows, of the ensemble of housing sectors and community centers in the entire settlement, the government was only to build the lowest-income housing sectors and even only partially. The rest, including major parts of the community centers, counting the community mosque, was to be built by providing "incentives" to the private sector at the right moment in development. Doxiadis hailed his scheme as a structure of "coordinating" public and private interests.[14] But "coordination" here is, in fact, a euphemism for managing displacement.

After conducting interviews with surviving refugees, Shahana Rajani and Shayan Rajani argue that Korangi's beginning were rooted in displacement from the start, even before the beginning of Doxiadis's scheme.[15] Most of the refugees "settled" in Korangi had already been forcibly displaced from an informal settlement called Quaidabad. This was named after the title *quaid-e-azam* (the great leader) given to Muhammad Ali Jinnah, Pakistan's first governor general and the leader of the Muslim independence movement the Muslim League. Jinnah, who died a year after partition, had been buried on the site, with the grave marked by a makeshift mausoleum in an army tent. Despite extended debate and proposals for a permanent grand mausoleum, the government continued to actively settle refugees from across the city on the grounds around the grave. By the time Ayub Khan seized power in 1958, the site had turned into a burgeoning settlement with resident shops and businesses, named Quaidabad after the beloved leader, whose makeshift tent-mausoleum still lies at its heart.

All that changed the day Ayub Khan cut the ribbon for Korangi (fig. 4.4). Sud-

Figure 4.4. General Ayub Khan at the ribbon-cutting ceremony of the Korangi-settlement scheme, 1959. Source: Ford Foundation Archives, New York, https://www.fordfoundation.org. This work is made available under the Creative Commons Attribution 4.0 International License (CC BY 4.0). To view a copy of this license, visit https://creativecommons.org/licenses/by/4.0/.

denly, Quaidabad was surrounded by army trucks. The refugee turned into the enemy as the aiding army transformed into a stay-behind force. The refugees, more than ninety thousand on the site, had only been a given a week's eviction notice. On the day of the move, placard cards with numbers of the new allocated houses in Korangi were hung around the necks of astonished residents. Within a week, the meaning of Quaidabad changed—its space transformed into a beachhead even while its territory remained the same.

A similar transformation occurred in Korangi. When the Quaidabad residents were dropped off at this remote site—the army trucks started moving two hundred families a day there—many found that the placards around their necks only pointed to open land some ten miles outside the city. What was there were just fifteen thousand small attached houses on three thousand acres (all funded by the United States Agency for International Development, or USAID) for more than five hundred thousand residents. There was also nothing much else that was promised: schools, industries, shops, hospitals, transportation, even sanitation facilities, like garbage collection and sewage connections, were absent. The rows of neatly lined houses, however, were enough to fill the background of the ribbon-cutting ceremony. The residents, who were forced to pay 1,900 rupees for the houses they were supposed to get, soon abandoned them, selling at a loss or simply vacating to return to new sites in the city near opportunities of work.

But the dispersal of refugees to Korangi and back across the city had set in motion a new regime of changing the meaning of land. Afterall, Korangi was, of course, not built on empty land. It was planned on shared indigenous land, with several villages that had intimate economic ties with the city providing vegetables, fruit, milk, and meat to different markets. As Shahana Rajani and Shayan Rajani document, the area around Korangi was a fertile land. "There were hundreds of acres of rolling orchards. Trees laden with mulberries, mangoes, guavas, dates, melons, papayas, and grapes dotted the landscape. Streams branching out of the Malir River braided between fields of crops." As one of Rajani and Rajani's interviewees, Karim—whose family had lived for three generations in Haji Gul Mohammad Goth, one of the villages on the site—recalled, "Korangi was not *banjar* (barren) as people like to believe.... It was *abad* (populated)."[16] This land around Korangi was acquired by the Karachi Development Authority in 1957 under the Land Acquisition Act of 1894. Yet it was not simply the power to forcibly acquire land that turned it from *abad* (populated) to *banjar* (barren); it was the nature of the space that was projected on it that made the instantaneous transformation possible.

This spatiality was inherent in the 1894 colonial legislation itself. The law gave government the wide-ranging power to acquire private land for public purposes, even without designating the scope of what is considered private or public. This ambiguity, and the limitless execution it afforded, drew on the larger crisis of the border that was simmering at the time in British India's North-West Frontier Province (NWFP)—an anxiety of control and invasion reflected in the very name given to these areas. The threat faced by the British was of a Russian land invasion through a territory whose alliances and political structure the colonial government had never been able to predict or control. Thus, the 1894 Land Acquisition Act was passed to not only acquire land in and around Karachi so as to establish reserve military garrisons to counter an unexpected Russian attack; it was also passed to expand that capacity in case of an emergency.

As Peter Hopkirk famously narrates, Central Asia, extending outward from NWFP, was a hotbed of dramatic British covert operations, where British spies, acquiring a tan and a beard, often tried to pass as lighter-skin tribesmen of Afghanistan.[17] The very administration of the NWFP and the operations launched from it depended on *not* marking a clear border—on exploiting the blurriness of the lines of empires, race, dress, and language, which were imagined and performed in distinct terms in the rest of British India. The blurriness and ambiguity of NWFP allowed for covert operations to be launched from it. The Land Acquisition Act in Karachi brought that ambiguity home. With it, Karachi could be turned from a port city into a garrison, and *abad* land turned into *banjar* land as need arose.

This transformative spatiality formed the key strategy of Doxiadis's plan. It was a quality resulting not just from the projected extension of Korangi but from the very ambiguity with which that extension was imagined. Doxiadis's plan was necessarily incomplete. Its very incompletion gave the government the ability both to not declare what was coming *and* to acquire land for its purposes. Thus, all land—no matter how *abad* or *banjar*—was transformed into covert space.

Such covert spatiality permeated every inch of Doxiadis's plan. Each individual house was planned on a grid. Just like the community facilities of the plan, owners were supposed to expand their houses over time with loans. Yet, at any time, the government could invoke that invisible grid so as to object to how and when those additions were laid out. The grid also functioned as a timing device. If the loan payment was not received on time, the part of the house built on that loan became susceptible to demolition. Indeed, in subsequent years, the numerous eviction and demolition drives in Korangi betray how the lines of the grid could expand to open a beachhead—even in the middle of one's home.

Thus, Doxiadis's grid was more than a planning tool. In fact, the gridded plan functioned with the logic of ambiguous border lines—from the partition to the NWFP—that could, at any time, be expanded or contracted to activate stay-behind forces.

Other Beachheads

The quintessential images of remembering the partition, which displaced more than ten million people and left millions dead or destitute, are Margaret Bourke-White's photographs for *Life* magazine. We can find them in countless history books from both sides of the partition, most famously perhaps in Khushwant Singh's historical novel *Train to Pakistan*.[18] I argue elsewhere that the ubiquitous resonance of these photographs stems from their ability to portray the refugees as utterly helpless subjects, displaced by historical forces larger than what they could shape or even comprehend. This framing allowed the state, particularly in Pakistan, to step in as the sole curator of the future.

We can see how Bourke-White's lens harbors this meaning. In the majority of these photographs, we see her taking a deliberative low or high stance such that the figures are cast against vast shadeless skies, highlighting the feeling of helplessness in the face of the unknown (fig. 4.5).

Bourke-White was determined to give specific meaning to the refugees, catching them in moments of desperation and disorientation. And yet the figures themselves sometime challenge Bourke-White's framing, resisting being thrown into the vastness of a nameless history. One of Bourke-White's most prominent photographs of the partition is of a boy sitting on top of a hill in Karachi with a vast refugee camp behind him (fig. 4.6). Bourke-White employed all the familiar strategies here as well.

The boy is captured at a moment of loss, holding his head in his hands with a look of desperation on his face. The camera is lowered to the extent that it frames

Figure 4.5. Margaret Bourke-White's opening photograph for "The Great Migration" in *Life* magazine, 1947. Source: Margaret Bourke-White, n.d., "The Great Migration," *Life*, November 3, 1947, in the LIFE Picture Collection / Shutterstock.

Figure 4.6. Margaret Bourke-White's photograph in "Partition of India" in *Life* magazine, 1947. Source: Margaret Bourke-White, n.d., "Partition of India," *Life*, November 3, 1947, in the LIFE Picture Collection / Shutterstock.

the boy's head against the vast, scaleless sky but still shows the chaos of the camp below. Yet this picture of destitution is disturbed by what seems like an unpredicted entry of another figure—another young face cropping up from behind the rock—in what otherwise seems like a perfectly framed moment of helplessness. This face returns the camera's gaze and, furrowing his brow, looks us in the eye, usurping the passiveness projected onto the refugees. It unsettles Bourke-White's framing of the partition and chases its echoes in countless official and popular publications.

The refugees were indeed destitute, but they were never silent. From the moment they entered the makeshift camps the government had set up for them, they organized and made demands, seeking to chart their own futures.

The second face in this photograph might be incidental, but, I would argue, it is not exceptional. It betrays precisely the split side of the politics of space deployed by the military government in later years. When space is deployed covertly, it also risks usurpation precisely by those who are meant to be controlled by it. The second face represents a premonition that the unstable spatiality of covert warfare, through which the military government would seek to control Karachi, would also open up the same possibility for others.

We see the state's hegemony over Karachi's spatiality unraveling as the Soviet occupation of Afghanistan came to a close in 1989. There, for over a decade, America and Pakistan had conducted a proxy war, engaging fighting groups that proclaimed themselves as mujahideen (holy warriors). As the war turned into a civil war, with retreating Soviet forces, many of these groups started establishing strongholds across the border in Karachi.

Already, the city had received many displaced Afghans, who had left refugee camps along the border in search of work. This long influx complicated the makeup of the city, especially its large population identifying as ethnic Pashtuns, who had migrated from the country's Northwest to Karachi under Ayub Khan's tenure. These people had traditionally been assumed to be constituents of the (public) Awami National Party (ANP), which challenged the major *mohajir* (refugee) political party, Muttahida Qaumi Movement (United National Movement), or MQM. But in the mid-1980s, the ANP's makeup and goals transformed radically with the influx of both Afghan migrants and mujahideen groups vying to be their representatives. And so the ANP started forming closely linked settlements in the Northwest of the city, with one prominent one on a hill called Manjhopir Pahari overlooking the strongholds of MQM.[19] Moreover, the new ANP foot soldiers, hardened by a decade of war, had brought back munitions that outmatched those of the MQM forces.

With shifting political alliances and precarious relationships to governance and power, small skirmishes turned into a full-fledged armed conflict—the scale of which had not been witnessed in the city before. In 1986, several Pashtun families were found murdered in their homes on Manjhopir Pahari overlooking the *mohajir* neighborhood of Qasba Colony. The ANP retaliated, firing rocket-propelled grenades and sniper bullets from the heights into the neighborhood below. What unfolded over the next decade was an elusive calculus of political alliances and criminal enterprise, which challenged both the logics of governance and geopolitics.

As the 1990s drew to a close, the MQM found itself in the favor of yet another military government—this time under General Pervaiz Musharraf. And this government would stay in power, and in US favor, for a long decade after the September 11, 2001, attacks in New York. Next, in 2005, after MQM enjoying years of power over ANP, the young newly elected MQM-supported mayor of Karachi Mustafa Kamal sought to undercut the ANP hold on the Manjhopir Pahari, the infamous hill overlooking *mohajir* neighborhoods. And he did so by borrowing from the planning playbook of Ayub Khan's government.

During the 1960s, as noted earlier, Ayub Khan's military government was pursuing its Korangi urban-development scheme. At the same time, the government, with USAID's help, cut through the few stubborn hills that cropped up from the desert surrounding Karachi so as to construct Pakistan's first high-speed road. Called the Super-Highway, the road ran some one hundred celebrated miles between Karachi and its distant sister city Hyderabad. Large stretches of highway appeared as if a gigantic hand of modernity had drawn a straight line between the two cities, leveling the hills. The Super-Highway symbolized the promise of modernity, development, and cosmopolitanism, which often led to proclamations of Karachi as the "Paris of Asia" in the 1960s.

It was this modernist vision from Karachi's storied past that Mayor Kamal invoked in 2005, and he did so to control the space of the present. Proposing a highway that cut through the ANP-controlled hill, the MQM government sought to connect the city's low-lying neighborhoods with the industrial areas beyond but also to disrupt the movement of ANP forces on the heights overlooking its headquarters. Compared to other infrastructural schemes in the city, Kamal's hill-leveling project was bulldozed through at a lightning pace.

Suddenly, Manjhopir Pahari had been bisected, and, from then on, it acquired the new name Kati-pahari (Split Mountain). At first, Kamal's project did undercut the ANP stronghold, interrupting the easy movement of munitions around the area. The project also allowed the *mohajir* population to encroach on the heights. Yet, very soon, the MQM once again lost its hold on power with the 2008 fall of Musharraf's military government.

At this point, the cleaved hill turned into an abyss, which started expelling the ghosts of the past. One side of the hill came to be occupied by the Pashtuns, and the other, by the *mohajirs*; bullets were now exchanged across the gap. Instead of a gateway to the future, the space in the hill became a political traffic jam of the present, exposing the logic of covert space that decades of national and geopolitical calculations had sought to control with their different strategies (fig. 4.7).

126 Chapter Four

Figure 4.7. Policemen stand guard to avoid any untoward incident at Kati Pahari Road as security had been tightened in the city due to violence on July 6, 2011, in Karachi. Source: Nadeem F. Paracha, "Visual Karachi: From Paris of Asia, to City of Lights, to Hell on Earth," *Dawn*, September 26, 2014, https://www.dawn.com/news/1134284 / Shutterstock.

Cold Borders

How should we understand the slice through the Kati Pahari? Is it a separation or a connection? It both prohibits movement and allows it. It forms a border and betrays the controlled porosity that all borders seek to implement. Yet it also betrays the far-reaching effects that porous borders—whether they take the shape of infinitely extending plans, cut mountains, or superhighways—produce in Cold War cities, like Karachi.

The linearly growing scheme for Korangi that Doxiadis proposed not only destabilized the meaning of land and property in the city but also turned the nation itself into an unfolding, unsettled space. The infinitely extended plan is perhaps better described as a cold border, which, in turn, opens the possibility of creating hot spots elsewhere. The lines of Doxiadis's gridded plan held within them the possibility of changing the meaning of ownership from legal to illegal at a whim. It didn't matter if you had never missed a loan payment; at a moment's notice, the state could always come to assess, with bulldozers and batons, if a wall was off the grid a foot here or there. Thus, the real goal of the displacements ushered onto the site could be *anything*—whether to undermine political strongholds or create property values elsewhere in the city.

Such wide-ranging potentials were just what the MQM-led city government sought to create by slicing Kati Pahari. More than dividing up the oppositional ANP stronghold, Kamal's project destabilized the broader political and spatial economies that had produced that stronghold in the first place.

In their struggle to claim a larger share of the urban turf, one of the major strategies pursued by both ANP and MQM was to take hold of *katchi abadis* (informal settlements).[20] Land agents associated with both parties would occupy land, divide it into gridded plots, and then sell these to their constituents. Later, at opportune political moments, the occupied land was "regularized"—that is, given legal status by the government. But before regularization, another spatial economy had to be mobilized—one that, I would argue, reverted back to the covert spatiality of Cold War planning.

In 1843, the British colonial government annexed Sindh and established Karachi as a military-reserve base from which to conduct operations into Afghanistan and Central Asia to curb the threat of a Russian land invasion. In so doing, the British classified the land in and around the city into three categories: *abad* (cultivated), *ghairabad* (uncultivated, at the moment), and *namumkin* (improbable or impossible to cultivate).[21] Over a century later, before establishing the Korangi housing scheme, the Ayub military government had declared the land around the site *ghairabad*, even though it was, as mentioned earlier, irrigated and cultivated. As the land pressure mounted in the proceeding decades, however, it wasn't just the land declared uncultivated that became a target for surreptitious planning but also the land declared *namumkin*, including that under roads, in mangroves, lakes, and creeks, around railway tracks and drainage channels, and on hills.

Kati Pahari—before it was cut through by a road—was one such "impossible" land site. ANP land agents started laying out plots on the site as there was an influx of migrants who had been displaced by the Pakistan Army's operation against Taliban groups in northwestern Pakistan. Between 2001 and 2010, the army conducted six major operations, with broad, unacknowledged "collateral damage," faced particularly by women and children.[22] The resulting influx created demand for sites like Kati Pahari.

At that time, MQM had a stronghold in the city government, but the ANP still found support from the Pakistan People's Party's (PPP) provincial government, which had opposed both MQM in Karachi and the military government in the center. And since the city's regularization agency, Sindh Katchi Abadi Authority (SKAA), was controlled by PPP rather than MQM, the SKAA allowed ANP settlements to be regularized.[23] MQM's and Mayor Kamal's strategy was to counter this expansion by deploying impossibility against impossibility: returning a portion of what was once deemed "impossible" land *back* to the category of impossibility—by running a highway through it.

The move, however, only showcased the larger tussle over who got to control impossible land in the city. By the early 2000s, MQM itself was regularizing its land agents' proposals along impossible land, including plots along railway lines and *nalas*, under roads, and on playgrounds and public parks. In 2007, the MQM-led government changed the long-standing arrangement of land conversion.

Upon annexing Sindh, the British colonial government had established a board of revenue (BoR), which controlled all land allotments in and around the city, declaring them *abad*, *ghairabad*, and *namumkin* as per its needs. To manage these allotments, the BoR divided the larger Karachi area into four functional categories: railways, garrisons, the port, and, the largest, Gadap—an area comprising of villages and farmland to the north, which supplied the city with its fruits, vegetables, meat, and milk.[24] Despite appearing to have fixed boundaries, these divisions followed an expansionist model, facilitating greater and greater extraction of resources from the province and larger and larger army operations to the north. The lynchpin of this transformation was Gadap, large portions of which could change categorization from *abad* to *ghairabad* to *namumkin* so as to put in place bigger army, railway and port infrastructures.

But as the pressure on land increased over time, it is this *namumkin* infrastructure—land under roads and around railways, creeks, ports, fisheries, and army garrisons—that became a valuable commodity. In 2001, the military federal government created the Sindh Local Government Ordinance (SLGO) to move the power of organizing land to the city and away from the provincial government—a domain historically controlled by its long-standing opposition, the PPP. Taking power in Karachi soon after, MQM seized the opportunity, dissolving the long-standing arrangement of provincial BoR control over city land and shifting it instead to eighteen towns of the city of Karachi itself, each under the control of an elected nazim (organizer).[25] Land agents, anticipating regularization, created new colonies on impossible land, already subdivided on grided plans in anticipation of government regularization.

The strategy of making the impossible possible worked. And it did so, on the one hand, because this strategy served more than just the exclusive political goals of one particular party and even satisfied the demand for cheap housing, which the government, both city and provincial, couldn't keep pace with. But, on the other hand, it worked because it mimicked the existing model of land transformation that the military itself already followed to advance its own interests in land.

The military's land-acquisition project started with the expansion of what was originally a small housing cooperative for military retirees, called the Pakistan Defence Officers Cooperative Housing Society (PDOCHS). The United States funded the first Afghan war against the Soviet Union in the 1980s primarily through the military regime of General Zia-ul-Haque. Leaning on the increased military budget, Zia turned the PDOCHS into the Defense Housing Association (DHA), a large commercial enterprise that sold land at discounted prices to military personnel—both active and retired—who could then, in turn, sell to the public at inflated prices. This transformed the nature of the military itself, making it, in the coming years, the largest real estate–holding company in the country, with DHA schemes and their ever-new "phases" opening up in all major cities. Today, DHA enclaves invite foreign developers to make Dubai-style marinas, luxury towers, malls, golf courses, commercial real estate, and private clubs across the country.

Inheriting British subdivision of land, DHA controlled prime oceanfront land in Karachi. But as the demand for land increased, it started opening new phases (DHA phases 6, 7, and 8 in particular) on reclaimed land in the early 2000s. This reclamation was also done by turning impossible land—in this case, vast tracts of mangroves, islets, and fishing villages—into possible land by dumbing garbage and construction material in shallow waters. With MQM losing its terrain in the next round of elections in 2009, the balance of power shifted once more toward the PPP provincial government. In 2011, Karachi land organization was once again shifted to the BoR model yet with previous districts divided into a wider arrangement. Yet despite the shift, the MQM- and DHA-led strategy of turning impossible land into occupiable land stayed at the forefront.

For example, in 2011, DHA started a new gated community, called the DHA City, north of Karachi, in the Gadap village and farmland zone. Even though the land itself was acquired by declaring it as *ghairabad* (barren), connecting it to other DHA developments (like the seafront phase 8 and the center city) nonetheless required unleashing a host of strategies for transforming *namumkin* (impossible) land to possible land, specifically to build new expressways along two major stormwater-drainage channels, the Malir River and the Gujjar Nala, that cut through the city.

Both the channels were surrounded by regularized and unregularized low-income housing, which were in strongholds of various political parties.[26] The third site included the Manzoor Colony Nala, which passed through the DHA, carrying its drain water as well to open into the Ghizri Creek at the mouth of the Malir River.

Here again, as late as 2011, the DHA deployed its tried-and-true military strategy: opening up surreptitious space within the houses, streets, and neighborhood, changing their status from legal to illegal overnight to gain access for its expressway. But this time, it would not be the lines of an invisible grid marked on official maps that transformed the status of whatever was built above them. Rather, it would be the flow of garbage and floodwater through the city that would come to serve as mercurial grounds for redefining space.

During the heavy monsoons of 2007, two problems—which had been growing with subsequent waves of Karachi's construction and population increases—came to a head: garbage and rainwater drainage. As garbage-filled drainage channels overflowed into the streets, the popular press was quick to blame illegal construction around the channels, seeing them as the primary reason for constricting the flow of rainwater drainage. This and a broken garbage disposal system in the city were seen as resulting from corrupt governance. But, as subsequent years of urban flooding would make clear, garbage disposal and rainwater drainage were themselves intertwined with the long legacy of spatial politics in the city.

In the early 2000s, informal garbage sorting and recycling started to emerge across the city on the streets. This emergence was not incidental but rather was largely driven by the influx of a large number of displaced Afghan migrants after the US-led troops invaded Afghanistan in 2001.[27] Previously unprofitable, such garbage and recycling sorting could now be capitalized with the infinitely cheap labor of refugee women and children. At this point in time, women could be seen burning shiny wrappers—from candy, biscuits, chips, and cigarettes—to collect the few grams of tin that imperceptibly coat them, though only at the end of a long toxic day. Hundreds of informal garbage-sorting sites emerged throughout the city. Reports of land agents paying the Karachi Development Authority's (KDA) garbage collectors to not pick up garbage from particular neighbors appeared in newspapers. Groups of small children roamed the street collecting garbage directly from homes.

Then, garbage added a new layer of ground on Karachi's surface, which could be manipulated to erase the distinctions between possible and impossible land. A new use of impossible land emerged—in the middle of roads, roundabouts, and under bridges and overpasses—as mounds of garbage were spread and sorted in every possible terrain of the city.

Garbage allowed select political groups that had previously been excluded from the politics of land in the city to enter it. And they did so through the curious duality of garbage being both an impermanent and a constant element, which could be collected from anywhere and dispersed and sorted anywhere. Garbage is mercurial. So were the political and economic alliances it enabled, cutting across binaries of governance and subversion. Escaping attempts to be tracked, these alliances were, too, described from a distance with the name of "mafia." Karachi was controlled, countless reports asserted, by both a land and garbage mafia.[28]

This was not just a marginal phenomenon. Like manipulation of land, garbage also provided a material medium for entities like DHA to claim new terrain. In the 1990s, Karachi and Sindh had seen a long drought with light monsoons. This was the time that DHA planners, without consultation with any of the other planning bodies in the city, were laying out plans for new phases in the DHA.[29] As Bashir Lakhani, a water-drainage engineer in Karachi, recalled, it was as if the DHA planners forgot that Karachi had a history of urban flooding during the monsoons, laying out the most expensive real estate in the city with meager or no rainwater drainage.[30] Lakhani had moved to Karachi from a US academic job, seeing endless consulting opportunities in this planning amnesia. True to his prediction, he was soon hired in an emergency by a panicked DHA leadership when monsoon rains returned with a vengeance in 2009. Embarrassingly, both elite and middle-class homes in DHA flooded, sharing the fate of poorer neighborhoods in the city. Lakhani's firm was brought in to lay bigger drains. But the damage had been long in the making. Not only was there not enough room on the roadsides to lay new drains, but also DHA had been constricting outlets to the Ghizri Creek mangroves with landfill. And it had used garbage and construction debris to do that.[31]

More than the impact of garbage clogging nearby drainage channels (such as those passing through Manzoor Colony), it would be this and proceeding land-reclamation projects by DHA that would produce devastating effects on the city's yearly flooding. Filling the area around the mangroves had not only narrowed the outlet of major drainage channels, like the Malir River, but also taken away the natural barrier against tide waters. The new drainage laid out by DHA since 2007, for phase 8, for instance, opened directly onto the beach. During high tides in the monsoon season, these drains become useless, pushing water back into the city rather than draining it away.

Yet DHA did not let the failure of its planning in the 1990s end its debris and garbage landfilling, turning the impossible land of mangroves into profitable real estate. Garbage could be deployed as a media strategy as well. We see another series of alliances emerging among DHA, the judiciary, and the provincial government between 2011 and the present.

In 2011, the Sindh Supreme Court passed a controversial judgment that gave the city greater and more expansive powers of eminent domain to clear illegal construction along *nalas* (drains). Since then, this ruling has been revived numerous times by the KDA—the main public works department working under the jurisdiction of the BoR—to demolish shops, bazaars, and homes, creating room for expressway access to high-value real estate, such as the DHA City to the north of Karachi. In 2020, the KDA launched new eviction and demolition campaigns around Gujjar Nala and along Manzoor Colony Nala—which passed through the DHA before opening into the Malir River—with only days' notice to the inhabitants. The justifications, once again, followed a narrative of garbage clearance. Years of unruly garbage circulation had clogged up the city's drainage channels, the official claim went, such that heavy equipment was needed at this point to clear them. This required, the KDA and DHA claimed, cutting thirty-feet swathes of land on both sides of the channels.[32]

Despite communal organization and protests across the city, the demolitions along the *nalas* moved ahead with the aid of armed police and army rangers—both notorious groups feared for their heavy-handed treatment of protests in the city. People found their houses cut in half, if not demolished altogether. But very soon, residents responded in the very language of planning and law that was launched against them.[33] Among other organizations, the Technical Training and Resource Center (TTRC)—started by a trainee, Muhammad Sirajuddin, from the long-standing community organization the Orange Pilot Project—discovered that only twenty feet of clearing was required on both sides of the channels for mobilizing the heaviest of cleaning equipment. The extra ten feet that DHA and KDA had demolished was not for the purpose of cleaning the channels. No explanation, on legal or planning grounds, could be found for the extra width. According to the housing activist Arif Hasan, the nexus of DHA, KDA, and the Sindh Supreme Court had used the notoriety of the garbage problem in the city to secure space for construction of two major expressways along the Gujjar Nala and the Malir River to connect DHA phase 8 with the DHA City to the north and DHA City to Karachi city center and the port in the South.[34]

As construction for the Malir Expressway moved forward, TTRC volunteers further mapped the flow of drainage channels from Gujjar Nala into Lyari River on foot. Here, too, they discovered that it was not illegal construction that was clogging floodwater drainage. Instead, it was the foundations of the new Malir Expressway and its many crisscrossing bridges that interrupted the river, without regard to its flow and drainage requirements.[35]

At this point, the Lyari Expressway was only half-complete. And so the TTRC, with the help of housing advocates and organizations, such as Karachi Bachao Tehreek (Save Karachi Movement) and Karachi Urban Lab, was able to put a stop to demolitions across the Gujjar Nala. This, however, only happened because the Gujjar Nala neighborhoods incidentally fell within PPP jurisdiction and could find the ear of the provincial government, which was not aligned with the goals of the DHA and other real estate stakeholders in the city. Other neighborhoods, such as Machar Colony, near Karachi Port, weren't so lucky. Today, inhabitants peer out from their half-demolished living rooms still waiting for the heavy equipment to arrive to clear the *nalas* of the garbage, which was, after all, the original excuse for demolishing their houses.[36]

Garbage is still a political issue. Voluntary cleaning drives from MQM and promises of clearing the city in a month by PPP still make headlines near elections. Newspapers still fill up with articles of corruption and inadequate governance with every flood. But as Sobia Ahmad Kaker and Nausheen H. Anwar argue, these attempts at parsing the situation through binaries of formal/informal, planned/unplanned, and corrupt/incorrupt do little for understanding, let alone managing, land, flood, and garbage mobilization in the city.[37]

Perhaps, as I have tried to show, a critical element in moving beyond these binaries in cities transformed under the shadow of the Cold War and its aftermath is understanding the politics of space, how space is defined, redefined, and unhinged from different sides through different means. In this history, incomplete refugee housing that can be demolished at a moment's notice, mountains that can be cut to redefine political strongholds, and garbage that can be left in drains to justify demolition drives all can act as instruments of design, deployed to change the status of space. Without understanding such politics of space, we cannot fathom how citizens can so smoothly be turned into enemies, and city's land, into hostile territory, how jurisdictions shrink and expand overnight, and how actions and operations are carried out across institutions and their supposed opposites.

Calling it corruption, mismanagement, or weak governance is to miss the point. Cities that have emerged out of the Cold War—or, indeed, are still living under the shadow of other wars since then that still rely on the political infrastructure created by the Cold War—are governed by covertness. Doxiadis's letter—full of militaristic bravado that turned citizens into enemies who needed to be subdued through covert operations—was not an exception to the rule. Instead, it betrayed how rules are made to appear and disappear in the midst of unsuspecting lives in spaces of the Cold War.

Five

AFGHAN REFUGEES AS POLITICAL ACTORS

SABAUON NASSERI *and* ROBERT D. CREWS

In late 1979 or early 1980, the Cold War came to the village of Rozay Qala. The inhabitants of this village in Afghanistan felt the destructive force of global politics when they became the target of a Soviet rocket attack. One of the survivors was Momin Gul, who recounted what transpired after a strike on his uncle's house: "We all wanted to go and see what had happened to the house and its inhabitants, but our parents wouldn't let us. Only my father went to help. When he returned, he sat in a corner. The only word he would utter was 'Nothing . . . nothing.'" He went on to recall, "I woke in the night and heard my mother and father weeping. Nobody had survived. The entire family disappeared in dust and ashes. The poor souls were burnt alive."[1]

Despite pursuing a policy of nonalignment, Afghanistan became an epicenter of Cold War violence in the late 1970s, forcing millions, like Momin Gul and his family, to seek refuge abroad. A coup d'etat by leftist revolutionaries in April 1978 and the Soviet invasion in December 1979 unleashed mass devastation. Fighting between the Afghan resistance movement (broadly known as the mujahideen) and the Soviet Army and its Afghan allies claimed an estimated one million lives. Soviet bombing campaigns; the scattering of landmines; the destruction of homes, livestock, and agricultural infrastructure; targeted assassinations; hunger; disease; and fear of foreign occupation—these were among the many factors that compelled millions of Afghans to flee the country, primarily for neighboring Pakistan and Iran. Afghans were also forced from or abandoned their homes under pressure from resistance organizations backed by the Americans, Saudis, Egyptians, Iranians, Pakistanis, and others. Fighting among mujahideen groups and violence against communities presumed to be their civilian clients were yet other causes of forced migration. By 1990, in addition to millions of internally displaced persons, the United Nations classified more than six million Afghans living outside Afghanistan as refugees. They made up perhaps as much as one-third of the country's prewar population.[2]

An examination of the case of the Soviet invasion of Afghanistan and its aftermath presents an opportunity to investigate Cold War conceptions of "the refugee." As in other settings, a number of competing actors and institutions advance differing understandings of the term, each in pursuit of their own interests. For the Soviets and the Moscow-backed government in Kabul, the refugee issue was a daunting and multifaceted challenge. The anti-Soviet coalition led by the United States also recognized the significance of this sizeable population, as did, of course, the neighboring countries that hosted millions of Afghans and who simultaneously opposed the Soviet occupation next door. For their allies in the Afghan resistance, they were of fundamental importance as well. Refugees became an essential resource—crucial for both their ideological framing of the war and for the material support that flowed through them. All parties sought to turn the refugee cause to their own advantage.

However, the Afghans who were themselves displaced by fighting had their own agenda—frequently conflicting and contradictory—and also their own ideas about what their actions meant. Many allied themselves with the agendas of the competing mujahideen parties through various informal and formal means. Others opposed them. The diversity of political views in Afghan refugee communities tended to mirror the broader society.

Nearly all parties to this conflict competed to define the place of the refugee within the wider contest over the future of Afghanistan. But there was one matter that the Soviets, Americans, Pakistanis, Iranians, international organizations, and even most Afghan rebel groups could agree on: these refugees should not be treated as substantive political actors with a voice in determining their political fate. In the Afghan setting of the 1980s and beyond, actors across the political spectrum capitalized on the image of the doleful and defenseless refugee as one key strategy, among others, to gain advantage in the war and, for Afghan parties in particular, to monopolize political power. Preventing several million Afghans from actively participating in the political contestation of the jihad was a central, if largely unexplored, aspect of the politics of the Cold War struggle in Afghanistan.[3]

As we will see, such efforts to exclude Afghan refugees from the political realm largely failed. For the mujahideen and their rivals alike, these refugee populations were a highly sought-after reservoir of popular legitimation. Insofar as the politics of Afghanistan circled back, in often conflicting and limited ways, to notions of democratic governance, various parties to the conflict continued to seek their active or, at least, passive assent. And yet—even as the Cold War powers and their regional allies shut down most opportunities for refugee political participation—Afghans themselves devised ways to affect the course of events in their home country. While formally excluded from the political institutions of the revolutionary government and the opposition alike, some displaced Afghans lent their support (informally, to one or another side) or withheld it (depending upon circumstances and their political leanings).

Thus, refugees did become political actors, through the limited avenues available to them. They did so in the choices they made about repatriation and, even more importantly, in recasting the values of Afghan society, which they achieved by circulating prose, poetry, and music that thematized the tragedy of their suffering in exile and that articulated their aspirations for the future.

Defining the Afghan Refugee

In practice, Afghan-refugee experiences were extremely varied. In Pakistan, the government devised formal policies and organizational structures to control them; in Iran, meanwhile, Afghans faced a very different environment with much less coordinated control. In Pakistan, Afghans settled in camps, as well as in informal settlements and urban areas, such as Peshawar, Quetta, Karachi, and Rawalpindi; in Iran, by contrast, initial reception in camps was soon followed by relocation to cities across the country, including Tehran, Yazd, Mashhad, Kerman, and others. Islamabad allowed numerous international organizations to provide medical and other services, while Tehran limited international access. Most Afghans in Pakistan tended to come from Pashtun and Baluch communities; those in Iran, however, were a diverse population hailing from the city of Herat in western Afghanistan, as well as Tajiks, Hazaras, Uzbeks, Turkmen, Nuristanis, Aimaqs, and others. Especially after 1983, refugees came from heterogeneous communities in the North.

In both Iran and Pakistan, though, mujahideen parties coordinated with the national governments with the aim of using refugees to advance the jihad in Afghanistan. And in both settings, Afghans clashed with locals on numerous occasions. In Iran, in particular—as the revolutionary state confronted a deepening economic crisis and multiple challenges due to the Iran-Iraq War—the government scapegoated Afghans. Despite having become essential to the Iranian labor force, Afghan refugees there experienced harassment and physical attacks as a regular part of daily life.[4]

Not long after the Soviet invasion of 1979, scholars of Afghanistan—working mostly from the disciplinary perspective of anthropology—identified discrepancies between how displaced Afghans understood their actions and how international organizations categorized them. In the view of the French ethnologists Pierre Centlivres and Micheline Centlivres-Demont, the typical Afghan refugee in Pakistan conceived of himself as "a 'two-fold' person, the *mohajer/mujahed*." On the one hand, many Afghan refugees believed that the exemplary conduct of the Prophet Muhammad—and especially his hijra, or migration from Mecca to Medina in 622—offered a model for all Muslims seeking to escape persecution. They thus took on the mantle of the *mohajer* (one who engages in hijra) to understand their own journey from their homes. On the other hand, many refugees also articulated a commitment to jihad—struggle in defense of the faith. Such fighters became "mujahideen" (singular: *mujahed*). Jihad, of course, became the leitmotif of the Afghan opposition that emerged in 1978 against the ostensibly "atheist" leftist government and its backers in Moscow. As Centlivres and Centlivres-Demont note, their typology of Afghan refugees' language for understanding their predicament contrasted sharply with the language of the international refugee conventions of 1951 and 1967, which fixed the identity of the refugee as a powerless figure in need of technocratic care.[5]

Despite these incongruities, the Afghan refugee became the site of various forms of international concern, expertise, and intervention on the part of the Union of Soviet Socialist Republics (USSR) and the United States, as well as dozens of nongovernmental organization (NGOs), the United Nations High Commissioner for Refugees, Afghan political organizations in exile, the revolutionary Democratic Republic of Afghanistan (DRA) government based in Kabul, and the governments of Pakistan and Iran.[6] What is more, not all Afghan refugees lived in the camps, which were the primary focus of the global superpowers, international NGOs, and Afghanistan's neighbors. For Islamabad and Tehran, Afghans initially were to be incorporated into ongoing projects to demonstrate the "Islamic" character of each state. In Iran, as Maliha Safri points out, Afghans received documents identifying them as migrants (*mohajerin*), not refugees (*panahandegan*). Similarly, Pakistani officials explained their reception of Afghans as a policy inspired by "the various Qur'anic injunctions on the treatment of migrants."[7] Despite the proliferation of these official (and scholarly) labels, Afghan-refugee perspectives remained quite varied and shifted over time.

Existing international protocols defined refugee status using the universal image of a helpless character. But the Cold War context now reinforced the trope of the Afghan refugee as pitiable victim, although for competing ideological ends. For example, the Afghan opposition and its partisans in Washington employed the refugee-as-victim figure as a rhetorical theme in their efforts to mobilize public support for rolling back the Soviet presence. Already in January 1980, the American ambassador explained to his Pakistani counterparts that "Pakistan should expect to benefit from world attention being focused on Soviet aggression, and ... it would be particularly beneficial to have [the] plight of Afghan refugees given full publicity."[8]

In this scenario, displaced Afghans were meant to evoke pity and righteous indignation. In October 1981, British prime minister Margaret Thatcher visited the Nasir Bagh refugee camp in Pakistan, accompanied by a retinue of international journalists. The purpose of her visit was to highlight the abject state of displaced Afghans. As the *New York Times* puts it, she "spoke of her sadness and anger at seeing the camp dwellers, who she said had been driven from their homes 'because the Russians invaded your country.'" Moreover, Thatcher used the camp as a backdrop to express "admiration" for what she portrayed as the innately anti-Communist disposition of the Afghan refugee: "You left your country because you refused to live under a godless Communist system which is trying to destroy your religion and your independence."[9]

Thatcher clearly signaled an affective ideological solidarity with the figure of the defiant Afghan *mohajer/mujahed*. However, this particular propagandistic framing never became the dominant mode of representing Afghan refugees. Even in Iran—where, from at least 1984, the government of Ayatollah Ruhollah Musavi Khomeini saw in Afghans the possibility of "exporting" the ideas of his revolutionary Shi'ism via Afghan Shi'i communities—state control over refugee politics was meant to diminish their capacity to act autonomously.[10] Despite the pronouncements of Thatcher and Khomeini, elites of all political persuasions in the conflict largely shared a commitment to denying the political agency of the Afghan refugee and to exclude these populations from the sphere of politics entirely.

The Refugee as Outsider

Backed by the United States and its coalition of anti-Communist allies, the mujahideen principally focused their struggle against the Soviets and their allies in Kabul on areas of military operations *within* the borders of Afghanistan, which they called the "fronts" of the jihad. In their newsletters and magazines published in Pakistan and Iran, mujahideen parties and activists highlighted their battlefield encounters with the Soviet and DRA enemies and, on occasion, with rival insurgent organizations. Photographs of men training artillery on enemy locations and of bands of men posing with rifles on craggy hillsides, as well as individualized portraits of martyrs who sacrificed themselves in combat, expressed the visual vocabulary of the jihad. Similarly, mujahideen memoirs and other accounts mirrored this focus on the "garden trenches," where fighters became "beautiful flowers of the *jihad*" and martyrs were like "butterflies drunk on their love of Islam and the homeland who eventually burned themselves in the bright candle and reached the summit of their love."[11]

Yet such mujahideen narratives spent little time *beyond* those trenches and depicted refugees as playing the role of merely spectators. In Pakistan, they became dependents of the seven mujahideen parties, through which Pakistan, the United States, and its allies distributed aid to refugees.[12] As Mohammad Tahir Aziz Gumnam declares in his contemporary chronicle of the jihad, "The best hero here is he who has carried out more and left the dirty problems of tribal issues aside from the holy jihad, leaving them to be judged by the desperate public and refugees."[13] The figure of the refugee reflected the gender and age hierarchies of the mujahideen imaginary. Some 75 percent of Afghan refugees in 1990 were female, which lent credence to the tendency in mujahideen media to present this entire population as feminized or elderly.[14] In such accounts, fighting for Islam and country was the active responsibility of daring young men, while female refugees and those too old for battle remained passive onlookers.

Neither the US-backed jihad nor the Soviet-backed Afghan Socialist project countenanced the agency of displaced persons. For their part, Soviet and DRA officials rejected the notion that anyone would willingly flee the political order inaugurated by the coup of April 1978. By their telling, this was a revolution led by the People's Democratic Party of Afghanistan (PDPA) and backed by the popular will. The policy of the Kabul government was to seek the repatriation of all who left the country.

Still, official DRA and Soviet media took pains not to blame Afghans who declined to return. Rather, this was the fault of the opposition parties who prevented displaced Afghans from returning to their homes. They also highlighted the duplicity of Pakistani and Iranian authorities: Afghanistan's neighbors were not aiding Afghans but were guilty of impeding their return from refugee camps and settlements. Greedy officials in Iran and Pakistan did not want to give up the material resources or political capital that hosting this population had yielded.

In such portrayals of the victimization of Afghan refugees, the culprits were not DRA or Soviet Army soldiers but the governments of the countries hosting displaced populations. In his retrospective review of Soviet operations in Afghanistan, Aleksandr Liakhovskii cites as paradigmatic an instance when "the authorities blocked the return to Afghanistan of 890 families from Zabul (Iran), 610 from the Nasar-Bagh camp, and 280 from the Savabi camp (Pakistan)."[15] Official sources frequently alleged that Pakistan and Iran colluded with the Afghan opposition to instrumentalize the cause of Afghan refugees to solicit international aid, which they siphoned off for their own purposes.[16]

DRA media outlets frequently highlighted the treachery of Pakistani and Iranian authorities. In May 1984, for instance, the *Kabul New Times* published an article featuring the testimony of a Pakistani policeman. Haq Nawaz, who had recently sought asylum in Afghanistan, claimed that the Pakistani government inflated the number of Afghan refugees for their own financial gain. The policeman condemned the unfortunate state of Afghan refugees. "Pakistani authorities working in camps," he claimed, "forcefully take away the rations allotted to the Afghans for themselves." In addition to being made to turn to crime for survival, the most vulnerable were compelled to sacrifice their dignity: "I have witnessed with my own eyes the Afghan 'refugee' women begging in Quetta, while the Pakistani government receives substantial aids [*sic*] in the name of Afghans, which they themselves use for their own sake." In DRA media, it was only the coercion of Pakistani officials that kept Afghans from acting on their desire to return home, not least of all because they faced hostility and conflict with the Pakistani population, which, in this portrayal, did not want the Afghans there any longer. "I would like to cite an example here related to the city of Paishee on one of the camps of Afghans. A number of Afghan fugitives robbed the houses of the inhabitants of the said city as a result of which a bloody confrontation took place between the Afghan 'refugees' and the inhabitants of the region. As a result of this confrontation one Pakistani was killed. Afterward, the government of Pakistan intervened in the case with hues and cries and was forced to move the Afghan 'refugees' camp 15 miles away from the city of Paishee to another region."[17] Such grim descriptions of the plight of Afghans emphasized the nefarious and duplicitous aims of neighboring states. By placing the term "refugee" in quotation marks, official media sought to undermine the opposition's claim that Afghan migrants genuinely merited this designation.[18]

The Soviet-backed DRA employed another, related trope in their propaganda campaign by portraying displaced Afghans as "misguided." Such a characterization questioned the refugees' loyalty, although it simultaneously acknowledged, however obliquely, their political agency. Building upon their denial of the legitimacy of the refugee status of Afghans resident in Pakistan, DRA authorities touted, in September 1982, a decree offering amnesty to Afghans abroad. The DRA-backed *Kabul New Times* reported on an announcement "recently distributed among the Afghan nationals living in miserable conditions in the so-called refugee camps in Pakistan despite the ban imposed by the counter-revolutionary bandit chiefs and the military regime of Islamabad on bringing printed materials into the camps." Insisting that these Afghans in actuality wanted to return, the article asserted, "These misguided Afghans now fully realise that they are living in exile, far from their country, leading a difficult and purposeless life, deprived of the warmth of their household and subjected to perpetual humiliation, while the revolution provides for them the means of work, education and participation in moulding the destiny of the society." The *Kabul New Times* expressed confidence that the collective delusion gripping "these co-called refugees" was being shed by the majority, who now realized "that US imperialism and the ruling elites of Pakistan and China are using them as cheap and convenient tools."[19]

Across the Cold War divide, Afghan-refugee politics became fodder for propaganda aimed at an international public and audiences at home. The resulting narratives dramatized the plight of displaced Afghans in ways that would advance the ideological agendas of their authors. In assigning blame for the suffering of refugees to their opponents, the leftist revolutionaries and mujahideen alike engaged in a form of deflection and avoidance of responsibility for the root causes of refugee displacement. At the same time, each of the parties to the conflict came to view this population as a crucially important constituency whose support might lend legitimacy to efforts to shape the future of Afghanistan.

The Refugee Camp as Catalyst

Tacitly acknowledging the political agency of Afghan migrants, both DRA agents and the mujahideen parties targeted them with propaganda. Both sides marked Afghans in Pakistan in particular for the dissemination of print, radio, TV, and other communications aimed at influencing their political choices. Among the most consequential of these was the question of whether or not to repatriate. For the DRA, the return of migrants was key to demonstrating the legitimacy of the revolutionary project. Consequently, Kabul promised amnesties and privileges for the return of Afghans, while exiled political groups opposed it.

In addition, the DRA launched disinformation operations—according to the Afghan Information Centre, a news organization run by opposition intellectuals led by Professor Sayyid Bahauddin Majruh and based in Pakistan—on both sides of the border. For example, in March 1987, the *Afghan Information Centre Monthly Bulletin* reported that the Kabul government had organized an elaborate ruse using government-backed fighters from a city on the Afghanistan-Pakistan frontier. "Militia families were taken from Jalalabad to the border during the night and transported back the following day in flower-covered buses and presented as refugees coming from Pakistan. Kabul government agents infiltrating the refugee camps were instructed to make a show of returning—packing, selling their belongings—and actually moving towards the border."[20] Yet such DRA-backed operations were countered by the mujahideen with their own programs to influence displaced Afghans. In fact, the mujahideen parties already had considerable leverage over the refugee camps since they oversaw the distribution of the identity cards that were necessary for the receipt of food, cash, and other resources (although it should be noted that many Afghan refugees bypassed the camps and settled in Pakistani cities). In the camps themselves, direct intimidation played a particular role as well. To remind refugees of their powerlessness, mujahideen party bosses issued threats, which circulated in handwritten night letters that demanded obedience.[21]

The language of these propaganda efforts insisted that being "political" was only available to a privileged set of actors. For instance, the activist Mullah Abdul Salam Zaeef recalls in his memoir how he had struggled to shift from a refugee to a fighter committed to jihad. In this instance, he had to overcome his family's opposition. Although his family moved from Kandahar to Quetta in 1984, he was still drawn to the battlefield despite his relatives' assurances that he could have a completely different life in Pakistan: "I could have a house, a wife and business, they said, if only I would stay in Pakistan and not return to Afghanistan."[22]

The political and religious views of the likes of Zaeef were not shared by Professor Majruh and his Afghan Information Centre. Yet even they employed analogous categories of analysis—dividing Afghans in Pakistan into "simple refugees in the camps," "the resistance fighters," and "commanders"—with a typology that suggests a hierarchy of political consciousness and engagement and a fairly strict division of political labor. Whereas mujahideen activists thought the camps were where Afghans might be made into docile clients of a particular party and their political and religious views recast by mujahideen media and by the material resources monopolized by party leaders, conditions evolved, and refugees gained exposure to new sources of information and political activism and expression. As Majruh himself began to notice, in the second half of the 1980s, his static portrayal of Afghan society abroad failed to match changing circumstances. Indeed, the life of the refugee camp now seemed a distinctive political arena of its own.

For some Afghan intellectuals, the refugee camps offered a singular opportunity to advance a nationalizing project—one that they had not managed to achieve within the borders of Afghanistan over the past half century. One such vision was presented by a group of exile scholars based at Peshawar University, the Writers Union of Free Afghanistan. In a pamphlet entitled *Life in Refugee Camps* (1985), the writers emphasize the role of the refugee camp as a catalyst of national unity. In their view, the camp created a new kind of Afghan identity. "Prior to the war in Afghanistan most Afghan ethnic groups were isolated from one another. Now one of the main benefits of living in camps is that people of different ethnic and linguistic backgrounds from various parts of Afghanistan are assigned to one camp. This will help them to understand each other better and find out more about one another's feeling, problems, and life-style. It is hoped that these . . . living conditions will help the process of nation state building of the Afghans in the future."[23]

Children in the camps were of particular importance to the Writers Union because they had only narrowly escaped being "indoctrinated with an education of communism, Marxism and atheism." Whereas Afghanistan under Soviet occupation had produced nothing more than "a generation of handicapped and disabled Afghans," the world of the camp was entirely the opposite. "Among the Refugee children," the pamphlet declared, education was addressing "the most serious problems of the future Afghan society!" Moreover, the camp provided stability and normalcy. It even encouraged family solidarity and filial devotion: "You will observe ... that despite hardships of various kinds refugee children are like children everywhere. They play games just like other normal children in countries at peace, and they also help their parents just to make life easier and more bearable for the family."[24]

By such accounts, the refugee camp then was not only a site of national consolidation and familial order but also a space where Afghans shored up their religious convictions. Like many other migrant organizations, the Writers Union of Free Afghanistan stressed that Afghans had sought "refuge" in an "Islamic country." Their fundamental aspiration was to "safeguard their religion intact." Since Islam was "a binding force" that united Afghanistan—a land "of many different ethnic groups with many languages"—the faith demanded special protection. Thus, millions of Afghans had made use of "their places of refuge as a base for resistance against the atheists." Unlike their fellow countrymen living under "the puppet regime in Kabul, Afghan refugees perform their religious obligations in complete freedom. Living in camps, they are free to worship the Almighty God."[25]

Afghan elites were forced to think more urgently about the future contours of the nation and the possibilities of repatriating millions of Afghans when, after coming to power in Moscow in 1985, the Soviet leader Mikhail Gorbachev signaled his intention of leaving Afghans to their own political devices. At this point, Afghan elites confronted the challenge of reworking the meaning of citizenship and patriotism in a new political order that appeared to be looming on the horizon.

Suddenly—with the prospect of national liberation—the status of Afghan refugees became a greater political priority. Put simply, neither side *knew* what the refugees who now might return actually wanted politically. It was true that, in keeping with the warring parties' consensus on the exclusion of refugees from Afghan politics, the Soviet and Afghan governments and the opposition parties conducted occasional surveillance on refugee camps. Still, they rarely sought out public opinion in a transparent and systematic way. Even for more secular and democratically leaning oppositional intellectuals, the collection of refugee views by surveys or other means does not appear to have been a major priority.

Then, in 1987, Professor Majruh undertook a survey to identify whether there was one single person that the disparate refugees might accept to unify opposition forces and rally support for a post-DRA government in Kabul. (The findings of his survey have appeared frequently in standard historical accounts of the Afghan jihad.) Majruh concluded that the survey demonstrated the popularity of the ousted king Mohammad Zahir Shah (r. 1933–1973)—a figure that the DRA government was also apparently considering as a potential intermediary who might negotiate an end to the war with the opposition.[26] According to Majruh, the former king polled at over 70 percent among men and around 50 percent among the smaller number of women whom his researchers interviewed. And, crucially, Majruh stressed that his findings showed a lack of popular support for the mujahideen leadership.[27]

What merits more attention in this context is Majruh's analysis of a spike in interest in politics among Afghan refugees in 1987. This corresponds to a moment when Moscow intensified efforts to extract the USSR from the country. In response to changes in the Soviet Union, the head of the DRA, Dr. Mohammad Najibullah, began to publicize the offer of a ceasefire and a campaign of "national reconciliation," likely to further divide and marginalize the opposition by accommodating some of its members. Writing in his *Afghan Information Centre Monthly Bulletin* in April 1987, Majruh observed that even "simple refugees" had been drawn into the political fray, principally by the agitation of opposition activists. "With the huge publicity about a settlement for the Afghan crisis, the political preoccupations among the refugees and fighters has [sic] increasingly come to the foreground. Among the Afghans in exile in Pakistan everybody is talking politics, the leaders more strongly than ever, but also the simple refugees in the camps and the resistance fighters and commanders. The political leaders in exile started the polemics." Majruh saw "a new development in the situation," noting an "increasing interest of the refugee population, resistance commanders and fighters in the political problems." All of this was manifest in "large gatherings" that attracted participants from camps along the Afghanistan-Pakistan frontier.[28] And while crediting the heads of the mujahideen parties with sparking this engagement, his account of these gatherings suggests that the displaced Afghans who attended these rallies came with their own convictions.

Refugees as Critics and Activists

Furthermore, Majruh noted that two infamous figures in the mujahideen constellation, Abdul Rasul Sayaf and Gulbuddin Hekmatyar, both staunchly rejected the return of Mohammad Zahir Shah as a potentially unifying national figure. In the spring of 1987, they organized rallies in refugee camps in the North-West Frontier Province and in Baluchistan with the aim, Majruh noted, "to make their stance approved by large public gatherings." Instead, Majruh asserted, "the people who attended did not seem to like anti Zahir Shah speeches, some loudly protested; in other cases the gatherings were simply disrupted or different speeches contrary to the intention of the promoters were delivered." Moreover, on April 11 in Miranshah in North Waziristan, refugees and fighters from different parties gathered in a large demonstration in which they shouted "pro-Zahir Shah slogans."[29]

Another turning point came on May 11 and 12, according to Majruh, when the BBC Persian and Pashto services published a very rare interview with the exiled king. Hearing the king had an enormous effect "on the refugees as well as the mujahideen," according to Majruh, who supported this claim by quoting an Afghan man from the Nasir Bagh refugee camp near Peshawar, who supposedly affirmed, "He was speaking. We heard his voice. That is quite different!" Although the man "did not much care about the contents of the interview," he "added enthusiastically: 'That was his voice, strong and clear. He is alive! He is ready. He has to come.'"[30]

During this same period, the BBC Pashto and Persian services received numerous letters from listeners in the Pakistani camps as well as in Iran, who sought to engage with the programs they had heard and to express their own views about Afghan politics and society. In 1990, Anthony Hyman, a British scholar of the

Figure 5.1. Speakers addressing Afghan refugees at a rally for King Zahir Shah in February 1989 in Peshawar, Pakistan. Source: *Noorullhaq*, February 1989, photograph. Courtesy of Afghan Media Resource Center and Library of Congress.

Figure 5.2. Afghan refugees attending a rally in support of King Zahir Shah in Peshawar, Pakistan. Source: *Muhammad Muqim*, February 1989, photograph. Courtesy of Afghan Media Resource Center and Library of Congress.

Soviet occupation of Afghanistan, published a small sampling of these letters, primarily from listeners in the North-West Frontier Province of Pakistan. Letter writers communicated a variety of views on subjects ranging from the return of Zahir Shah and the mujahideen to the activities of Muslim clerics in exile in Iran and Pakistan. Others commented on corruption, nepotism, women's rights, the political uses of Islam, and changing marital practices.[31]

One refugee listener called for the exiled Zahir Shah—a "wise and senior politician"—to return to power. This listener invoked the "legendary story of a King who thinks that the old whitebearded people are useless in his kingdom, and orders that they are to be got rid of at once." Yet when this kingdom went to war, the king now realized that he needed "to find a senior wise old man to guide the course of the war." Given the fact that "most of our experienced, wise and senior politicians have been killed by the present regime," the letter pointed out, "the only person who now lives is Mohammad Zahir Shah," whom the "Afghan nation desperately wants . . . to put their ruined house in order." The story quoted in the letter highlighted the wave of political assassinations that had engulfed the country and its diaspora in Pakistan during those years. Few intellectuals and high-ranking officials survived the assassinations, but Zahir Shah was among them. Another challenged this perspective, arguing that "Zahir Shah himself is responsible for the current situation of Afghanistan." "During his reign of 40–50 odd years," the listener observed, "nepotism was the order of the day. He kept the Afghan nation in the dark and paid no attention to its welfare. This injustice bred grievances and the Russians were on hand to exploit them."[32]

Other letter writers complained of conditions in Pakistan and called for repatriation while criticizing Afghan leaders in exile as upstarts and frauds who exploited "the feelings of Afghans under the guise of Islam or jihad." These were the same people, one letter asserted, who "didn't have a donkey back home, and now own cars." Another called the mujahideen party leader Hekmatyar a "snake in the grass" and accused him of assassinating Professor Majruh a few months earlier (an accusation voiced by many at the time and later).[33]

Continuing with this critique of right-wing mujahideen, a group of women wrote from Quetta to complain that they had had to leave Kabul. The reason was that, in Kabul, they had faced persecution at the hands of a Shi'i group, Resalat, which had targeted women for a "Prophetic Mission" under the banner of the Iranian revolutionary leader Ayatollah Khomeini.

> At this moment, through this Organisation, which calls itself Islamic, tens of our innocent sisters are in Pule Charkhi prison [in Kabul]. If we had not left, perhaps we too would be there, thanks to the actions of the same Organisation. I beseech you to send these words to the members of the Islamic Resalat Organisation to stop such anti-humanitarian acts and have pity on our young girls, and to stop their wrong deeds which in their own eyes are Islamic. [Tell them] not to cause the death or imprisonment of our young girls with their statements or pictures of Khomeini. It must be mentioned that it is a blatant interference [in Afghan affairs] to kill the Russians and substitute Khomeini for them, as for us both are foreigners.
>
> The people of Afghanistan must, without foreign interference, establish a government of their own choice.

In a letter that may also have come from a woman, a listener protested the fact that clerics (*akhonds*) "are maintaining that all bareheaded people are the enemies of Islam." "I appeal to you," the letter urged, "as an impartial broadcasting organisation in this known world to help spare the lives of thousands and thousands of Afghans by exposing to the Afghan people these guardians of the middle ages." And from Qom in Iran, a group of Afghan women implored the BBC to aid the cause of "a group of humiliated people, or to put it simply the victims of a feudal system" and to condemn the recent "idiotic statement" by a mujahideen leader,

Yunus Khalis, who "said in an interview that women in Afghanistan have no right to vote." "Tell the silly, uncultured Khalis on our behalf," the women complained, "that the caravan of humanity is forging forward. Gone are the days when you can look at women as the morsels of your passion. We will fight for our rights in Afghanistan till our last breath."[34]

Such source materials that allow us to track the politicization of Afghan refugees in their own voices are rare. Yet there are other forms of evidence that show how refugees employed collective action and how they did so outside of the limiting frame of the hapless victim, the constraints of the refugee camp, and even the strictures imposed by mujahideen activists and the police and military of their host countries. And reports of organized violence—and even pitched battles—between armed refugees and Iranian and Pakistani authorities, as well as between them and local communities, reveal a significant avenue of political action.[35]

Another is suggested by a 1990 survey by the German ethnologist Bernt Glatzer, who interviewed refugees from Kunar Province in Bajaur District, Pakistan, about their reluctance to return to Afghanistan after the Soviets had withdrawn the previous year. Respondents to Glatzer's queries emphasized uncertainty about local security and economic conditions, as well as about political stability in Kabul given the events of 1978 and 1979.[36] In Kunar, Glatzer finds, sharp divisions then emerged within communities—and even within families—about whether or not to leave the area.[37] Compelled to weigh how their decisions would be received within communities on both sides of the border, Kunaris expressed particular anxiety about others' perceptions of their political loyalty. Some locals who had not left Kunar for Pakistan, for example, were tainted with the brush of collaboration with the leftist government and the Soviets. Even those who opted for Pakistan at a later date labored under the burden of these suspicions. And for those considering return from Pakistan, resettling too soon might betray insufficient devotion to the legacy of the jihad and the nation. Thus, choices that Afghans made about repatriation were, in fact, another form of political engagement.

The Politics of Music, Poetry, and Prose

Yet another kind of political activism emerged in the 1980s when poets and singers—in camps and informal settlements in Pakistan and in cities across Iran—began to produce and circulate their own narratives about the present and future conditions of displaced Afghans and their homeland. Poetry was central to this project. Zuzanna Olszewska points out that Afghan refugees' "experiences of exile

... have been intertwined with poetry, both oral and written, as their longest-standing, most portable, and most durable artistic tradition—and ... as a means of continuous critique, reflection, world-building, and intervention in social life."[38]

In Pakistan, these musicians and poets were largely excluded from the media channels of the mujahideen parties. Yet for many, their independence proved an advantage, aided by access to new cassette technology.[39] Commenting on the evolution of poetic conventions among Pashto speakers, Professor Sayyid Bahauddin Majruh notes that "in the resistance and among the refugees the number of those who devote themselves to poetry has markedly increased. If they know how to read and write they print collections of their poems; if not, they sing them, record them on audiocassettes, and try to distribute them."[40]

In Iran, by contrast, the Shi'i resistance parties, especially in the early 1980s, exerted greater control over Afghan cultural production and became patrons of "resistance poetry."[41] Often educated in Iranian seminaries, Afghan poets in Iran produced new works influenced by their clerical training and the wider context of living in a society being remade by revolutionary martyrdom and war (with Iraq). Meanwhile, in Pakistan, again according to Majruh, women in particular used the traditional twenty-two-syllable poetic form of the *landay* to comment on the condition of exile: "The only thing [about *landays*] that has changed is the hierarchy of the themes. Love and eroticism are praised less, while religious outpourings, the call to holy war, nostalgia for the ancestral land, the sense of honor, and the glorification of heroism dominate."[42] These sources offer traces of an archive that neither the Afghan elites in exile nor their backers nor the government in Kabul could appropriate.

Among the numerous themes that writers, poets, and musicians developed, a few stand out for closer examination. One of these thematic strands focuses on the tragedy of displacement and the suffering of exile. Among the women's poems collected by Majruh, one laments,

> The woman in exile never stops dying.
> Turn her face, then, toward her native land so that she may breathe her last.

Another expresses nostalgia for the landscape of the country's capital:

> Tears are streaming down my face.
> I cannot forget Kabul's snow-topped mountains.

More provocatively, one of the *landays* recorded by Majruh addresses God directly in expressing a woman's determination to return to her homeland:

> God, do not let any woman die in exile!
> With her last breath she will forget Your Name so as to think only of her native land.

A related subject of such poetry treats exile as a site of resistance. Refugee women often used *landays* to urge their men to return to the battlefield, promising steadfast and passionate devotion until their return.

> Go and fight in Kabul, my love,
> For you I'll keep both my body and my mouth intact.[43]

Others warned that a lack of courage would bring not just shame but also the lover's rejection:

> A martyr is like lightning that glitters and is then snuffed out.
> He who dies at home does nothing other than defile the bed.

Another poem reads,

> Dust for you, but never my mouth again:
> You hid when the men went off to battle.[44]

Female poets thus engaged in informal, but consequential, agitation on behalf of the resistance struggle. The composition of *landays* became a vehicle for Afghan-refugee women to bolster the jihad and to transform the future of Afghanistan.

Longing for the homeland and a more harmonious future was another poetic preoccupation. While there are several words for "country" in Persian and Pashto—such as *sarzamin, kishwar, mumlakat,* and *hewad*—refugee poets and singers often returned to another term: *watan*. Similar to the Iberian word *patria* analyzed by Benedict Anderson, *watan* can "gently stretch from 'home village,' through 'hometown' and 'home-region,' on to 'home-country.'"[45] Refugee poetry relied on this word because it lent itself to writing about a spectrum of Afghan experiences: from birds and streams in one's village to war and the destruction of cities to longing for Afghanistan's soil.[46]

Much of this poetry and other writing avoid ethnicity or political animosity for one or another group, instead often speaking of brothers killing brothers. Even when concerned with localities and dialects, these works posit the possibility of unity and fraternity within patriotism.[47] Some poets also pointed to a future secured by the fraternity of all Afghans. Such writing expresses a longing for return to a homeland, where one can find dignity and security—but also a context in which their views mattered.

Yet, simultaneously, a variant of this political sentiment emerged—one that focused on the liberation of marginalized and persecuted ethnic and religious communities. Since even the nineteenth century, the Pakistani city of Quetta had been a center of exile and settlement for the Hazara ethnic group of Afghanistan. From Quetta, the popular singer Sarwar Sarkhosh focused on the historic struggle of the Hazara people to attain equal rights and to chart their own political destiny—an epic challenge that persisted in the face of the Saur Revolution of 1978 and the Soviet invasion. Performed and recorded in Quetta, Sarkhosh's songs recall a lengthy history of Hazara suffering—of mass killing and enslavement under Amir 'Abd-al Rahman in the late nineteenth century—and Sarkhosh called on his people to embrace this fight as a moment of liberation for all Hazaras.

> The Hazara people are a brave people,
> That defend the land like a lion.
> The history of this land is written with blood.
> The people . . .
> These brave people have broken their shackles,
> With the cry *Allahu akbar* [God is great].
> The people . . .[48]

Sarkhosh was a leading figure in a wider movement to map out a new position for Hazaras, to change perceptions within the community and within Afghan society at large. Among Hazaras as well as other communities, songs composed by refugees in Pakistan and Iran circulated across borders, passing through the interior of Afghanistan and throughout the diaspora, making refugee gatherings a privileged site for the reimagination of Afghan politics.

Afterlives

The Soviets finally withdrew from Afghanistan in 1989. And yet the political actors who defined the jihad era largely continued to prevent the return from exile dreamed of by millions of Afghans. At the same time, the poet and scholar Mohammad Kazem Kazemi (b. 1968 in Herat) could still express hope and determination in his celebrated 1991 poem "Return."

> How could I not return, when my battle trench is there?
> How? Oh, the memory of my brother's grave is there.
> How could I not return, when the mosque and the mihrab,
> the sword which waits to kiss my head, all of these are there?
> A time to build, a time to pray, were all that I had here;
> my fight for freedom and my cries of "God is great!" are there.[49]

For others, the war had changed Afghanistan too much. In his poem "In Mourning for Justice," Hadi Arussang (b. 1950 Kabul)—a member of the revolutionary PDPA, which had seized power in 1978, and, later, an amateur poet writing in the Netherlands—writes about the destruction and unrecognizability of the nation he once knew:

> The white-haired mother of the era
> wept, shedding tears bitterly
> Those, on whose grave she lay
> told of life's secret and mystery
> I inquired: Mother, who rests here?
> She answered: My child, "justice" has died
> Behold, the grave of my children is here
> the harvest of my white hair and body
> Here lies "fairness," deceased last year
> she embraced "truth" and took her in tow
> Here lies "faith" within the prophets' religion
> villains and murderers did her so.[50]

Arussang imagines Afghanistan as a feminine spirit woven from diverse qualities, including justice, truth, and faith. Directing attention away from material destruction and toward the spiritual scars of war, the writer conveys sorrow in these lines, revealing how the absence of these qualities has reshaped his relationship with his "mother" country.

From the eminent Kazemi to the amateur Arussang, Afghan artists, singers, and writers have played a key role in expressing the aspirations of a population whose displacement did not end with the conclusion of the Cold War. They have distributed their poems through the internet as well as in-person gatherings.[51] The poetry and short stories of Parween Faiz Zadah Malal (b. 1957 in Kandahar), for instance, explore the intimate experiences of Afghan refugees in Pakistan. Written in Karachi in 1995, her story "Hate" features a mother who makes money by collecting and selling discarded paper, taking the reader into the unnamed protagonist's daily struggle: "Early in the morning she and her little son left their tent and collected paper in the city's bazaars and alleys until late in the afternoon. When the evening drew near, they stopped by a shop to sell the paper they had collected during the day." But we learn that this struggle is knotted with other forms of precarity that only someone familiar with the refugee experience can communicate, with Malal adding, "As the clouds piled up, a feeling of anxiety grew within her. On rainy days, they could not walk far, and there was a risk that a heavy rain would soak all the paper." So we learn about the protagonist's struggle, in which the vicissitudes of weather could ruin her day's income. On the occasion when there is no dry paper to sell, she is left to muster the courage to beg for food for her son: "Her heart was split in two; on the one hand was a mother's love and affection, and on the other was shame and fear."[52]

Malal's writings are far removed from those of the 1980s written by Afghans taken with grand ideas of martyrdom. In her work, battle and heroism are replaced by a focus on labor as struggle, the shame of being a hungry wanderer, and a longing for her son to receive an education. The story still contains the familiar thematic strand of a return to the embrace of one's country "as the flames of exile and migration" burn in the protagonist's heart, getting "her thinking about returning to her homeland."[53] Unlike the jihad era, however, Malal is not prioritizing a desire to die in her native soil but rather the significance of homeland as a place that can provide education, bread, and therefore dignity and tranquility.

Similarly, in her poem "Like a Desert Flower," Malal likens the refugee's hope for return and peace to thirst and exhaustion, lamenting the loss of a sense of home curated by a woman's touch.

> Like a desert flower waiting for rain,
> like a river-bank thirsting for the touch of pitchers,
> like the dawn
> longing for light;
> and like a house,
> like a house in ruins for want of a woman -
> the exhausted ones of our times
> need a moment to breathe,
> need a moment to sleep,
> in the arms of peace, in the arms of peace.[54]

As shown in the uncertain future of the child in Malal's story, a second and third generation of Afghans have grown up in Pakistan and Iran still bearing the label of Afghan refugees (in Iran, *mohajerin-e Afghan*) but now without the enthusiasm of politicians who saw in them a weapon in a global conflict.[55] These artists continue to reflect on their ongoing displacement and seemingly unending violence in the country of their ancestors. Yet they do so while also critiquing their status as people who inhabit countries that are not their own and whose chances for education, work, housing, health, and safety have steadily declined since the Cold War powers retreated. As one Afghan rapper in Iran lamented (sometime after 2001),

> We too were human, so why were we exploited
> We became laboratory mice, in every corner of the planet
> In the neighboring country, the filthy Afghan
> In the queue of their bakery, we became the last one.[56]

Another, writing anonymously, addressed fellow Afghans directly about the horrors of trying to reach Western Europe:

> What terrible days I saw on this path
> What great youth drowned in the river
> My words are true, o compatriot
> There is a lot in my heart, how can I declare
> Between Greece and Turkey, drowned many a compatriot.[57]

The continued displacement of millions of Afghans after 1991 stands out among the many underappreciated legacies of the Cold War. A number of Afghan orphans educated in religious schools in and around refugee settlements would gravitate toward the Taliban when they emerged in the early 1990s and fill the ranks of a movement that sought to transform the country in their image.[58] While millions returned home, the American invasion and occupation beginning in 2001 unleashed new waves of exodus, repatriation, and flight again. Since the American withdrawal and the Taliban return to power in August 2021, at least 1.6 million have fled the country, adding to the 5.8 million Afghans who remained displaced in neighboring countries. Moreover, under pressure from Pakistani authorities, another 669,000 returned—or were deported—from Pakistan by August 2024.[59]

Thus, the figure of the Afghan refugee as a site of national and regional political contestation outlived the Cold War. Pakistani and Iranian policies toward Afghans living in these countries—as well as violence against them and the ever-present threat of deportation—have continued to entangle the politics of these three countries.[60] Since 2001, successive Afghan governments have staked their legitimacy, at least in part, on the promise of providing for the repatriation of Afghan refugees at last. But, just as in the early 1990s, the inability of Afghan authorities—and, from 2001 to 2021, of their international backers—to provide security and lay the foundations for a stable economy dashed such plans.

During this same period, Afghan-refugee communities—increasingly self-identifying in varied contexts in Europe and North America as a "diaspora"—have challenged the labels of powerlessness and helplessness imposed from without. Crucially, after 2001, a number of Afghans who left as refugees managed to return as allies of the United States. American-backed exiles became essential intermediaries in Washington's twenty-year occupation. Moreover, from the safety of Europe and North America, many of these figures enjoyed a privileged position to intervene in Afghan politics but without the risk of living in the conditions of insecurity like their compatriots. Most Afghan refugees across the world engage in grueling labor. But some sit securely in the diaspora, seeking to influence or one day reenter Afghan politics.[61] Their position in the very countries where they find themselves refugees and marginalized "simultaneously enables them to play, in a flash, on the other side of the planet, national hero."[62] All this has had immeasurable effects on Afghans in Afghanistan as well as those living in Iran and Pakistan. And from Indonesia to Germany and the United States, Afghans—like many other migrant and refugee communities from the Middle East, Africa, and Latin America—now confront increasingly militarized borders and xenophobic Nationalist politics in countries that have largely forgotten the legacy of Cold War displacement in Asia.

Epilogue

AFTER CRUELTY
The Last Subject of Cold War Humanism

AISHWARY KUMAR

The problem of the Twentieth Century is the problem of the color-line.
—W. E. B. Du Bois, *The Souls of Black Folk*

The important point for liberalism is not so much where the line is drawn, as that it might be drawn, and that it must under no circumstances be ignored or forgotten.
—Judith Shklar, "The Liberalism of Fear"

It is quite conceivable, and even within the realm of practical possibilities, that one fine day a highly organized and mechanized humanity will conclude quite democratically—namely by majority decision—that for humanity as a whole it would better to liquidate certain parts thereof.
—Hannah Arendt, *The Origins of Totalitarianism*

It is by now clear, despite the pervasive denialism that marks the contemporary political condition, that we have entered a planetary age. It is an age inaugurated by the convergence of the voracious human will to colonize land and expand in space, on the one hand, and the increasingly destructive unfolding of natural events and transhuman forces that are altering the physical face of the planet, on the other. The effects of this convergence are not being tempered, let alone ameliorated, by the worsening norms of moral and political conduct in global affairs. Quite the opposite: international institutions and law—whose power to mine, extract, railroad, and police the earth was defined, *at their very origin*, by punitive imperial interests and juridical visions drafted in nineteenth-century capitals of European nation-states—continue to haunt the planet today. The colonial origins and neocolonial restructuring of international legal and economic institutions have only aggravated the disparity and neglect that, for over three centuries, afflicted the human condition. That Euro-American desire for sovereignty over the globe now casts, in even more brutish and brazen forms, a long and dark shadow over the future of the planet itself.[1]

One deceptive name for this postimperial shadow is the "Cold War." Notwithstanding the ideological weight and obfuscating moralism that the term carries, the Cold War, in starkly human terms, was a bloody theater mounted worldwide through the postwar rearrangement of land and sea by those great European powers that were, by the middle of the twentieth century, weakened by their greed overseas and yet not weakened enough to stop leaving a trail of displaced postcolonial populations in their wake. For over four decades after the end of the Second World War, the Cold War became a gladiatorial fight set up to redefine and decide, once and for all, the meaning of liberty and of *human freedom* for the globe. But this was a fight at once so bloody and farcical that it excluded from the world of ideas that very swathe of humanity that had just wrested back the idea of freedom—and its profoundly moral and constitutional practice—from the Europeans.[2]

Some of the most exemplary thinkers of human freedom were to be found, by the second quarter of the twentieth century, not in mainland Europe but instead in the anticolonial bloodlands of the Global South. By the 1960s, this constellation was transformed further, pulled radically back into the Black Atlantic by those thinkers who, in the sacrificial prime of the 1960s civil rights *revolution*, converted the racialized landscape of the American South into a stage for their own militant retelling of the modern epic of freedom and tyranny. This intellectual shift occurred not because Europe (or the West) had set the South and its moral imagination free. If anything, decolonization in Asia and Africa proved as deceptive as the Civil War had in America a century earlier: both epochs had changed the world but not its interpreters. Despite the mid-twentieth-century wave of self-determination and civil rights victories, the ideals and institutions of postwar democratic practice continued to be warped by a racial philosophical mindset and brutal military infrastructure whose coordinates still ran through the capitals of postimperial Europe.

The southern theory of political freedom emerged despite Europe's foot-dragging withdrawal from the Global South, not because of it.

Much of Cold War humanism and the study of the humanities in Euro-American institutions that grew out of this postimperial stasis have remained trapped in the warp of this farce. On the one hand, Cold War humanism trafficked in the myth that Europe had ceased going to war and that there was indeed, after the Second World War, something like a *postwar*. This myth of peace, put in place by postwar military treaties and alliances, seemed to be true, but only because the postwar battlefields were to now be increasingly found in the decolonized regions of the Global South: that savage hemisphere where the violent puzzles of human freedom and dehumanizing inequality were being solved by the barbarians themselves and with which Europe—either in its thinking of independence or in its violent demise—had purportedly nothing to do. On the other hand, Cold War humanism gave political theory of the Global North credit for thinking about care, welfare, and justice even though the intellectual firepower behind these questions—the moral commitment to an archaeology of freedom in the face of tyranny, archaic and new—had shifted dramatically to the South.

For all this, as the contributors to *Cold War Refugees* have shown in uncompromising detail, the price of this farce—the disjuncture between the *intellectual* and the *political* and the asymmetry between *theory* and *practice*, which underwrite Europe's philosophical amnesia—was no less tragic. The Cold War was, after all, not merely a chapter in the global history of ideas, much less a struggle merely over the contours of late modern humanism and its ends. Neither its promise of perpetual peace (liberalism) nor total equality (Communism) ever rang true in the Global South. It wasn't surprising, then, that its end would fail to bring upon the southern horizon the promised freedom from global war. Instead, it would only reinforce a cold historical fact: that the Cold War was a brutish affair whose human price, for a long time, felt cheap and distant to the Global North simply because much of it was paid for in Asia and Africa.

This global inequality is what James Baldwin calls, in his searing critique of postwar American power, "the price of the ticket." An intellectual history of that price, which cut away a vast swathe of humanity from the very idea of being human, is yet to come.[3] *Cold War Refugees*, with its unsparing retelling of that story and its contributors' painstaking attentiveness to historical facts and numbers, makes that intellectual history unavoidable.[4]

In what follows, I make a beginning toward that genealogy of the human—and *the price of human freedom*—from the South. My primary concern in this epilogue is not to reiterate and reinforce what the preceding chapters have already argued and accomplished (even if I do refer to them where necessary to substantiate my point). Rather, my aim is to probe, in all its moral and political depth, *the weight of inequality* and the histories of dispossession that the pervasive condition of modern statelessness continues to carry in itself, especially as its shapes change under pressure from the mutating strains of late liberal democracy. In doing so, I hope to bring into sharper conceptual focus this book's commitment to asking not simply why the figure of the refugee matters now—for this concern is not new—but, instead, why we are unable to get past cycles of moral indifference and political violence against them worldwide. Who—or *what*—is it that we attack when we attack the refugee?

I argue that this cycle perpetuates itself—and that the law willfully neglects this last *infrahuman* subject of neoliberal jurisprudence—because of an obdurate moral and juridical split in our conception of the *figure* of the refugee. We see *internal frontiers* and segregationist legislation within modern nation-states—in the form of their racial apartheid or caste laws—as belonging to a different, almost unrelated, juridical order, distinct from interstate delusions or international visions of border making, line drawing, and partitions. Both orders are equally arbitrary, equally violent, equally formed and stained by the planetary history of colonization and slavery. And one relentlessly haunts the other. Yet we see these as two different orders: one as a strain of "the social question" at home (a question driven by primal human compulsions and "need," of which Hannah Arendt writes in her treatise *On Revolution*) and the other as an international, political, and legal question (with the refugee seen as a figure in the punishing story of human greed—a subject worthy of punishment). This modular *judgmentalism*—or epistemic prejudice—is the legacy of the Cold War. But its ideological anchors are dug deep into the moral psychology of both archaic nationalisms and ultramodern racisms of the last two centuries.[5]

It is to this nexus that the constellation of thinkers in the brilliant firmament of the American civil rights tradition would respond, poetically and uncompromisingly, in the second half of the twentieth century. And it is in their wake that I argue that the cruelty of *segregation* (perpetrated within borders) and the compulsions of *statelessness* (faced beyond borders, or, better still, on the outer edge of borders) are morally inextricable and legally conjoined. For unlike snobbery, from which it ensues, cruelty is not the province of the smug affluent alone; it is the kingdom of the disdainful misanthropes. Only societies in which to be born poor or to seek

Figure E.1. W. E. B. Du Bois (1868–1963). How must we deepen our archaeology of "the color line" that Du Bois spoke of at the turn of the twentieth century now that the pernicious force of that line has penetrated even deeper into the twenty-first? What might come after it? Source: W. E. B. Du Bois Papers, Robert S. Cox Special Collections, University Archives Research Center, UMass Amherst Libraries, University of Massachusetts.

refuge elsewhere amounts to having committed a crime worthy of hatred can the weaponization of hunger—killing unprotected populations on the borders by starvation and famine—be deemed perfectly permissible under the law. Only societies with life-numbing inequalities can let refugees drown—in full and plain sight of the law—just a few miles off their coast, punishing strangers for their own misfortunes at home. This is perhaps why such a wide range of states—countries as starkly different in their economic and political stability as Greece and the United States, as incommensurable in their political beliefs and histories as China and Italy—are nonetheless so dramatically and equally consumed by their indifference toward refugees, asylum seekers, and religious minorities (to which all these states and their majorities respond with laws of detention, deportation, and disposal).

This paradoxical nexus of segregation and statelessness, caught in a relation of force and counterforce—one packing human bodies together and the other abandoning them altogether—is what W. E. B. Du Bois compresses, with unmatched diagnostic—and, if you will, *prophetic*—power, in his formula of the global "color line." It is in Du Bois that *force* first appears, in its most primal form, as an attribute of *color* and color appears, in its most veiled form, as an attribute of force. And it is Du Bois, who begins with this archeology of the line in his 1903 classic *The Souls of Black Folk* and then deepens it in his 1920 essay "The Souls of White Folk" in *Darkwater: Essays from within the Veil*, to whom we must always turn for the intellectual and moral history from the South I propose here.

A Planet of Migrants

The scale and sweep of the forces that today imperil the planet might seem unfathomable. But their origins are of recent vintage, unleashed by the massive industrial depredation and militarized partition of the globe by European powers that marked the beginning of the capitalist and colonial age. This does not mean these forces have not started to dangerously tower beyond the standard rules and norms that the modern world had invented to measure its life, liberty, and happiness, if such a measure of life were possible. The truth is these forces now brush past the profoundest extremes of technological imagination about what the human is, where its boundaries—old and new—are, and what life as such might soon become.

To speculate about humanity's afterlife—*the human after the exhaustion of life*—is no longer an exercise in mystical theology. It has now become an urgent experiment in philosophical realism.[6] Humanity—the moral and political figure or law-abiding species upon which modern jurisprudence had built the language of natural and human rights and upon which our ethics and politics of shared fate and common finitude had come to rest for over three centuries—has been pushed across the threshold of scientific certainty, righteous individualism, and mystical comfort of the earlier ages. Humanity seems to have found itself bound again into one common, uncertain, and planetary fate, although the sharing of these commons remains divisively and violently unequal.

Speculations about planetarity tend to quickly devolve into abstract rhetorics of sharing and the commons. But they are empty without a critique of its history. After all, things that are today shared under duress, when they are shared at all, have *never* been equally given or held in common. Neither natural resources nor moral sentiments have ever been equally given to—or seen as being equally bestowed upon—the world. What is deemed sharable, including human freedom, has always been unequally inherited—often marked by segregation and hierarchies of birth, skin, and hemisphere.

It is a matter not of insignificant historical detail that the earliest language of liberty in the Atlantic world found its first constitutional expression among the slaveowners of the American South. It was the enslavers who first laid claim to the language of liberty, which to them meant their invincible right to own other human beings as property. "*Rights* was their favorite word," Judith Shklar writes of the slave-owning masters in a sharp ironic moment in her genealogy of American conscience.[7] What is even today experienced as life lived in proximity with others—separated by a barbed wire fence, a postwar freeway, a militarized strait, a racialized peninsular, a relentlessly surveilled waterfront, or an invisible latitudinal line—has never felt like a life equally worthy of living on both sides of the color line. Worse, like the plantations of the South, life itself never seemed equally bearable or livable to everyone on the planet that emerged from that predatory economy.[8] To be sure, today, the global color line is vacillating and unstable, pushed to the ends of the earth. But its unlivable disparity and cruelty have by no means disappeared from the heart of the modern social contract.

If anything, the human body today encounters the extremes of what the "unlivable" looks like even more unequally than it did when the planet was mildly cooler and income inequality, more tolerable. None of this makes the deep history of inequality and heat, which today push millions of people into migrancy worldwide, excusable. But it is equally true that human beings respond to this inequality not by more openly and voluntarily sharing things that belong, at least in principle, to the commons. Instead, they respond—even and especially under conditions of liberal democracy—with even more brutal, segregationist legislation and democratically sanctioned judicial barbarism, all directed against those strangers, aliens, and migrants who, uprooted from their homes or dispossessed of their land or expelled by their own national states, need the commons the most. Now as ever before, what belongs to the commons, at least in principle, remains accessible to the powerful and the vulnerable only unequally. The rhetoric of planetarity is no substitute for an equality that must be freely shared.

This brings us to the starkest reality about the contemporary human condition, of which the *refugee* has emerged over the last century as the most unrelieved figure. In a world where every human being seems—or is deemed self-evidently to be—

equally mortal, equally capable of being injured, and equally perishable as others, the disappearance of the refugee from the world has come to be seen as even less worthy of being mourned. The human that perishes without even being mourned or even counted—that is the *last subject of modern humanism*, by which I mean the refugee is not simply a function of asymmetrical juridical power—or total domination—of some over many; it is also the figure of *mutation in the human* as such.

So normal and pervasive has this inequality become worldwide that it would almost seem that humanity has survived on earth precisely because of this violent inequality, this absolute command of a few over the many in a manner reminiscent of an earlier archaic age, not despite it.[9] And in the act of staring unflinchingly at this moral inversion, perhaps even recognition of what the human has become—under the stress of an unequal planetarity—might lie our capacity to look at our cruelty in its face and overcome our desire for it.[10] "We first become aware of freedom or its opposite in our intercourse with others, not in intercourse with ourselves," Arendt writes.[11] If she is right, then there is no freedom worthy of the word on an unequal earth; there is only the license to violate others in its name.

At its heart, *Cold War Refugees* is a global story of this unforgiving kinship between inequality and violence and of the insoluble bond between dispossession and democracy, forged at their very origins in the anticolonial South. It is also an uncompromising prehistory of that with which, more than three decades after the formal end of the Cold War, we are now confronted: the weaponization of unbearable planetary heat against over 150 million human beings, who will be forced to leave the unlivable, blistering parts of the globe—many of them from the neocolonial and paramilitarized regions of the Global South—only to be met by armed police and naval guards on the borders of the southern United States and the shores of Mediterranean Europe. These are borders policed by armed forces with unprecedented technological capabilities, along with a brazen will to violate international laws of amnesty and asylum. Their arbitrary, lawless sense of righteousness on land and sea alike are so infinite that they in fact seem, as if pulled out from Walter Benjamin's worst nightmare, "mythic" beyond limits.[12] Thousands every year are left "unprocessed," their wait for a visa or search for paperwork suspended in an abyss, which increasingly looks like a strip of quarantined land in the desert. Neglect has become the compulsive fuel of this righteous humanism of care and its security apparatus.

This contemporary implosion of the postwar regime of human rights into a "jurisprudence of neglect"—which I call the *neodemocratic condition*—is barely happenstance. If anything, it is a symptom of the slowly metastasizing degeneracy of sovereign power into autonomous spheres of detention and surveillance that invoke national security in principle but, in practice, have become completely independent of the judicial limits imposed by those national states themselves. Such implosive sovereignty—the independence of paramilitary law from sovereign guarantees of life—was all that remained in the Global South during and after the withdrawal of European imperial states in the middle of the twentieth century. And while there were exceptions to this late-colonial pathology of sovereignty, their mechanics were going to always be inadequate to the task of national restoration in the former colonies and theaters of war. The postwar tumult that produced the mass of stateless populations in Asia and Africa and turned them into refugees was not an aberration. Instead, it was a function of the bloody and botched decolonization overseen by European powers on three continents, beginning just as the Cold War set in.

Neglect and Freedom

By the late 1940s, well before decolonization swept the Global South, the stage was already set for this postimperial stasis. What would come to define the Cold War most fundamentally was not an eradication of conventional interstate military conflict but instead the consolidation of a global police and *paramilitary logic*, as Yumi Moon subtly shows in her introduction. Such a force would achieve a level of juridical independence—*the sovereignty to punish*—that civil institutions, even inside of nation-states, have rarely had in modern times. "The nation-state, incapable of providing a law for those who had lost protection of a national government, transferred the whole matter to the police," Arendt argues in *The Origins of Totalitarianism*. And this meant that, for the first time in Western Europe, the police now held "the authority to act on its own, to rule directly over people; in one sphere of public life it was no longer an instrument to carry out and enforce the law, but had become the ruling authority independent of government and ministries." Most strikingly, Arendt observes, the power of the police and "its emancipation from the law and government grew in direct proportion to the influx of refugees."[13]

It is in the paramilitary law that the time of decolonization meets and merges with the postwar epoch. Or better still, *it is through its police logic that the Cold War aggressively mutates into global civil strife*. And in so becoming, this mutant blurs the classical boundaries between international border forces and domestic police apparatuses in the postcolonial South, on the one hand, and promises of immigration and doctrines of deportation in the postimperial North, on the other.

In the first half of 2023 alone, the United Nations Refugee Agency reported that 2,500 migrants, trying to cross the Mediterranean, went missing or perished in the sea.[14] Those who survive or wash ashore are met not by civil guards but armed police with modern weaponry and neocolonial attributes. *Cold War Refugees* is a textured hemispheric understory of this archaic brutalism and its doctrine of neglect that has shaped our neodemocratic condition—a condition that historians continue to almost casually brush under the more celebratory term "decolonization" and that political scientists had long ago moved on from under the pretext of the more pressing concerns of the "Cold War."[15]

Neglect here is not passive abandonment. It is a structure of violence built on the theologico-juridical will to punish by making the border police exempt from all political control, an island of sovereign jurisdiction unto itself. It is a function of sustained punishment, a painstaking craft of making the inequality of the stateless hurt. Sometimes, neglect amounts to making the stateless disappear altogether, either through institutionalized indifference toward those who perish on the seas or through an exhaustive countermeasure: the science of settlement—*ekistics*—and sheltering the refugee. That is, neglect can sometimes involve giving the refugee temporary shelter, if only to launch them into the abyss of an unending wait for the paperwork that might testify to their humanity. In that sense, neglect is less a consequence and more a counterpart of the modern biopolitical logic, which sees keeping life safe and bodies usable as the sovereign purpose of politics.[16] It is also an inversion of the sanctity granted across religious traditions to the preservation of life as such, which, since Thomas Hobbes, has morphed in the modern age into the founding logic of sovereign power—both in the protective guarantees that sovereignty provides and in the penal rights over life it claims in general.[17] And this has tragically meant that the late modern doctrine of neglect can express a society's civic or political will to punish the stateless—through legitimate *majoritarian decision* and its inverted jargon of religious piety and purity—only under liberal democratic conditions, because no choice as such exists under tyranny.

Neglect is now the unspoken doctrine of the neodemocratic condition. It has no preservative function, only a punitive one. In fact, neglect does not even carry with it a society's interest in oppressing the illegal immigrant, the asylum seeker, or the refugee. Its only interest resides in discarding and bussing them off to their doom or letting them drown on the high seas or airdropping them back in lands they had fled in terror, thus shredding the very border between war and peace, refugee and citizen. In its abyss of moral bottomlessness, it is not only the classical definition of the citizen—and thus of the *stranger*—that neglect today leaves obsolete. It is also the juristic notion of classical civil war that it renders unusable for our time.[18] For political neglect is the infiltration of barbarism into citizenship itself, rendering all conventional theories of fratricidal combat and hostility pointless. It is a war without end.

For too long, the Cold War has been celebrated, in some quarters, for eliminating war altogether, even if only through its introduction of radioactive weaponry into modern warfare and its use of deterrence based on fears and hopes of mutually assured destruction. At the most fundamental level, *Cold War Refugees* offers a tragic reminder that, in fact, the Cold War neither exorcized the counterrevolutionary specters haunting the long decolonization in Asia and Africa nor marked the definitive end of European imperial hubris on those continents.[19] Instead, from the very beginning, it masked the long aftermath of decolonization for what it was: a civil war of colonial origins with global sweep, which would never really cease to smolder. If there is a twentieth-century example of what Hannah Arendt might have called a "global civil war"—a sort of moral and military grey zone where war and revolution, violence and justice, and, above all, racism and humanism become ideologically indistinguishable from each other and, under the sheer burden of their joint brutalities, engulf the entire planet in it—the Cold War is quite literally that cold bloody specter, *the antirevolutionary counterpart to decolonization*.[20]

Arendt comes close to identifying the morphology of planetary conflict that might produce this new paradigm of statelessness. "A world war appears like the consequences of revolution, a kind of civil war raging all over the earth as even the Second World War was considered . . . with considerable justification."[21] Beyond doubt, the Second World War, for all the human and material price it extracted, did carry the revolutionary air of self-determination to Asia and Africa. Despite her formidable insight about this kinship between war and revolution, however—and to be sure, one turns into the other as frequently in the real world as it does in humanist visions of the world—Arendt barely pauses to note that it took merely the *threat* of liberation within their own colonies to spur the victorious, freedom-loving, "revolutionary" European powers of the Second World War to unleash their entire military might against their colonial subjects. In fact, the revolutionary and victorious powers of the Second World War quickly morphed into executors of a barbaric and counterrevolutionary suppression of independence in the colonies.

That this reversal is a phenomenon to which Arendt is oblivious perhaps reveals her failure—or studied unwillingness—to fully theorize what a twentieth-century civil war with global sweep—only, now, with America's humane constitutional tradition behind it—would look like.

More crucially, however, Arendt misses entirely why this cold war had come to be called what it came to be called, if only to force the world to forget what it truly meant in the colonies. "In its bare reality, decolonization reeks of red-hot cannonballs and bloody knives," wrote Frantz Fanon in his unsurpassed indictment of a failing humanism that, with its one hand, ratified a Universal Declaration of Human Rights (1948) and, with its other, soon sanctioned the most violent assaults on the very notion of life and living in the colonies.[22] But it is only when its ideological hubris (or, to marshal Judith Shklar, its postimperial "hypocrisy") is breached from Asia that Cold War humanism appears on our horizon in its true planetary gambit: as a politically unstable backstop to human liberation, its (ideological) content and (geopolitical) form built around the neocolonial and sometimes neo-Socialist scaffolding that took shape in the Global South under *anticolonial* and, at the same time, *antirevolutionary* pressure. In its tragic moments and in unfortunate places, the long anticolonial dream would itself morph into a soul-crushing counterrevolutionary force.

The Cold War, then, which was pegged on the wobbly balance of this strife in Asia and Africa, was not a world-making story of human freedom ideologically conceived in Europe and globally realized in liberal ideals and institutions championed by postwar American imperialism overseas. Nor did its end mark the worldwide triumph of neoconservative values rooted in virtues of the market, let alone the "end of history," as Francis Fukuyama had ambitiously declared.[23] Instead, the opposite was true. The war was given its global structure as much by the universalist promises of liberal democracy and ambitious international legalism as by the unpredictable geopolitical contingencies created by mass dispossession and movements of displaced populations upon whose bodies the helpless language of human rights grew.

In turn, with its moving frontiers and strategic linchpins, the Cold War itself dramatically restructured ideas of democracy and internationalism, of jurisprudence and political thought, and of the moral contours and shapes of postwar liberalism at large.[24] And all this occurred even as war continued to be waged through barely covert means, with unmitigated racial brutality at home and vicious racial prejudice abroad. The ideological mutations in Cold War humanism, the rising concern with care and welfare as a function of human freedom, all occurred in the midst of sustained weaponization not only of human hunger and child poverty—economic inequality turned into military strategy—but also in the regulated torrent of invention, sale, supply, and use of weapons that were designed to biologically deform the genetic constitution of the human as such.

The irony, of course, is that when added as a descriptor of war, the adjective "cold" forces a conceptual backslide and reverses its meaning. It insinuates into the notion of war at once a rhetorical fallacy and a legal fantasy. It achieves the first—*rhetorical fallacy*—by falsely intimating that this was a war that did not really happen, that this was a war that cannot be located or traced back to the postcolonies, as if its trail had forever been left cold. It unleashes the second—*legal fantasy*—by suggesting that this was the war that coldly outlawed, through moral calculus and nuclear deterrence, all future possibility of war as such. It is a testimony to Western liberal amnesia and of its narrative power that this fantasy has managed to sometimes entirely write off the presence of European powers—if not of postwar international coalitions—from the scene of twentieth-century revolutionary wars in postcolonial theaters, some of which smoldered on and reached genocidal proportions. It was there that much of the Cold War's human price was extracted in the service of a fading imperial consensus, which the aging, inept, and senseless bureaucratic machinery of European colonialism directly fueled.

This is why each chapter in *Cold War Refugees* is so careful to disinter the movements of that ghosted transcontinental war. Each contributor does so to reanchor those movements into the wider world and inscribe Asia at the heart of a planetary story. As the chapters show, the Cold War was not one monolith of a bipolar conflict between two world powers divided by incommensurable visions of human freedom. It was, instead, a global civil war that produced more borderlines, more settlements, and more refugees than any other nonevent or ghost war in modern history. Ultimately, this ghost war coldly rejected the vision of an equal, shared life on the planet even as it raged on in the name of liberty and life. And it coldly entrenched a racialized disparity across the globe in whose tentacles, at the beginning of the century and in a moment of prophetic anticipation, Du Bois had already seen the surreptitiously rising power and deepening militarization of the color line.

Cruelty and Transcendence

Today, in light of our most recent experiences, cherished concepts of life and humanity (which emerged in the wake of the modern scientific revolution and its philosophical anthropology) seem inadequate and impoverished, if not entirely drained of their moral stability and social legitimacy. This exhaustion is not merely a function of philosophical anxiety about the human form and its future but a consequence also of cold realities of the recent past. Exhaustion does not mean that notions about creaturely life in general and the human being in particular have lost any of their punitive scaffolding and police logic. It only means that, having once put the "citizen-subject" at the center of the modern moral, juridical, and political universe,[25] the humanist vision of life—and its separation of the human from nature, of machines from sentient creatures—today seems overwhelmed by relentless pressure from humanity's own insatiable appetite for space and violence. This has destabilized the very ontology—which is to say, border—between the human and nonhuman, persons and things. Political cruelty is, at its core, this *force* that reduces persons to things.

Exorbitant demands are now made upon the planet and upon human beings by destructive drilling, policing of land, and even interstellar ambitions in space. Such demands are exacerbated by militarized segregations on sea, where hundreds perish every year on rickety crammed boats, left to set sail and capsize in full view of a morally shambolic global legal system. All these conditions pose devastating ethical and legal questions about the limits of being—and remaining—human. How much violence can a form and *figure* of life bear until it simply ceases to be? And if life as such turned into a strife with the unlivable and the barely alive, what would be left of the human? What might become of life when the human is finished with itself and others and done with (leaving) the earth?

Paradoxically, life—and the living—can often find itself trapped in conditions that are "unlivable." For the truth of the matter is that the unlivable, too, is lived; it too must be stared at and survived, even if in inexcusable proximity with death. Consider a refugee trapped in a boat, unsure of reaching southern Europe, *willing to drown in order to live*. Such a figure perhaps demonstrates the unlivable in international law. And yet, in our political imagination no less than our moral psychology, something still marks out and separates the subject who lives on the threshold of the unlivable from the subject who is either brutalized by the law directly or violated in full view of it. The distinction is not that these two deformed figures of the living are subject to cruelty differently from each other or that they are violated in varying degrees—sometimes they might even be cared for or tended to. Instead, the distinction is that the brutalized subject, even if it perishes, still finds itself within the web of the law, while the subject who survives at the threshold of the unlivable, one who perishes on the high seas, does so in *oblivion*.

Is there one figure that truly embodies the history of this unbearable suffering and its familiar oblivion? One in whose tragic resilience we might still be able to recover the seeds of a new political and ethical responsibility? One who would reveal a force that might even help us salvage the rough drafts of a democracy without violence or, better still, of a politics that might leave violence behind? What might that figure be?

Perhaps this is the profoundest task that *Cold War Refugees* undertakes. It is certainly the most demanding task it sets for us. For the book seeks nothing short of returning the figure of the refugee to the moral center of global affairs, calling them back from the margins and borders of liberal democratic thought, where it has languished as a helpless bearer of human rights guaranteed by those nation-states that have already abandoned them. As each chapter in this book shows, the refugee is not simply a figure of statelessness. It is the figure of the last human stuck at the limit that we have been calling the unlivable. As if trapped in a tragic fight for survival and a dizzying flight for transcendence at one and the same time—now from heat and now from war—this last subject might have morphed into a refugee on its own warming planet. Its physical, moral, and psychological limits are tested, on the one hand, by shrinking spaces for habitation on land and, on the other, by the rapid unraveling of previously settled boundaries between artificial intelligence and sentient life. Meanwhile, technocratic brutalism has not only made the slow liquidation of populations theoretically possible, as Arendt had already warned in the 1950s. It has also rendered a large swathe of humanity practically disposable.

One might argue that human beings have entered the age of cruelty—an age whose hubristic delusions and violent compulsions are mandated not solely by the gods but bolstered by machines, sanctioned not by the political theology of kings but by the postconstitutional fantasies of neodemocratic supremacist majorities. Perhaps human beings never leave one age entirely when they enter another. It is just that the current age is marked not only by the archaic, ritualized, sacrificial violence of the earlier ages but by a new theologico-juridical will to make the living pay the price just for trying to survive on an unequal, segregated earth.[26] In one fundamental way, older theologies of sacrifice have indeed survived and even thrived in the global age of mechanical reproduction and artificial intelligence—as a collective and organized will to extract a price from the most vulnerable human beings for humanity's self-inflicted wounds, sometimes by walling them off from humanity altogether.

Along the lines of this resurgent segregationist war, *Cold War Refugees* proceeds one chapter, one region, one peninsula, and one port city at a time. Each contribution probes in startling detail how systematically, to paraphrase Arendt, "the condition of rightlessness was created before the right to live was challenged."[27] Examining how laws of design follow political history, for example, Ijlal Muzaffar, in his chapter, rewrites the postcolonial narrative of imperial design, whose broad strokes have been prevalent since Paul Rabinow's *French Modern*.[28] Muzaffar does so by offering a scrupulous archaeology of Cold War ekistics, the science of settlement—with its view of space scaffolded in five dimensions, constituted around humankind, society, shell, nature, and network—in Pakistan, of which the Karachi Development Authority emerges as the linchpin. Looking at the spatial transformation of the port city under neocolonial conditions—its drafts and sketches generated under the geopolitical dynamics of the Cold War but whose effects were felt on every livable and wasteful dimension of the city—Muzaffar carves out a space for writing a labyrinthine counterhistory of violence. This is a slow-burning violence that becomes invisible and endemic *after* the historian's genocide has passed—a violence whose subject is not the citizen alone but also the permanently unsettled refugee, trapped in a land of cold, vacillating borders, in a city built around moving settlements and unsettling colonies inside the postcolony. Thus excavated, even the waterfront returns from the topographical edge (where the city literally ends) back to the center—an *internal frontier*—of its tenuous identity. Could it be that it is now the sea, contra Carl Schmitt, that shapes the segregationist logic and law of postcolonial lands?

Racialized segregation is seen as the partition running through or inside of sovereign borders, quarantining even those human beings who, at least formally, are construed as citizens by birthright. But even citizens by birthright, if born of a wrong race or caste or skin, are not safe from the paramilitary law and its apparatus of detention and expulsion. For this is the very logic of paramilitary law that has gone independent of sovereign and even constitutional guarantees of life: its will to segregation within borders is governed by the same structure of penal power that makes the refugee waiting outside the borders illegal. Urban segregation may seem distinct from the general criminalization of migrancy. But this is so not because it belongs to another order—or because it is meant to evoke another scale of strife—but because it is simply the more obstinate, more pernicious side of the same apparatus. If rightlessness is a consequence of the sovereign state making a criminal out of the refugee, then segregation is the sovereign state abandoning and making an outlaw out of the citizen inside of them. And both compulsions demand sacrifice or, worse, as Grégoire Chamayou puts it in his galvanizing account of migrancy, a "manhunt."[29]

This unity of penal logic binds the national-social and international legal regimes into one punishing whole, entrenching the global color line across sovereign borders and states. Since the end of the Cold War, this logic has only deepened its footprint on the planet. Racial segregation is the quiet vacillating face of the civil strife that the earth today faces. And like a classic civil war, it will yield no new political formation when it is done, only a deformed idea of the human. We can grasp the contours of this theologico-juridical entrenchment of a worldwide web—at once religious and racial—only when we are willing to understand that "segregation" now observes no limits of either legal order or of terrestrial scale set upon it by the modern nation-state. Instead, it drives the logic of a global civil war, waged in full view and with the full might of the law mobilized against citizens and refugees equally, on land and sea alike.

Arendt is strikingly prescient about this inextricable relationship between expulsion and segregation, between eviction and immobilization at one and the same time. "The first loss," she points out, "which the rightless suffered was the loss of their homes, and this meant the loss of the entire social texture into which they were born." But the second loss, she observes, was the end of government protection, which truly undid the hope that at least an abstract, formal sanctity of human life could be guaranteed by international law. "Treaties of reciprocities and international agreements have woven a web around the earth that makes it possible for the citizen of every country to take his legal status with him no matter where he goes. . . . Yet, whoever is no longer caught in it finds himself out of legality altogether."[30]

Here appears the most oblique but unifying thread of *Cold War Refugees*—one that runs through every chapter in this remarkable volume. Looking out from Asia, where much of humanity today lives, the classical distinction between civil conflict and world war has always been hard to maintain. After all, the World Wide Web of postwar legality was put in place there by the withdrawing powers of the European colonial age. The result was that theologies of transcendence, which in an earlier age involved moving collectively past suffering and sharing the commons in the name of liberal universalism, democratic solidarity, or even religious redemption, were already ensnared into an archaic logic of cruelty on a planetary scale.

The postwar global order, built on the presumption and promise of this redemption—an overcoming of suffering and evil delivered through humanitarian universalism—had never rung deafeningly true in the Global South. But for some time now, its web has been threatened by another cruel delusion, another mad attempt at transcendence. This new drive is no less religious, no less sacrificial, no less sanctimonious. What makes it especially pernicious is the sheer array of tools and technologies at the command of the predatory overlords, who lead it with religious, neofascist zeal. The story of statelessness under late liberalism—and the Cold War humanism that birthed it—is also the story of cruelty in the age of technological reproduction.

Oligarchies: At the Edge of Oblivion

Across epochs and ages, humanity has expressed its timeless quest for transcendence through monastic rigor, through pursuits of excellence and happiness, and through sacrifice of worldly things and beings. Those earlier pathways of seeking transcendence, religious or otherwise, however, are not the antithesis of the new cruelty but its counterpart. Consider the intergalactic delusion of those who, while insisting on erecting lethal walls on earth and floating barbed wires on sea—both designed to physically hurt and trap immigrants and their children—would themselves rather live on another planet. They would rather take flight from land altogether if they could, docking their ships on an untraceable island or planet. But even before they leave, they are compelled to make movement treacherous and lethal for those who will have to stay behind on an unequal earth.

This oligarchic escape activates the religious grammar of an earlier age but feeds on the unprecedented technocratic power of its own. This *theological-technological* bond is the running underside of the age of cruelty, not its final solution. God knows, as the Hannah Arendt of *Eichmann in Jerusalem* might write today, the worst is still to come. Expulsion and flight, legalized banishment of "illegals" and the oligarchic will to leave earth—both these compulsions are supported by democratically elected governments across the globe. And they are today equal parts of what we glibly call the humanitarian crisis, if only because they have both been equally constitutive of the modern political world, of its humanist vision and its juridical apparatus. "Only with a completely organized humanity," after all, Arendt writes in a memorable line in *The Origins of Totalitarianism*, "could the loss of home and political status become identical with expulsion from humanity altogether."[31] The tragedy of an "organized humanity," of course, is that its juridical institution, its political stability, and its moral legitimacy have been, from the beginning, tethered to the nation-state. And the total collapse of the national-social state, therefore, however desirable it might seem to some on the global Right and Left, will never be accompanied by anything short of total devastation of the human, of the reduction of the "person" into just another "thing," teetering between moral and artificial life.

If these remarkable chapters in *Cold War Refugees* collectively tell us a deeper, colder story of our wars on the figure and idea of the human, it is that the refugee—who is exemplary of this deformation of the human—might be our first postplanetary universal: *the anticitizen*. It is this figure that today bears on its body both the sovereign memory of colonial empires of the past and the frightening intimations of "techno-feudal" islands of the future.[32]

Even at the edge of this oblivion, the resemblances between the past and future are striking, if only because their genealogies are so profoundly entangled. Neither the colonial capitalist nor the techno-feudal overlord faces any limits on their openness to militarized violence. Both use expulsion as a punitive device to push humanity out of habitable zones on the planet: the capitalist to extract labor; the overlord to make (or steal) data out of the tragic patterns of human flight. Both approach the laws of earth on scales meant for "great spaces" (*Großraum*) rather than small-room (*Kleinraum*) activities of mortal human beings.[33] Both invest their theoretical energy in rescaffolding the globe—first, through railroads in the "heart of darkness" in colonial Asia and Africa, then through ports and docks in the postcolonial world, and, finally, since the end of the Cold War down to the techno-feudal epoch, through mazes of undersea cables and pipelines.

If we thought islands would disappear off the surface of earth, swallowed by rising seas and then off human consciousness itself, we were wrong. Islands are where refugees to Europe, which first produced them, try to land and survive. Islands are where decolonization today meets its Cold War ghost. And as this book shows, the Cold War was nothing if not the counterpart of this specter of decolonization in Asia. While decolonization forced European colonial powers to leave the Global South, the Cold War entrenched the North's neocolonial infrastructure in the farthest, remotest islands of the planet, even as the powers themselves seem to have departed. The colonial and Cold War epochs are separated in time, but, between the two, there remains a tragically linear continuum—their fates bound by the history that they (and their ideologues) seek to overwrite, their logics wound along the line Du Bois had begun excavating at the turn of the last century.

Decolonization formally put an end to the British and French colonial projects in Asia and Africa in the middle of the twentieth century. This left behind neocolonial mandates and protectorates, straits and settlements, refugee colonies and apartheid townships across three continents. At times, the violence in the postcolony was barely distinguishable from the brutalities of the colonial overlordships that preceded them. Half a century later, at the end of the 1980s, the Berlin Wall fell, which was deemed to mark the mythic end to the Cold War. And this, in turn, formally opened the floodgates to neoliberal consolidation in global governance, whose paradoxical effects play out today with a nearly uncontrollable intensification of antiglobalist and neoconservative compulsions.

Yet, as *Cold War Refugees* makes devastatingly clear, only from Europe do these epochs seem so dramatically different in their attributes and pathologies. Only from Europe does it seem that the world has generally stopped going to war (or that an invasion of one country by another is an exception to the rule). Elsewhere, beyond Europe—where much of the world today lives—politics has failed to move on from the smolders of colonial violence and police lines. If anything, the sacrificial energies of anticolonial politics let loose a suicidal strife in the postcolonies. Human and natural history were to get catastrophically entangled with each other in a manner sometimes so barbaric that they might have undone the founding moral certainties and technological assumptions that have anchored the idea of the human itself. The refugee today is that figure and effect of the entanglement between human will and technological counterforce. The refugee is the vanishing mediator—*the last man*—between dignified survival and pure power on a punishingly hot planet.

Whatever else might be said of Francis Fukuyama's zealous claim in *The End of History and the Last Man*, written in the heady early days of Cold War triumphalism, the fact is that the world now does live with the distinct possibility that the Hegelian metaphor of the "last man" might indeed become a reality in the foreseeable future.[34] If there are any lessons to be drawn from conservative storytelling about the end of the Cold War, it is an inverted one: that far from being over, the specter of the subject left stranded on the planet alone—the haunting possibility of being the last man on earth—today lives on like a bad colonial dream—a dream that in truth began with Euro-American vengeance on land and sea and one that has never really ended.[35]

Only now, in place of a colonial penal officer, the anticitizen—this last subject of Cold War humanism—awaits the catastrophic arrival of a planetary winter that will mutate life itself, if not altogether annihilate it. The disheartening truth also is that there is little moral high ground separating the colonial from that which came after it. The political universe has simmered to a point where a vast part of humanity, even in democratic parts of the globe, if given a choice between extinction and equality, might well choose extinction with a sacrificial glee—with a theologically charged suicidal delirium even—rather than choosing to live in an equal world. With his searing poetic insight, James Baldwin connects this drive to extinction with the raging anxieties of white—which is to say, *colonial*—fear of living in an equal world. "This cowardice, this necessity, of justifying a totally false identity and of justifying what must be called a genocidal history," he writes in "On Being White . . . and Other Lies," "have brought humanity to the edge of oblivion: because they think they are white."[36]

The New Segregation

In their remorseless commitment to inequality, both decolonization and the Cold War were moving parts of a violent continuum. Neither the revolutionary breeze of self-determination in Asia nor rhetorics of liberal universalism in Europe managed to conceal this shared love of inequality and predilection for judicial barbarism. The chapters above powerfully testify to how the Cold War set in precisely at this moment of late-colonial barbarity. It first appeared as a dispersed, slow-burning, racialized extension of a reluctant, bloody decolonization, unleashed by white fear in Asia and Africa and then, ideologically, as an indissociable counterpart to colonialism itself—each exactly like the other in its logic of rulemaking, in its persistent brutalism, and in its cruel, lawless jurisprudence, which would continue to split the planet along an earth-wide color line. As Phi-Vân Nguyen shows above in her groundbreaking chapter on Vietnam (and India's dubious role in the war there), even the doctrine of nonalignment championed by the newly independent nation-states flattered only to deceive.

It is not by chance that their aftermaths looked barely different. By the late 1950s in Asia and Africa, the ageing nineteenth-century version of colonial power amassed by imperial Europe was replaced by the penal power and apparatus of various revolutionary and neocolonial stripes, often with calculated spatial design and overt European sanction. Just forty years later, that same logic was replicated, with barely any difference, in the countries of the Eastern bloc after the Berlin Wall fell.

Indeed, in the 1990s, the brutal strife in Eastern Europe, punctuated only by ever worsening tales of ethnic cleansing and systematic torture of populations, gorily mirrored Europe's counterrevolutionary repressions in Asia and Africa earlier in the century—one whose fires had never ceased to burn and whose military infrastructure had never ceased fire. There has never been, to reformulate the terms of Tony Judt's influential account, a "postwar" outside of Europe.[37] Let me put this even more starkly: *there has never been a military or moral postwar outside of Europe precisely because of Europe.* This is a radically new story that requires a genuinely global vision, as Yumi Moon intricately lays out in her introduction to *Cold War Refugees*.

From the very beginning, celebratory chroniclers of both decolonization and the Cold War have employed the same devices for justifying the imperial reordering of the globe. Their protagonists have deployed similar strategies in the battlefields and refugee camps: expulsion and torture; forced dispossession and resettlement of populations; arbitrary drawing of lines, which, in some places in British South Asia, were several miles thick and belonged to nobody (and were therefore fair hunting ground for everyone); targeted starving of migrants and malicious rigging of grain trade; and sudden military withdrawals. The wounds of these tactics are indelible, fueling a system of archaic, brutal inequality that has outlived the worst excesses of colonial misanthropy. The Cold War has left a morbid shadow on the government of the living (and the barely living) in Asia. Its aftermath haunts the continent like a specter. But for that reason alone, its effects are no less real, no less burning. And only because we write its history rarely ever from Asia as its hot center that we deem that this is a cold specter of a finished war.

Underwriting this amnesia is an *inequality*, at once of epistemology and economy, now betrayed by surges in planetary heat and ocean levels, even as fantastic technologies of war obscure the decapitation of life and make invisible the place of Big Tech in the new oligarchic economy of barbarism. The refugee economy is an economy ruled by islands of oligarchic power that operate beyond the pale of national sovereignty and its norms—an economy that makes itself disappear in plain sight using the very liberties guaranteed by nation-states.[38] Meanwhile, refugees, the most fortunate among whom will be absorbed into the vast economy of invisible and punishing labor at wages lower than the minimum guaranteed by law, perish trying to reach islands and shores in numbers difficult to keep a statistical or moral measure of in even a remotely humane way.

Such moral decomposition in the age of global lawfare is also the story told by

Cold War Refugees. Henceforth, our philosophical history must contend with these futures of the human—and the humanity of this *thing* we are left with—mired in techno-politics and resurgent theologies alike. Such futures, indeed, might come after the end of this life and perhaps after the end of the earth as we know it. There is after all, on the one hand, the irreversible and catastrophic warming of the planet that imperils the very survival of human life. There is, on the other hand, the unfolding spectacle of a delusion and quest for afterlife, immortality even, of a will to transcendence that is reminiscent of an archaic political theology—one that runs in the direction opposite of the looming extinction as if it were in denial about this coming catastrophe while being inextricably related to it. These are marks of an insatiable will to technological domination and dreamy habitation on distant planets, whose surfaces are yet to even show any proof of life.

This ultrahumanist will to domination today fuels a new regime of moral and artificial intelligence that has mutated the boundaries of the human and the ends of earth as such. Even extinction seems just another frontier of the will to capture and conquer space. But the theologico-juridical vectors of this will—the will to make laws and draw lines for all of humanity all the while seceding from it—is barely new. Not for the first time in the past century has humanity traced its path back into "world alienation," as Arendt called it in 1958, in the wake of the first Soviet space missions and American atomic explosions, describing it as humanity's "twofold flight from the earth into the universe and from the world into the self, to its origins."[39] Both movements occur simultaneously; both constitute humanity equally, with equal grandeur and violence. For humanity, it has always been a theologically charged and sacrificial flight to origins, Arendt might well have added—one that has plagued the human condition from its beginning. It is a flight shorn not one bit, even today, either of its earlier creativity—What else were the atomic explosions proof of?—or of its timeless temptation to vengeance.

And yet, for all its ambition to become equal to the universe and God himself, the ultrahuman will to transcend the finitude of earth is, unfortunately, no less segregated, no less hostile, and no less punitive than it was in an earlier age, especially toward those "undesirables" and "displaced persons" who must still inhabit it to be able to live. Among other things, Du Bois was masterful in identifying the global color line—cutting right across Asia and Africa, through the racialized, militarized depths of the Pacific and the overpoliced macabre that is the contemporary Mediterranean—as the decisive twentieth-century impasse.[40]

It is an anchorless, placeless impasse (an *aporia*, pace Derrida), but not because human beings did not ever cross it. Thousands have, even if they have barely survived their fragile capsized boats and empty liberal solace. It is an impasse because *the color line is a moral blockage lodged at the very heart of the liberal democratic vision of equality*. Should we leave it free to gnaw at civilization—in the manner liberal humanism has for the best part of the last century, as Du Bois anticipates—it would metastasize. Pushed too far, the color line would become a threshold, beyond which humanity itself—victim, perpetrator, and bystander alike—might become something monstrously unrecognizable to itself.

We simply cannot let that line metastasize into a normalized threshold or an oblivious fold of cruelty—one that we cross in our sheer indifference every time an innocent child is found dead, his face buried in sand on Europe's policed shores, his only crime being born Kurdish or Muslim or just nothing other than stateless. "The important point for liberalism is not so much where the line is drawn, as that it must be drawn," Judith Shklar writes in a moment of striking resonance with Du Bois, "and that it must under no circumstances be ignored or forgotten."[41] It is important that there be a line, in other words, even if this line is mostly an exception that proves the neocolonial logics of rule with which we are left to contend.

Violence without Theory

While giving us a powerful textured prehistory of this barbarism, *Cold War Refugees* also retraces, through the decidedly cosmopolitical chapter on Afghan imaginaries, the long aftermath of the postwar impasse confronting us. The chapters here also remind us that, for all its universalism, what we today call planetarity marks the return of an unforgiving inequality among human beings rather than the dissolution of their segregated differences into a purportedly common fate. As Sabauon Nasseri and Robert D. Crews demonstrate, Afghan refugees—now citizens of the world audaciously hoping to remake lives elsewhere—do not stand as examples of the endurance of global institutions. Instead, they exemplify the indomitable stamina and sheer human will needed to withstand the disdain of contemporary neocolonial institutions, all the while fighting a concerted indifference that is equally political and militarized in scale.

Far from deploying instruments of total domination, Nguyen indicates in her probing analysis of India's dubious moral aspirations to emerge as a continental power in Southeast Asia, neocolonialism—in and of the South and North alike—has often sought power through passivity: stalling of help or, worse, sudden withdrawal, leaving vast populations at the mercy of bigoted elites. Eight hundred thousand Vietnamese migrated from the North to the South of the country in roughly ten months between July 1954 and May 1955. In that sense, militarized indifference observes no political or moral limits, because it draws its lines only to brutally destroy them, sometimes within the ambit of the law and more often through strategic recession. If military invasion is unequivocal war, *military withdrawal*—as the American departure from Afghanistan showed as recently as 2022—is pure power. Both produce the condition and sense of statelessness among those who have already been rendered homeless by invasion and war in their own land. Only now, their utter desolation and despair can be met with a vengeance altogether of a different—or indifferent—kind, one to which international law is capable of offering no response.

Military withdrawal, then, is *violence without a theory*, an effect of the worst chasm between power and responsibility. The reasons and conditions for waging "just and unjust wars" find themselves at the center of Western moral and legal philosophy from Immanuel Kant down to Michael Walzer.[42] This is because even the most brute exercise of military power assumes some sense of obligation toward its victims. By contrast, there is absolutely nothing in the modern political tradition, beginning with Machiavelli, that lays down rules to leave war, except that suddenly leaving war, whether out of moral anxieties or military concerns or simply strategic impatience (as Nguyen demonstrates in the case of the French), unleashes an abandoned display of power for its own sake. Leaving behind straits and settlements and islands in disarray can itself be a formidable show of colonial and neocolonial force. This withdrawal without framework and without responsibility—*militarism without war*, as it were—is one of the great blind spots of postwar jurisprudence. Its tenets were put in place neither for the first time nor the last—but indeed, they were articulated most arbitrarily—at the end of the Second World War and through the early years of decolonization in Asia and Africa.

Whatever else it was, then, this untheorized violence of Cold War humanism was not a doctrine. It was even less of a moral line that the colonial powers (including America) might have found hard to transgress; on the contrary, pace Shklar, this was *violence without the line*. It was also the beginning of a twofold flight of the idea of the human from the earth—set in accelerated motion by the horror of the atomic explosions, on the one hand, and the international declarations made by postwar states to uphold human rights, on the other.

Of that paradoxical legalism and the universal rights that it bestowed upon the inhabitants of an unequal earth, thinkers of modern constitutional thought, like Judith Shklar in America and Bhimrao Ambedkar in India, had never been too hopeful. In fact, it was precisely the legal "web around the earth"—the racialized, juridical color line—that produced the specter of recurring statelessness among vast populations in the Global South. "We became aware of the existence of a right to have rights (and that means to live in a framework where one is judged according to actions and opinions) and a right to belong to some kind of organized community," Arendt posits in that decisive passage of *The Origins of Totalitarianism*, "only when there suddenly emerged millions of people who had lost and could not regain these rights because of the new global political situation. The trouble is that this calamity arose not from any lack of civilization, backwardness, or mere tyranny, but on the contrary, that it could not be repaired, because there was no longer any "uncivilized spot on earth, because whether we like it or not, we have really started to live in One World. Only with a completely organized humanity could the loss of home and political status become identical with the expulsion from humanity altogether."[43]

These rightless millions were sometimes rendered stateless, sometimes segregated. The tragedy of the latter, of these segregated millions, Ambedkar would tell Gandhi in 1931, was not that they had no homeland even in their own home but that there was no *language* to theorize their rightlessness. For the segregated lose not simply their abstract legal personhood; they lose their *civil rights*: the very fabric, the common social bond—which is to say, political speech—that might hold their humanity and homes together. In their case, "what is unprecedented is not the loss of a home but the impossibility of finding a new one."[44] What is impossible to overcome is not just the loss of dwelling but the loss of a sense of being useful to the world, of being of any use to fellow human beings. The segregated thus lose their humanity not as refugees from elsewhere but instead as outcastes—*pariahs*—in their own home, at the very heart of the national social state that promises to give them shelter (even if it leaves them with no land). Modern statelessness and a segregated, civic rightlessness could indeed be, if only under very specific certain conditions, distinct calamities. But the nature of their expulsion would still be similar. Unlike the stateless, the segregated might have a state. And yet they might still not have even the barest of protections under its laws, thus reduced to abject rightlessness—*homelessness*—by the perversion of the domestic law itself. One name for this calamity without refuge, *shelter without amnesty*, is caste.

Inasmuch as there is a jurisprudence of caste—perhaps the most ancient of all moral and punitive canons—this jurisprudence is held together by a science of shelter, a sort of scaffolding ekistics for a reason, then, which also explains Ambedkar's radical claim that with millions of outcastes turned into mere fractions at once by the lawless monstrosity of untouchability and the legal sanction of caste, India has barely ever been a society. To Ambedkar, its civilization was founded less upon an aspiration to a moral life and more upon the concealment—or *amnesia*—of an original felony. The outcaste, devoid of personhood and dignity, is simultaneously beyond the intricate legality and lawless excesses of caste. Precisely because of this aporia, Ambedkar argues, the outcaste's fate might be worse than even that of an enemy combatant trapped on the most brutal of battlefields. Which explains, too, why victims of caste atrocity, left without shelter, are rarely seen in the same legal terms as refugees.[45] They live in the unlivable, abject state of rightlessness but are not yet expelled from the law fully enough to be deemed stateless. Caste is that cruel juridical anomaly: no law exists for its redress because it is the law. It is violence without a legal theory.

The real calamity of the pariahs—Arendt might concur—is "not that they are deprived of life, liberty, and the pursuits of happiness, or of equality before the law and freedom of opinion—formulas which were designed to solve problems within given communities—but that they no longer belong to any community whatsoever. Their plight is not that they are not equal before the law, but that no law exists for them; not that they are oppressed but that nobody wants even to oppress them."[46] The analogue of this catastrophe is to be found, ironically, in the idea of human rights. The idea failed not because of the lack of theoretical imagination of its signatories but because its globalist framers placed their faith in the ability of states to guarantee human rights—the very states that had already abandoned their subjects, turning them into a disposable mass of rightless, superfluous humanity.

Today, planetarity—a vision of the world that takes as its frame of reference an entire globe devoid of that incurable, forgotten inequality—clamps back in place again, steadily but not slowly, invisibly but not impalpably, a new regime of borders and islands on earth. The mundane social realities of this unraveling planetarity, perhaps for the first time in recorded history, bend our politics and morals away from the punitive borders of sovereign states and empires—as was characteristic of the modern age—and thread them along the warming curvature of the globe. But it is by no means clear who the citizen-subject of this age would truly be. Even more perplexing is the question of who rightfully belongs to this age. To whom does this age—one of shrinking governments and expanding islands, anchored by data

Figure E.2. Judith Shklar (1928–1992). Among all the postwar thinkers of the modern liberal experiment, Judith Shklar stood in singular solitude for her refusal to think of human freedom along any "line" that wasn't first made to pass through the South. "Putting the South first" was fundamental to Shklar's moral psychology and, even more, to her archaeology of political cruelty. Like Bhimrao Ambedkar and Frederick Douglass before her, she was fearless in her critical constitutionalism, willing to call out caste as a system of lethal fear in a manner few liberals even today can. Source: HUD 366.04, p. 48, Harvard University Archives. Courtesy of Harvard Yearbook Publications.

cables, optical fiber, and nuclear waste of an earlier era—now rightfully belong? *Who is the new subject of the right to earth?*

Amnesia and the Island

As early as 1927, Ambedkar had launched, in the Bombay Presidency, a militant anticaste movement for access to public waterworks as a civil right of the outcastes. Even then, it has remained difficult to fully contend (from inside the modern legal tradition for much of the twentieth century) with the fact that the most timeless struggles for human dignity, on land or sea, have always involved water. If anything, for much of the modern age, the sea has stood as an analogue of a lawless nature, an antithesis of the terrestrial, humane rule of law. And there, the island too has since sat—tethered precariously to the vast blues of the planet as a necessary reminder of the oblivion that water is (and a cautionary tale of what the earth itself might become if not for laws of the land). The island is the living void, a remainder of the law, and thus a discarded fragment of life that is forgotten precisely because it is so easy to punish it—and its people—for indescribable crimes. The island is an inanimate pirate.

For the breathtaking simplicity of its violence, as if written for schoolchildren, Carl Schmitt's *Land and Sea* today reads like a troubling if still profound testimony to this enigmatic place of the sea—and of the fabled Leviathan—in the modern political imagination. "How can I dare tell," Schmitt asks, "in an adequate way, of the two wonders of the sea, of the most powerful of all living beasts and of the most cunning of human hunters?"[47] The normalized indifference toward refugee boats capsizing in the Mediterranean barely miles off mainland Europe today is indissociable from this enigmatic imaginary of the sea that sits at the bottom of modern political consciousness—the sea as the home of exemplary beasts at once sovereign and indomitable (beasts from whom, since Hobbes, all lessons of sovereignty have been drawn), on the one hand, and, on the other hand, the sea as the discarded birthplace of the law for the globe at large, upon which—and this is why it is discarded from the republic—no law as such holds. *Cold War Refugees* shows, with an unwavering eye to detail, how this enigma is further entrenched, lodged even deeper in the heart of the postwar global imagination. Excising it requires a new planetary alignment of Cold War history—and the place of the Atlantic and Pacific in it—away from the modes in which it has been until now written.

Not without reason, these modes of resolute, searing counterhistory seem to appear on the islands. When liberal democratic politics can only stare at the unlivable, frozen into inaction by its own indifference, it is poetry that must respond to it, as it has often, with lyrical intensity, in the stanzas of those who come from the islands, refusing to be erased by history. A radical vison of the sea is opened, for example, by the Puerto Rican Jewish poet Aurora Levins Morales in "Red Sea." Her poetry of refugee freedom offers a vison of the ocean freed of debt and bondage, if only because, as she writes, "we cannot cross until we carry each other."

> This time we are tied at the ankles.
> We cannot cross until we carry each other,
> all of us refugees, all of us prophets.
> No more taking turns on history's wheel,
> trying to collect old debts no-one can pay.
> The sea will not open that way.
>
> This time that country
> is what we promise each other,
> our rage pressed cheek to cheek
> until tears flood the space between,
> until there are no enemies left,
> because this time no one will be left to drown
> and all of us must be chosen.
> This time it's all of us or none.[48]

If to be a part of humanity means to be bound together by a common fate, Morales reminds us, then, this bond does not have to be forged by the pernicious exclusions, banishments, and chains of the law. Humanity, after all, has also always been forged around that other equally common, equally mortal, and equally fatal striving—the striving to seek *refuge* elsewhere, somewhere, anywhere that is not ruled by the endless cycle of debt and death.

The sea is also a reminder of this other humanity—the humanity in us that came *before the law* and might still come *after its cruelty*, the humanity that was *anarchic without being lawless* and that might still open itself to becoming a community—a country even—without being barbaric. And yet the sea, from where these last splinters of human hope might emerge, still seems like a groundless ground, a limitless limit, a "flood of tears," where the war between nature and humankind has never ceased. For all the chatter about trade, traffic, and corridors, for all the arguments about sovereignty and possession, for all the treaty negotiations about rights and rites of passage that it today generates, the sea remains a zone of barbaric abandonment—the space where death ceases to trouble the law.

In the Samoan imaginary that she simply calls, in a flourish of revolutionary irony, "Atlas," the poet Terisa Siagatonu cuts open the lacerating violence of this enigma.

> If you open up any atlas
> and take a look at a map of the world,
> almost every single one of them
> slices the Pacific Ocean in half.
> To the human eye,
> every map centers all the land masses on Earth
> creating the illusion
> that water can handle the butchering
> and be pushed to the edges
> of the world.
> As if the Pacific Ocean isn't the largest body
> living today, beating the loudest heart,
> the reason why land has a pulse in the first place.
>
> The audacity one must have to create a visual so
> violent as to assume that no one comes
> from water so no one will care
> what you do with it
> and yet,
> people came from land,
> are still coming from land,
> and look what was done to them.
> When people ask me where I'm from,
> they don't believe me when I say water.
> So instead, I tell them that home is a machete
> and that I belong to places
> that don't belong to themselves anymore,
> broken and butchered places that have made me
> a hyphen of a woman:
> a Samoan-American that carries the weight of both

colonizer and colonized,
both blade and blood.⁴⁹

Thus begins, with these devastating two stanzas, Siagatonu's epic poetry of strife—and *amnesia*—that plagues the idea of being human without land, of that fragment of humanity that leaves the island in order to live and that descends upon land from water. This human being—the last subject to arrive on land—comes from the unlivable island that simply does not exist in terrestrial consciousness; it is simply not seen as a part of the worldwide legal web Arendt wrote about in the middle of the last century. Thus, one receives, in an utter daze, the redemptive exemplarity of the Samoa for our time, the indomitable will of its American citizens, who, because they come from nowhere and because they sail from beyond the farthest horizon of American consciousness that the Pacific can absorb, are neither stateless nor rightless, simply *hemispheric*. They come from water, which renders them incommensurable with the terrestrial imaginary—the *violence*—that frames the ideals and institutions of American citizenship.

If we could place at the heart of our political thought this other, incommensurable swathe of humanity from the islands as fellow persons seeking a humane sanctuary state—as opposed to what Daniel Heller-Roazen calls "absentee persons," that subhuman species of the islands subject to the brutality of a sovereign, militarized, suburban America—how radically could the theory of liberal democracy (and of humanism as such) change?⁵⁰ If we placed at the heart of our moral thinking not our pejorative denunciation of those displaced persons "clamoring" for land but instead our firm solidarity with those who tread the perilous sunbathed path of migration from sea just to get to land, how could our vicious and collective refusal to give asylum change? Above all, how might our moral history and imaginary of homeland itself alter, curving away from the terrestrial xenophobia whose bloody rhetoric, stained by theologies of white supremacy, was set in place by the colonial nineteenth century?

There are, let us note, two *figures* and *imaginaries* of the island. Sometimes, as Moon shows above, this imaginary is built on a peninsula, cut arbitrarily along the imaginary curves of a punitive latitudinal line, the crossing of which is a matter of life and death. On the one hand, there is the island that belongs to those who have always lived in the vast unnoticed blues of the Pacific and southern Indian Ocean—as if they come from nowhere—and who must now leave the rapidly submerging islands (and thus their very dignity) behind so as to come ashore on lands where they shall never belong but whose violence they shall always bear on their bodies. The island of Terisa Siagatonu's imaginary splits open the wounds of this anticitizen surviving an unequal earth—a people who have never had any part of landmass for themselves because they come from "nowhere" and because the neo-colonial atlas has never seen them arrive or depart, alive or dead.

On the other hand, there is the heavily surveilled, watchful island of the yacht docks and data centers, of detention camps for uncharged terror suspects and metallic shelters for unprocessed refugees, who must confine themselves in cells constructed out of decommissioned ships and barges (such as the one the United Kingdom pressed into housing service for legal asylum seekers in 2023).[51] This other island is the *archipelago of inequality*—the entrenched sea link of unprecedented oligarchic disparity and technological power concentrated in the hands of the few who are determined to alter the fate of the planet. In his unsparing work *Techno-feudalism*, Yanis Varoufakis paints a radical picture of capitalist demise and the splintering of its global value system into feudal attributes. The planet, he argues, is now governed, for all practical purposes, not through the financial system overseen by sovereign nation-states—whose age of manufacturing might have already passed—but through island-like fiefdoms ruled by tech giants, who simply process data and identity, acting less like manufacturers of value and more like rentiers who hoard it.[52] This is the other island that dots an unequal earth. This inverted island of late techno-capitalism is a fiefdom where nobody ever arrives or docks without being seen and where no refugee is to be washed ashore or be caught on its white sands, alive or dead.

It is in this haunting sense that inequality has today made a return—unprecedented in its segregationist structure, legitimized by an indifferent planetarity talk, and unsure, as Siagatonu devastatingly reveals, of what to do with the islands. The questions her revolutionary irony leaves in its wake are no less haunting than the inequality of the modern humanist calculus—and its blind *atlas*—that she lays threadbare.

Can we be excused for doubting that there is anything to be said anymore to the blind, murderous indifference of Cold War humanism? To the hijacking of human dignity by the most depraved, who now need but a keyboard and screen? Is there anything—perhaps just a word—that might cut through this impenetrable wall of moralism that today hides its own monstrous appetite for insult? Whose rhetoric of dignity excludes those who die on seas just miles off Europe's fabled coastlines, left to drown in the familiar oblivion of organized, tactical neglect? What is the word for this urbane depravity that sees no deprivation around it? And where will it take us in the end? How, if at all, would nation-states themselves lower their cruel walls?

When I say "neglect," I don't simply mean abandonment of citizens deemed so barely human that, to paraphrase Arendt, "nobody wants to even oppress them." By "neglect," I mean a sacrificial architecture whose sole aim is the management of populations (rather than redistribution of public goods); a technocratic competence backed by an archaic theological energy; a brutalist awareness of space, design, and matter scaffolded around a merciless religious zeal; and, above all, a collective willingness to punish citizens and strangers alike, fueled by a majoritarian pursuit of power that is delusional in its quest for a corrupted—or, as Benjamin might say, "rotten"—transcendence. This appetite for power is infinite. And yet it frequently takes on the language of monastic renunciation, substituting the shared vulnerability among human beings with an ascetic disregard for life itself—one's own life and that of the other. They do not believe her when she says she comes from water, Siagatonu reveals. But perhaps they do when "I tell them," she says, "home is a machete." This is the poetics of counterpower—a lyric of brutal hope—that is still to come. But it is already a testament to the obstinance with which jargons of sacrifice haunt Cold War humanism.

As *Cold War Refugees* testifies, there are two sacrificial vectors along which postwar power has grown and gnawed at humanity in the Global South. One vector is the delirious randomization of historical time—the complete breakdown of any sense that humanity has ever been secular or modern. The other vector is the complete embrace of a religious charge taken to a fanatical extreme—only this time, by its side is a new language, a new competence and skill, and, most importantly, a new love of technology. As Jacques Derrida cautions, religion and technology have always been meant to travel happily together.[53] And when they combine thoughtlessly, there is very little that separates a society that despises the refugee or the migrant from a society that hates its own outcastes, minorities, women, waterborne, and even the infirm. Such a society simply signs up to a murderous consent, setting its eyes on those who are most vulnerable, most capable of being injured, most easily allowed to perish. This is what we might call, following Achille Mbembe, "the society of enmity."[54]

Ends: Of Flight from Earth

The number of people migrating on account of climate events, the World Bank's *Groundswell* report estimates, will be 216 million by 2050. The very nature of human mobility and arguments about the right to move—in effect, the future of human freedom as such—are now unthinkable unless we reconceptualize the relationship between politics and the planet, between borders and heat. Whether it is overcrowding in the megacities of the rapidly industrializing South or the endemic violence associated with racially segregated housing in the developed North, nothing aggravates the partitions of the globe more glaringly than the disparity that human beings are confronted with when they face increasingly unbearable heat. Every inequality is today magnified under the stress of a warming planet. Every escape route that a migrant takes as she becomes a refugee might flow directly from the suffering unleashed by changing oceanic currents. Far from a safe dwelling, home itself, as Siagatonu writes, must be a machete—a curved, cutting, sacrificial shot at life.

Power, meanwhile, now comes not only from domination over earth. Its fantasies, potentialities, and ambition extend to outer space and other planets. Marked by the desire to supersede earth and turn the globe into just another frontier of human will and of what it can next conquer (or where it will forever perish), the rhetoric of planetarity—despite its resemblances to colonial and neocolonial universalisms of an earlier age—today threatens to render modern conceptions of the border wholly irrelevant. Yet it does so, tragically or otherwise, not by liberating itself from the *logic of the border* but precisely by reenacting and intensifying the effects of a theologico-juridical drama, reminiscent of the worst traits of religion's earlier tryst with capitalist modernity.

Although some would have us believe otherwise, planetarity—the moment at which the earth becomes a mortal, perishable thing—is not an epochal break with earlier regimes and laws of suffering. Instead, it is an epochal intensification of the pain inflicted upon mortals that, in an earlier colonial era, accompanied the Kantian dream of "perpetual peace." Only now, Cold War peace has given way to cold borders over the high seas. And the last subjects of this theologico-juridical order of things, permanently estranged from their homelands and thrust out frequently onto the sea that they must cross, are barely containable within the limits of the nation-state. The populations of the planetary age are overwhelmingly stateless. And this is so even as citizens within sovereign states are left morally placeless and unresponsive, unable to offer any meaningful response other than mere solace to those who arrive on their borders seeking a home on a "planet of slums."[55] The refugee is this figure of arrival on a segregated planet, constituted as much by its own statelessness as it is by its universality, trapped no less in its rightlessness as it is in its ubiquity, superfluity even. The refugee, I argue, is our first postplanetary universal: a remnant of an exhausted modernity and a memory of its endless violence. It is the exemplary anticitizen from our future.

Today, what we need is an ethics of migration in active synchrony with the question of technology. We need this synchrony simply because, on the one hand, new technologies enable new forms of surveillance of those who want to move across borders and thus directly assist in their detention and killing and, on the other, because, while turning migration into a prohibitive paramilitary question, technology is itself implicated in encouraging another form of migration: extraterrestrial flight fueled by the belief that an affluent chunk of humanity can leave the earth itself. Investigating the coming forms, compulsions, and duress of human movement—which is to say, of *refugees still to come*—requires that we pay attention to the language of international institutionalism and its rhetoric in times of war and peace alike. But it also demands a new international focus on the depredations of those armed asymmetrically with new unregulated technologies.

When one reads *Cold War Refugees*, one notices a series of questions waiting to be asked. Where are the limits to the law, if any, that today governs the great spaces on earth (and thus, in a tragic irony, also determines the shapes of planetary segregation)? How did the disposability of human life—and the regime of penal power that now sees in the refugee less an asylum seeker and more an enemy hostage—come to be braided with the disregard for the planet's future at large, even as this disregard now finds its expression in the desire to leave the earth? And then there is the recognition this book leaves us with. No matter how many or how few manage to leave earth (before the earth abandons humanity), human beings are now bound to inhabit a planet of refugees. It is to the postwar history of this abject equality—one that is forged across national boundaries not by redistribution of public goods by the equality of exposure to extinction—that *Cold War Refugees* so forcefully draws our attention.

Probing this relationship between disposability and transcendence, between lawlessness and the law, requires an archaeology of not only the natural rights tradition from its European vantage—there is only that much this history now explains—but also the conditions of its reformulation in the wake of Europe's imperial expansion into the Global South from the eighteenth century onward. It demands not only charting commercial and philosophical liberalism's complex relationship to anthropological notions of movement and unrest but also probing the structure of anxieties around technology and its effects on warfare and identity and, above all, the system of normative values anchored in exhausted ideas about human agency.

Are those who move, migrate, and seek refuge across the seas less worthy of the right to live? Has technology deformed the punitive impulse of modern sovereignty and international legislation so irreversibly that states can now respond to movement—which is the foundational principle of human freedom—only by criminalizing those who come from the seas? And what of those who seem, on the surface of the seas, free to move? Are they really free? Or have we moved entirely past the humanist burden that we once carried of at least trying to make human freedom equal and equality of human beings self-evident?

Cold War Refugees shows the value of cold history in reanimating these questions of freedom and violence, tracking, one chapter at a time, how inextricably planetary anxieties about the human today are linked to the punishing counterrevolutionary violence of colonial feuds and decolonization in Asia and Africa. Only now, three quarters of a century later, at stake—in the checkered global history of rights and migration, in the rapacious international division of land and sea, in Euro-American delusions of sovereignty over the entire planet whose beginnings are so often located in Hobbes's seabound imaginary that is the *Leviathan* (1651) but whose intensity had not subsided until as late as the end of the Cold War—is not merely the virtues of citizens and the criminality of migrants or the brutalism of racial, caste, and religious segregations or the institutional fate of civic identity and civil rights. At stake are the moral and biological frontiers of the human as such—a *figure* torn between sentient intelligence and artificial, mechanical life.

It might be paradoxical, but this violent tear in the idea of the human, its "twofold alienation," as Arendt calls it, does echo the general history of humanity and its striving for immortal transcendent deeds.[56] Only now, cruelty and transcendence have mutated into one whole so that humanity's most powerful oligarchs try at once to wall off refugees *and* to take flight from the planet, leaving humanity out in another dark, cold, but by no means unfamiliar oblivion. Of that oblivion, the Mediterranean is today the primal scene. "The sea rises, the light fails, lovers cling to each other, and children cling to us," James Baldwin writes in his crushing meditation on faith "Nothing Personal." "The moment we cease to hold each other, the moment we break faith with one another, the sea engulfs us, and the light goes out."[57] Perhaps the refugee today is a remnant of this failing light of humanity at sea. It might also be the last bearer of human freedom before the light goes out entirely.

Notes

Introduction

1. "Christmas Miracle at Hungnam: The Epic Evacuation That Changed Korea Forever," *National Interest*, October 10, 2021.

2. Amnesty International, "Afghanistan's Refugees: Forty Years of Dispossession," June 20, 2019, https://www.amnesty.org/en/latest/news/2019/06/afghanistan-refugees-forty-years.

3. Peter Gatrell, "Refugees: What's Wrong with History," *Journal of Refugee Studies* 30, no. 2 (2016): 170. Gatrell offers a valuable overview of these Asian refugees in Gatrell, *The Making of the Modern Refugee* (Oxford: Oxford University Press, 2013), chaps. 6–7.

4. Yến Lê Espiritu et al., *Departures: An Introduction to Critical Refugee Studies* (Oakland: University of California Press, 2022).

5. That chapter briefly discusses Western regulations applying to refugees from Eastern Europe and the refusal to accept the millions of refugees from Communist Asia, and it attributes this exclusion to the imperial practice of population control originating in the West's period of colonization and empires. Matthew Connelly, "The Cold War in the Long Durée: Global Migration, Public Health, and Population Control," in *The Cambridge History of the Cold War*, ed. Melvyn P. Leffler and Odd Arne Westad (Cambridge: Cambridge University Press, 2010), 3:366–488.

6. Angelina Y. Chin, *Unsettling Exiles: Chinese Migrants in Hong Kong and the Southern Periphery during the Cold War* (New York: Columbia University Press, 2023); Evyn Lê Espiritu Gandhi, *Archipelago of Resettlement: Vietnamese Refugee Settlers and Decolonization across Guam and Israel-Palestine* (Oakland: University of California

Press, 2022); Dominic Meng-Hsuan Yang, *The Great Exodus from China: Trauma, Memory, and Identity in Modern Taiwan* (Cambridge: Cambridge University Press, 2021); Phi-Vân Nguyen, "Victims of Atheist Persecution, Catholic Solidarity and Refugee Protection in Vietnam: 1954–1958," in *Refugees and Religion: Ethnographic Studies of Global Trajectories*, ed. Birgit Meyer and Peter van der Veer (London: Bloomsbury, 2021), 51–57; Nguyen, "A Secular State for a Religious Nation: The Republic of Vietnam and Religious Nationalism, 1946–1963," *Journal of Asian Studies* 77, no. 3 (2018): 741–71; Jana K. Lipman, *In Camps: Vietnamese Refugees, Asylum Seekers, and Repatriates* (Oakland: California University Press, 2020); Glen Peterson, "Forced Migration, Refugees and China's Entry into the 'Family of Nations,' 1861–1949," *Journal of Refugee Studies* 31, no. 3 (2018): 274–79; Justin M. Jacobs, "Exile Island: Xinjiang Refugees and the 'One China' Policy in Nationalist Taiwan, 1949–1971," *Journal of Cold War Studies* 18, no. 1 (Winter 2016): 188–218.

7. Laura Madokoro, *Elusive Refuge: Chinese Migrants in the Cold War* (Cambridge, MA: Harvard University Press, 2016), 11–16. See also ibid., chap. 5.

8. Department of State, Special Committee on Migration and Resettlement, "Draft of Letter Prepared by the State Department for the Signature of the President, to the Secretary of War. Presumably Sent between July 18 and July 27, 1943"; "Working Draft: Displaced Populations and Groups in Korea," September 28, 1944, RG 165, entry 463, box 140, sec. 3: Refugees, National Archives and Records Administration, College Park, MD (hereafter cited as NARA).

9. Gatrell, *Modern Refugee*, 3–4.

10. Bei Gao, *Shanghai Sanctuary: Chinese and Japanese Policy toward European Jewish Refugees during World War II* (New York: Oxford University Press, 2013); Marcia Reynders Ristaino, *Port of Last Resort: Diaspora Communities of Shanghai* (Stanford, CA: Stanford University Press, 2001); Kevin Ostoyich and Yun Xia, eds., *The History of the Shanghai Jews: New Pathways of Research* (Cham: Palgrave Macmillan, 2022).

11. H. F. Arthur Schoenfeld, a career diplomat, chaired the committee and Dr. Eleanor Lansing Dulles, an economist and sister of John Foster Dulles, who served as secretary of state in the 1950s, held the position of secretary. Department of State, Special Committee on Migration and Resettlement, "Minutes of the Fifteenth Meeting," November 4, 1944, RG 165, Civil Affairs Division General Records, Security Classified General Correspondence, 1943–July 1949, box 113, sec. 3: Committee on Migration, NARA.

12. Lori Watt, "The 'Disposition of Japanese Civilians': American Wartime Planning for the Colonial Japanese," *Diplomatic History* 41, no. 2 (2017): 392–414.

13. On the coordination with the War and Navy Departments, see "Letter from Dean Acheson, Assistant Secretary to Admiral William D. Leahy," November 30, 1944; "Letter from Dean Acheson, Assistant Secretary to Henry L. Stimson, Secretary of War," RG 165, Civil Affairs Division General Records, Security Classified General Correspondence, 1943–July 1949, box 113, sec. 3: Committee on Migration, NARA.

14. Department of State, Special Committee on Migration and Resettlement, *Dis-*

placed Populations and Groups in Korea (October 26, 1944); "Recommendations to Military Authorities with Respect to Displaced Groups in Korea (October 26, 1944)"; *Displaced Populations and Groups in the Netherlands East Indies (October 26, 1944)*; "Recommendations to Military Authorities with Respect to Displaced Groups in the Netherlands East Indies (October 26, 1944)"; *Displaced Populations and Groups in Japan (July 14, 1944)*; "Recommendations to Military Authorities with Respect to Displaced Groups in Japan (July 15, 1944)"; *Displaced Populations and Groups in the Philippines (July 11, 1944)*; "Recommendations to Military Authorities with Respect to Displaced Groups in the Philippines (July 11, 1944)"; *Displaced Populations and Groups in the Japanese Mandated Islands (July 12, 1944)*; "Recommendations to the Military Authorities with Respect to Displaced Groups in the Japanese Mandated Islands (July 14, 1944)"; *Displaced Populations and Groups in Formosa (May 20, 1944)*; "Recommendations to Military Authorities with Respect to Displaced Persons in Formosa (May 22, 1944)," RG 165, Civil Affairs Division General Records, Security Classified General Correspondence, 1943–July 1949, box 113, sec. 3: Committee on Migration, NARA. No similar papers on mainland China and Manchuria were found in the Special Committee's files. This absence could be attributed to the expectation that the Republic of China would regain sovereignty over these areas or that they would be occupied by the USSR after Japan's defeat. The fact that the Special Committee did produce papers on Taiwan indicates the potential for a US military presence there, though ultimately the United States did not actually occupy the island. On the US consideration of the postwar occupation of Taiwan, see Department of State, "Papers Concerning Miliary Government in Formosa," June 3, 1943, RG 165, Civil Affairs Division General Records, Security Classified General Correspondence, 1943–July 1949, box 46, sec. 1: Military, NARA.

15. "Treaty between the United States and China for Relinquishment of Extraterritorial Rights in China and the Regulation of Related Matters, Singed January 11, 1943," Foreign Relations of the United States: Diplomatic Papers, 1943, China, Office of the Historian, Department of State, accessed October 31, 2024, https://history.state.gov/historicaldocuments/frus1943China/comp12.

16. E.g., see Department of State, Special Committee on Migration and Resettlement, *Displaced Populations and Groups in Korea*, p. 7; *Displaced Populations and Groups in the Philippines*, p. 6.

17. The committee estimated that a total of approximately 970,000 Japanese civilians would be displaced in the aforementioned Asian regions, the majority of them in Japan's formal colonies and mandates: 250,000 in Taiwan, 600,000 in Korea, and 80,000 in the Japanese mandated islands. The rest were in the islands under Japan's occupation: 30,000 in the Philippines and 10,000 to 15,000 in the Dutch East Indies. Lori Watt suggests that a total of 3.2 million Japanese civilians, as of August 1945, were outside of the Japanese archipelago. Watt, *When Empires Comes Home: Repatriation and Reintegration in Postwar Japan* (Cambridge, MA: Harvard University Asia Center: 2009), 2.

18. Department of State, Special Committee on Migration and Resettlement, *Displaced Populations and Groups in Formosa*, pp. 7–8.

19. The committee advised that the military authorities issue new identification cards to Koreans who had lost their cards, utilize police records to identify Koreans among the Japanese, and prepare to eventually submit their information to the governing authorities responsible for Korea. Department of State, Special Committee on Migration and Resettlement, *Displaced Populations and Groups in Japan*, p. 8; *Displaced Populations and Groups in Formosa*, p. 3.

20. In Japan, official Japanese sources reported a significantly lower number of Chinese nationals (27,000 in 1936) in Japan. However, the Special Committee considered 225,000 Chinese to be partially confirmed by reliable sources. Department of State, Special Committee on Migration and Resettlement, *Displaced Populations and Groups in Japan*, pp. 4–5.

21. They were considered Dutch citizens by birth while residing in the colony but would become Chinese citizens if they moved back to China, while if they moved to a third country, they had the right to choose their status as either Dutch or Chinese nationals. Department of State, Special Committee on Migration and Resettlement, *Displaced Populations and Groups in the Netherlands East Indies*, pp. 8–9.

22. Department of State, Special Committee on Migration and Resettlement, *Displaced Populations and Groups in the Netherlands East Indies*, p. 17.

23. Department of State, Special Committee on Migration and Resettlement, *Displaced Populations and Groups in the Netherlands East Indies*, pp. 10–11.

24. Department of State, Special Committee on Migration and Resettlement, "Recommendations to Military Authorities with Respect to Displaced Groups in the Netherlands East Indies," pp. 1–2.

25. Department of State, Special Committee on Migration and Resettlement, *Displaced Populations and Groups in the Japanese Mandated Islands*, p. 9; *Displaced Populations and Groups in Korea*, p. 10.

26. Finally, the United States regarded both Japanese and non-Japanese displaced groups in Asia as a potential labor source. The Special Committee advised military authorities not to disperse displaced groups if they were already part of the workforce and recommended assigning the displaced groups to labor units after assessing their qualifications and willingness to work. It was likely that using displaced persons as a labor resource was a shared principle among the Allied forces because the USSR employed skilled workers and technicians, including Japanese civilians, in government agencies and factories. In Korea, the United States did not actively utilize the displaced groups as a workforce or maintain labor units consisting of displaced persons or refugees, although young refugees from northern Korea were often employed as "houseboys" on US miliary bases. Further research is needed to fully understand how the United States implemented this labor policy in different regions of Asia. Department of State, Special Committee on Migration and Resettlement, *Displaced Populations and Groups in the Netherlands East Indies*, pp. 16–17.

27. Department of State, "Letter from Minister Schoenfeld to Major General J. H. Hilldring," March 12, 1945, RG 165, Civil Affairs Division General Records, Security Classified General Correspondence, 1943–July 1949, box 113, sec. 3: Committee on Migration, NARA; Department of State, Special Committee on Migration and Resettlement, "Minutes of the Fifteenth Meeting," p. 5.

28. Department of State, Special Committee on Migration and Resettlement, "Minutes of the Fifteenth Meeting," pp. 4–5.

29. Sara Halpern, "A Problem of Some Delicacy: Chinese Sovereignty, Jewish Refugees, and the West, 1945–1946," in *The History of the Shanghai Jews: New Pathways of Research*, ed. Kevin Ostoyich and Yun Xia (Cham: Palgrave Macmillan, 2022), 179.

30. Gatrell, *Modern Refugee*, 89–90.

31. Gerard Daniel Cohen, *In War's Wake: Europe's Displaced Persons in the Postwar Order* (New York: Oxford University Press, 2012), 4.

32. Cohen, *In War's Wake*, 6–7. On a brief discussion on expellees, see "Report on Industry and Trade," United States President's Famine Emergency Committee Records, box 26, folder 1, pp. 4–5, Hoover Archives, Stanford University.

33. Watt, "Disposition of Japanese Civilians," 402–9.

34. On the screening operations of the DPs in Europe, see Cohen, *In War's Wake*, chap. 3.

35. Cohen, *In War's Wake*, 5, 1–2.

36. Emmanuel Comte, "Waging the Cold War: The Origins and Launch of Western Cooperation to Absorb Migrants from Eastern Europe, 1948–57," *Cold War History* 20, no. 4 (2020): 461; Cohen, *In War's Wake*, 46; Peter J. Verovšek, "Screening Migrants in the Early Cold War: The Geopolitics of U.S. Immigration Policy," *Journal of Cold War Studies* 20, no. 4 (Fall 2018): 165.

37. Kim Po-yŏng, "Han'guk chŏnjaeng sigi yi sŭng-man ŭi pan'gong p'oro sŏkpang kwa hanmi kyosŏp," *Ihwa Sahak Yŏn'gu* 38 (2009): 191–93.

38. David Chang, *The Hijacked War: The Story of Chinese POWs in the Korean War* (Stanford, CA: Stanford University Press, 2020), 4–6.

39. On a critical review of refugee law and regulations, see Espiritu et al., *Departures*, chap. 1.

40. UNHCR (Office of the United Nations High Commissioner for Refugees), *Convention and Protocol Relating to the Status of Refugees* (Geneva: UNHCR, 2011), 14, https://www.unhcr.org/media/28185.

41. UNHCR, *Convention*; Madokoro, *Elusive Refuge*, chap. 1.

42. For a critical review of humanitarianism and international organizations on refugee relief, see Espiritu et al., *Departures*, chap. 3.

43. Rebecca Hamlin, *Crossing: How We Label and React to People on the Move* (Stanford, CA: Stanford University Press, 2021), 1–2.

44. Espiritu et al., *Departures*, 71.

45. Department of State, "Draft of Letter Prepared by the State Department for the Signature of the President, to the Secretary of War: Presumably Sent between July 17

and July 27, 1943; Referral to in Memorandum of July 17, 1943 from the Secretary of State to the President"; "Memorandum for the President (July 17, 1943)"; "Paraphrase of Telegram Sent from the Secretary of State to the American Consul, Algiers (July 27, 1943)," RG 165, Civil Affairs Division General Records, Security Classified General Correspondence, 1943–July 1949, box 140, sec. 3: Refugees, NARA. In July 1943, the secretary of state sent a letter on the refugees in Spain to the secretary of war in preparation for receiving the approval of President Roosevelt on the relief of the refugees in Spain.

46. UNRRA (United Nations Relief and Rehabilitation Administration), "Letter from A. H. Feller to John H. Hilldring (September 8, 1944)"; FEA (Foreign Economic Administration), "Letter from Leo T. Crowley to John H. Hilldring (October 24, 1944)"; UNRRA, "Letter from Herbert H. Lehman to John H. Hilldring (October 10, 1944)," RG 165, Civil Affairs Division General Records, Security Classified General Correspondence, 1943–July 1949, box 140, sec. 3: Refugees, NARA. Following this discussion, UNRRA opened a refugee camp in Philippeville, Algeria. The camp was ready for occupancy on October 1, 1944, with a capacity to accommodate approximately forty thousand refugees.

47. SHAEF (Supreme Headquarters, Allied Expeditionary Force), G-5 Division, Displaced Persons Branch, "Subject: Talisman Plan (August 12, 1944)"; "Memorandum No. 14: Control of Displaced Person (August 12, 1944)," RG 165, Civil Affairs Division General Records, Security Classified General Correspondence, 1943–July 1949, box 140, sec. 3: Refugees, NARA.

48. SHAEF, "Memorandum No. 14," p. 1.

49. Regarding the role of the Intergovernmental Committee on Refugees, the document states, "The Intergovernmental Committee on Refugees will continue its responsibility for persons who have been obliged to leave their homes for reasons of race, religion, or political belief, and cannot or do not desire to be repatriated." SHAEF, "Memorandum No. 14," p. 5.

50. Department of State, "Specific Comments and Recommendations on SHAEF Outline Plan for Refugees and Displaced Persons (August 5, 1944)," RG 165, Civil Affairs Division General Records, Security Classified General Correspondence, 1943–July 1949, box 140, sec. 3: Refugees, p. 1, NARA.

51. Gatrell, *Modern Refugee*, 95.

52. Hannah Arendt, *Origins of Totalitarianism* (1951; repr., New York: Harcourt Brace, 1973), 279, 284, quoted in Gatrell, *Modern Refugee*, 95.

53. Hannah Arendt, "We Refugees," in *The Jewish Writings*, ed. Jerome Kohn and Ron H. Feldman (New York: Schocken Books, 2007), 264.

54. Edward Said, *Reflections on Exile and Other Essays* (Cambridge, MA: Harvard University Press, 2000), 181–82, 184.

55. Yang, *Great Exodus from China*, 3, 5.

56. Vinh Nguyen, "Refugeetude: When Does a Refugee Stop Being a Refugee?," *Social Text* 37, no. 2 (2019): 117.

57. For a critique of Cold War liberalism along these lines, see Mimi Thi Nguyen, *The Gift of Freedom: War, Debt, and Other Refugee Passages* (Durham, NC: Duke University Press, 2012).

58. Nguyen, "Refugeetude," 123.

59. On refugees and their sociopolitical construction of space and place, see Liisa Malkki, "National Geographic: The Rooting of Peoples and the Territorialization of National Identity among Scholars and Refugees," *Cultural Anthropology* 7, no. 1 (February 1992): 24–44.

60. Malkki, "National Geographic," 25.

61. Giorgio Agamben, "We Refugees," *Symposium* 49, no. 2 (1995): 118; emphasis original.

62. Odd Arne Westad, *The Global Cold War: Third World Interventions and the Making of Our Times* (Cambridge: Cambridge University Press, 2005).

63. On this point, see Heonik Kwon, *The Other Cold War* (New York: Columbia University Press, 2010), 6.

64. Liisa Malkki, "Speechless Emissaries: Refugees, Humanitarianism, and Dehistoricization," *Cultural Anthropology* 11, no. 3 (1996): 378.

Chapter 1

1. For a recent historiographical analysis, see Philip Catton, "'It Would Be a Terrible Thing If We Handed These People Over to the Communists': The Eisenhower Administration, Article 14(d), and the Origins of the Refugee Exodus from North Vietnam," *Diplomatic History* 39, no. 2 (2015): 331–58. For an account claiming its central role in the United States' involvement in South Vietnam, see Seth Jacobs, *America's Miracle Man in Vietnam: Ngo Dinh Diem, Religion, Race and U.S. Intervention in Southeast Asia, 1950–1957* (Durham, NC: Duke University Press, 2005); Jacobs, *Cold War Mandarin: Ngo Dinh Diem and the Origins of the America's War in Vietnam* (Lanham, MD: Rowman and Littlefield, 2006). For a more nuanced analysis of this nascent partnership, see Edward Miller, *Misalliance: Ngo Dinh Diem, the United States and the Fate of South Vietnam* (Cambridge, MA: Harvard University Press, 2013).

2. Kathryn Statler, *Replacing France: The Origins of American Intervention in Vietnam* (Lexington: University of Kentucky Press, 2007); Fredrik Logevall, *Embers of War: The Fall of an Empire and the Making of America's Vietnam* (New York: Random House, 2012). For a longer perspective, see Mark Philip Bradley, *Imagining Vietnam and America: The Making of Postcolonial Vietnam, 1919–1950* (Chapel Hill: University of North Carolina Press, 2000).

3. For a more recent analysis on the evacuation, see Peter Hansen, "The Virgin Heads South: Northern Catholic Refugees in South Vietnam, 1954–1964" (PhD diss., Melbourne College of Divinity, 2008); Hansen, "Bắc Di Cư: Catholic Refugees from the North of Vietnam, and Their Role in the Southern Republic, 1954–1959," *Journal of Vietnamese Studies* 4, no. 3 (2009): 173–211; Jason A. Picard, "'Renegades': The Story of South Vietnam's First National Opposition Newspaper, 1955–1958," *Journal of Viet-*

namese Studies 10, no. 4 (2015): 1–29; Picard, "'Fertile Lands Await': The Promise and Pitfalls of Directed Resettlement, 1954–1959," *Journal of Vietnamese Studies* 11, nos. 3–4 (2016): 58–102; Phi-Van Nguyen, *A Displaced Nation: The 1954 Evacuation and Its Political Impact on the Vietnam Wars* (Ithaca, NY: Cornell University Press, 2024).

4. Arie M. Dubnov and Laura Robson, eds., *Partitions: A Transnational History of Twentieth-Century Territorial Separatism* (Stanford, CA: Stanford University Press, 2019).

5. Christopher E. Goscha, *The Road to Dien Bien Phu: A History of the First War for Vietnam* (Princeton, NJ: Princeton University Press, 2022).

6. Brett Reilly, "The Sovereign States of Vietnam, 1945–1955," *Journal of Vietnamese Studies* 11, nos. 3–4 (2016): 103–39; Reilly, "The Origins of the Vietnamese Civil War and the State of Vietnam" (PhD diss., University of Wisconsin–Madison, 2018); Shawn McHale, *The First Vietnam War: Violence, Sovereignty, and the Fracture of the South, 1945–1956* (Cambridge: Cambridge University Press, 2021).

7. Alec G. Holcombe, *Mass Mobilization in the Democratic Republic of Vietnam, 1945–1960* (Honolulu: University of Hawai'i Press, 2020); Alex Thai Vo, "From Anticolonialism to Mobilizing Socialist Transformation in the Democratic Republic of Vietnam, 1945–1960" (PhD diss., Cornell University, 2019); Vo, "Nguyễn Thị Năm and the Land Reform in North Vietnam, 1953," *Journal of Vietnamese Studies* 10, no. 1 (2015): 1–62.

8. The idea of the DRV being an archipelago state first appeared in Christopher E. Goscha, *Vietnam: Un État né de la guerre, 1945–1954* (Paris: Armand Colin, 2011).

9. Ramesh Thakur, *Peacekeeping in Vietnam: Canada, India, Poland, and the International Commission* (Edmonton: University of Alberta Press, 1984), 104.

10. Christopher E. Goscha, *Thailand and the Southeast Asian Networks of the Vietnamese Revolution, 1885–1954* (London: Curzon Press, 1999).

11. McHale, *First Vietnam War*; François Guillemot, *Dai Viêt, indépendance et révolution au Viêt-Nam: L'échec de la troisième voie (1938–1955)* (Paris: Les Indes savantes, 2012), 574–77. On their integration into the SVN, see Nu-Anh Tran, *Disunion: Anticommunist Nationalism and the Making of the Republic of Vietnam* (Honolulu: University of Hawai'i Press, 2022).

12. Robert F. Randle, *The Settlement of the Indochinese War* (Princeton, NJ: Princeton University Press, 1969); James Cable, *The Geneva Conference of 1954 on Indochina* (New York: St. Martin's Press, 1986).

13. Paul Ély, *Mémoires: L'Indochine dans la tourmente* (Paris: Plon, 1964), 1:181–83.

14. Pierre Grosser, "Une 'création continue'? L'Indochine, le Maghreb et l'Union française," *Monde(s)* 12, no. 2 (2017): 71–94; Grosser, "La France et l'Indochine (1953–1956): Une 'carte de visite' en 'peau de chagrin'" (PhD diss., Institut d'études politiques, 2002).

15. Zhai Qiang, "China and the Geneva Conference of 1954," *China Quarterly* 129 (March 1992): 103–22; Tao Wang, "Neutralizing Indochina: The 1954 Geneva Conference and China's Efforts to Isolate the United States," *Journal of Cold War Studies* 19,

no. 2 (2017): 3–42; Chen Jian, "China and the Indochina Settlement at the Geneva Conference of 1954," in *The First Vietnam War: Colonial Conflict and Cold War Crisis*, ed. Mark Lawrence and Frederik Logevall (Cambridge, MA: Harvard University Press, 2007), 240–62; Christopher E. Goscha and Karine Laplante, eds., *L'échec de la paix en Indochine, 1954–1962* (Paris: Les Indes Savantes, 2010).

16. Pierre Asselin, "The Democratic Republic of Vietnam and the 1954 Geneva Conference: A Revisionist Critique," *Cold War History* 11, no. 2 (2010): 168.

17. Randle, *Indochinese War*, 235.

18. United Press International, "French Abandon Province South of Hanoi to Vietminh," *New York Times*, June 30, 1954.

19. Reuters, "Tonkin Lines Shortened: Southern Area Evacuated," *Christian Science Monitor*, July 1, 1954; Henry Lieberman, "Vietnam Premier Protests French Pull-Back in Delta," *New York Times*, July 3, 1954; Lieberman, "French Give Up South Zone of Vietnam's Delta to Reds," *New York Times*, July 2, 1954; United Press International, "French Abandon Province"; "Evacuation Rush Strikes Namdinh: Red River Defense Keystone in State of Confusion as French Troops Leave," *New York Times*, July 3, 1954.

20. Lieberman, "French Give Up."

21. "Indochina Going," *New York Times*, July 4, 1954.

22. Catton, "Terrible Thing," 349.

23. E.g., Jacobs, *Cold War Mandarin*; James M. Carter, *Inventing Vietnam: The United States and State Building, 1954–1968* (Cambridge: Cambridge University Press, 2008).

24. "Geneva Agreements: 20–21 July 1954; Agreements on the Cessation of Hostilities in Viet-Nam, 20 July 1954," UN Peacemaker, accessed February 10, 2025, https://peacemaker.un.org/sites/default/files/document/files/2024/05/kh-la-vn540720geneva agreements.pdf. The main accounts of the conference are Cable, *Geneva Conference*; Randle, *Indochinese War*. For recent findings since the opening of Communist archives, see "New Evidence on the 1954 Geneva Conference on Indochina," February 17–18, 2006, CWIHP Document Reader, Wilson Center, Washington, DC, https://www.wilsoncenter.org/publication/the-1954-geneva-conference.

25. Catton, "Terrible Thing."

26. Robert B. Frankum, *Operation Passage to Freedom: The United States Navy in Vietnam, 1954–1955* (Lubbock: Texas Tech University Press, 2007). On the British participation, see Philip Catton, "The Royal Navy's Vietnam War: H.M.S. Warrior and the Evacuation from North Vietnam, September 1954," *Historical Research* 83, no. 220 (2010): 358–77.

27. Jessica Elkind, *Aid under Fire: Nation Building and the Vietnam War* (Lexington: University Press of Kentucky, 2016); Delia T. Pergande, "Private Voluntary Aid and Nation Building in South Vietnam: The Humanitarian Politics of CARE, 1954–1961," *Peace and Change* 27, no. 2 (2002): 165–97; John Ernst, *Forging a Fateful Alliance: Michigan State University and the Vietnam War* (East Lansing: Michigan State University Press, 1998). On Catholic solidarity more specifically, see Jacobs, *America's Miracle*

Man; Phi-Vân Nguyen, "Victims of Atheist Persecution: Transnational Catholic Solidarity and Refugee Protection in Cold War Asia," in *Refugees and Religions: Ethnographic Studies of Global Trajectories,* ed. Birgit Meyer and Peter van der Veer (London: Bloomsbury, 2021), 51–67.

28. Henry Lieberman, "Battle for Allegiance Goes On in Indochina," *New York Times,* August 8, 1954; Lieberman, "'Go South' Slogans on Buildings Spur Mass Exodus from Hanoi," *New York Times,* August 21, 1954; "Red Agents Begging Vietnamese to Stay," *Washington Post,* July 25, 1954; "Soviet Bloc Scores U.N. Refugee Plan," *New York Times,* October 6, 1954.

29. Jacobs, *America's Miracle Man,* 136.

30. Thomas A. Dooley, *Deliver Us from Evil* (New York: Farrar, Straus and Cudahy, 1956).

31. For a discussion of the figures, see John Prados, "The Numbers Game: How Many Vietnamese Fled South in 1954?," *VVA Veteran,* January–February 2005; Đặng Phương Nghi, "Về số người công giáo di cư từ Bắc và Nam sau Hiệp định Genève," Văn Tuyển, 2002, http://vantuyen.net/index.php?view=story&subjectid=20311/; Phi-Vân Nguyen, "Réfugiés, religion et politique: La signification du regroupement de 1954," in *Travail, migrations et culture au Viêt-Nam, du début du 19e s. à nos jours,* ed. Éric Guérassimoff, Thi Phuong Ngoc Nguyen, and Emmanuel Poisson (Paris: Maisonneuve Larose, 2020), 185–201.

32. On the Koreans displaced during the war, see Yumi Moon, "Northern Refugees and the Rise of Cold War Nationalism in South Korea, 1945–1950," in this volume; Janice C. H. Kim, "Pusan at War: Refuge, Relief, and Resettlement in the Temporary Capital, 1950–1953," *Journal of American-East Asian Relations* 24, nos. 2–3 (2017): 103–27. On people leaving East Germany, estimates vary. Paul Maddrell counts 2.75 million refugees and therefore excludes persons who were expelled, while Konrad H. Jarausch estimates a total of 3.5 million who left East Germany altogether. See Maddrell, *Spying on Science: Western Intelligence in Divided Germany, 1945–1961* (Oxford: Oxford University Press, 2006), 54; Jarausch, *The Rush to German Unity* (Oxford: Oxford University Press, 1994), 8.

33. FTNV (Forces terrestres nord-Việt Nam) Secteur Grand Haiphong, "Evacuation des civils" Étude du Groupement des unités de points sensibles relative aux Opérations "à chaud," January 29, 1955, Fonds Indochine (hereafter cited as 10H), 1039, Service Historique de l'armée de Terre, Vincennes, France (hereafter cited as SHAT).

34. Mission de liaison armée de la CIC (Commission internationale de contrôle), April 29, 1955, 10H, 5784, SHAT.

35. Note récapitulative sur l'exode des populations du Nord, May 1955, Phủ thủ tướng (hereafter cited as PThT), An Ninh, 14.754, Trung tâm lưu trữ quốc gia II (hereafter cited as TTLT2).

36. "Evacuation des civils," Étude du FTNV, Secteur Grand Haiphong, Groupement des unités de points sensibles relative aux Opérations à chaud, January 29, 1955, 10H, 1039, SHAT.

37. For an analysis of their perceptions, Nguyen, *Displaced Nation*.

38. Vijay Prashad, *The Darker Nations: A People's History of the Third World* (New York: New Press, 2007).

39. Jeremy Adelman and Gyan Prakash, introduction to *Inventing the Third World: In Search of Freedom for the Postwar Global South*, ed. Adelman and Prakash (London: Bloomsbury, 2022), 11.

40. Cindy Ewing, "'With a Minimum of Bitterness': Decolonization, the Right to Self-Determination, and the Arab-Asian Group," *Journal of Global History* 17, no. 2 (2022): 254–71.

41. Olivier Campeau, "La perception française de l'Inde durant la guerre d'Indochine, 1947–1954: Une étude de cas du mouvement anticolonialiste sur la scène internationale avant Bandung" (MA thesis, Université du Québec à Montréal, 2014); Lorenz Lüthi, *Cold Wars: Asia, the Middle East, Europe* (Cambridge: Cambridge University Press, 2020), chap. 11.

42. Ministry of External Affairs of India, *1953–54*, report, accessed January 6, 2022, https://mealib.nic.in/?pdf2480?000; Michael Brecher, *India and World Politics: Krishna Menon's View of the World* (New York: Praeger, 1968).

43. Monica Kim, *The Interrogation Rooms of the Korean War: The Untold History* (Princeton, NJ: Princeton University Press, 2019); Robert Barnes, "Between the Blocs: India, the United Nations, and Ending the Korean War," *Journal of Korean Studies* 18, no. 2 (2013): 263–68.

44. K. S. Thimayya, *Experiment in Neutrality* (New Delhi: Vision Books, 1981), 211.

45. Goscha, *Vietnam*, chap. 9.

46. Dirk Moses, "Partitions, Hostages, Transfer: Retributive Violence and National Security," in *Partitions: A Transnational History of Twentieth-Century Territorial Separatism*, ed. Arie M. Dubnov and Laura Robson (Stanford, CA: Stanford University Press, 2019), 257–96.

47. Moses, "Partitions, Hostages, Transfer," 278–80.

48. Prashant Bharadwaj, Asim Khwaja, and Atif Mian, "The Big March: Migratory Flows after the Partition of India," *Economic and Political Weekly* 43, no. 35 (2008): 40.

49. Gilles Boquérat, "India's Commitment to Peaceful Coexistence and the Settlement of the Indochina War," *Cold War History* 5, no. 2 (2005): 218.

50. A. Lakshmana Chetty, "India and the 1954 Geneva Conference," *Proceedings of the Indian History Congress* 39, no. 2 (1978): 621. See also Ton That Thien, *India and South East Asia: 1947–1960* (Geneva: Droz, 1963), 131. Krishna Menon declared he was responsible for drafting the six-point proposal. See Brecher, *India and World Politics*, 44.

51. I borrow this expression from Boquérat, "India's Commitment," 220.

52. Indian Parliamentary Group, *V.K. Krishna Menon*, Eminent Parliamentarians Monograph Series 3, nos. 13–16 (New Delhi: Lok Sabha Secretariat, 1991). While the superpowers imagined India could take part in the conference, they eventually decided not to extend their invitation to make sure that China would not feel undermined by

the presence of another Asian power. See Zhang Sulin, "The Declassification of Chinese Foreign Ministry Archival Documents," *Cold War International History Project Bulletin*, no. 16 (2008): 13, Wilson Center, Washington, DC, https://www.wilsoncenter.org/sites/default/files/media/documents/publication/CWIHPBulletin16_p1.pdf.

53. Laurent Césari, "La Négociation sur l'Indochine à la conférence de Genève (1954)," *Relations internationales* 135, no. 3 (2008): 7–24.

54. Boquérat, "India's Commitment," 221.

55. Quoted in D. R. Sardesai, *Indian Foreign Policy in Cambodia, Laos, and Vietnam, 1947–1964* (Berkeley: University of California Press, 1968), 93.

56. Boquérat, "India's Commitment," 225, 219.

57. Thimayya, *Experiment in Neutrality*, 217.

58. On Nehru declaring that the Geneva ceasefire reflected the five principles of peaceful coexistence, see Sardesai, *Indian Foreign Policy*; Bhaskarla Surya Narayana Murti, *Vietnam Divided: The Unfinished Struggle* (Bombay: Asia Publishing House, 1964).

59. Brecher, *India and World Politics*; Ministry of External Affairs of India, *1954–55*, report, 50, accessed January 6, 2022, https://mealib.nic.in/?pdf2481?000; Ton, *India*, 126; Sardesai, *Indian Foreign Policy*.

60. ICSC (International Commission for Supervision and Control), *First Interim Report of the International Commission for Supervision and Control in Viet-Nam: August 11, 1954 to December 10, 1954*, External Affairs Supplementary Paper 55/1 (Ottawa: Canada External Affairs, 1955), 20–21, https://gac.canadiana.ca/view/ooe.b1642467/1; Murti, *Vietnam Divided*, 74.

61. Thakur, *Peacekeeping in Vietnam*, 118; Sardesai, *Indian Foreign Policy*, 54.

62. ICSC, *First Interim Report*, 17.

63. Sardesai, *Indian Foreign Policy*, 132. The Canadian representatives considered publicly denouncing the violations and the ineffectiveness of the commission, but the risk of withdrawing entirely from its role and the priority given to the de-escalation of the tensions to avoid a nuclear war led them to give up this possibility. See Douglas A. Ross, "Middlepowers as Extra-regional Balancer Powers: Canada, India, and Indochina, 1954–1962," *Pacific Affairs* 55, no. 2 (1982): 185–209.

64. ICSC, *First Interim Report*, 17.

65. ICSC, *First Interim Report*, 3, app. 7, no. 7.

66. ICSC (International Commission for Supervision and Control), *Second Interim Report of the International Commission for Supervision and Control in Viet-Nam: December 11, 1954 to February 10, 1955*, External Affairs Supplementary Papers 55/4 (Ottawa: Canada External Affairs, 1955), 2, app. 3.

67. It did not even need the support of the Soviet Union. See Mieczysław Maneli, *War of the Vanquished* (New York: Harper and Row, 1971), 40.

68. "Lettre n.3483/CMC du Général de Brigade Brebisson, Chef de la mission française de liaison au Général d'armée, Commissaire général de France et Commandant en chef de l'Indochine, Enquête de la Commission internationale à Luu My, 16 mars 1955," 10H, 5783, SHAT.

69. ICSC, *Second Interim Report*, 2, app. 6.
70. ICSC, *First Interim Report*.
71. Murti, *Vietnam Divided*, 76.
72. "Lettre n.3483," attachment, Rapport de la Commission internationale de contrôle, March 15, 1955.
73. "The Cause and Consequence of the Geneva Armistice, Tran Van Chuong," Wesley Fishel Papers, 1191, Michigan State University Library (hereafter, MSU), 4.
74. Carlos P. Romulo, *The Meaning of Bandung* (Chapel Hill: University of North Carolina Press, 1956), 21.
75. "Embassy of Vietnam: Press and Information Service, Volume 1 No. 7, 22 April 1955," Wesley Fishel Papers, 1193, MSU.
76. "Phim đồng bào di cư chiếu tại Bandoeng," *Thời Luận*, April 23–24, 1955.
77. Raymond Aron, "Bandoeng: Conférence de l'équivoque," *Le Figaro*, May 27, 1955. To see another denunciation of Communist colonialism, see the intervention of Ceylon's delegate at the Bandung Conference in Romulo, *Meaning of Bandung*, 27.
78. This declaration came from Carlos Romulo, a Filipino diplomat. See "Vietnam Presse n. 1581, Ingérence ou non-ingérence?," June 14, 1955, PThT, An Ninh, 14.731, TTLT2.
79. *Major Policy Speeches by President Ngo Dinh Diem* (Saigon: Press Office Presidency of the Republic of Viet Nam, 1956), 8.
80. Đảng Cộng sản Việt Nam, ed., "Chỉ thị của Ban bí thư số 04–C/TW về việc gây một cuộc vận động lập lại quan hệ giữa hai miền Bắc và Nam giới tuyến quân sự tạm thời, 29/1/1955," in *Văn Kiện Đảng* (Hanoi: Nhà Xuất Bản Chính Trị Quốc Gia, 2001), 16:35. On campaigns for unification, see Đảng Cộng sản Việt Nam, ed., "Điện của ban bí thư gửi xứ uỷ Nam Bộ, liên khu uỷ V và ban cán sự Trị-Thiên (Liên khu uỷ IV chuyền) về việc phổ biến Tuyên bố của chính phủ lập lại quan hệ bình thường giữa hai miền Nam Bắc, 9/2/1955," in *Văn Kiện Đảng* (Hanoi: Nhà Xuất Bản Chính Trị Quốc Gia, 2001), 16:48–51; Đảng Cộng sản Việt Nam, ed., "Chỉ thị của bộ chính trị số 26-CHƯƠNG TRÌNH/TW, Tình hình hỗn loạn ở miền Nam và nhiệm vụ công tác cụ thể của chúng ta ở miền Nam Việt Nam, 15/6/1955," in *Văn Kiện Đảng* (Hanoi: Nhà Xuất Bản Chính Trị Quốc Gia, 2001), 16:381.
81. "Biên bản Đại Hội nghị các trại định cư thuộc các tỉnh miền đông Nam-Việt (Biên Hòa, Thủ Dầu Một, Tây Ninh, Gia Định, Baria, Vũng Tầu, Saigon, Cholon)," July 8, 1955, PThT, An Ninh, 14.747, TTLT2.
82. Ngô Đình Diệm, "Lời tuyên bố truyền thanh của thủ tướng chánh phủ ngày 16-7-1955 về Hiệp định Genève và vấn đề Tuyển cử," in *Vấn đề thống nhất lãnh thổ Việt Nam* (Saigon: Nhà in thông tin, 1960), 31–32.
83. Ngô Đình Diệm, "Lời tuyên bố ngày 22-7-1954 của thủ tướng chánh phủ về Hiệp định Genève," in *Vấn đề thống nhất lãnh thổ Việt Nam* (Saigon: Nhà in thông tin, 1960), 29.
84. "Thủ tướng Ngô Đình Diệm tán thành tổng tuyển cử đề thống nhất lãnh thổ nhưng với bốn điều kiện," *Dân Việt*, July 21, 1955.

85. "Les étudiants manifestent leur mécontentement envers la CIC," July 13, 1954, 10H, SC 55–177, ECPAD (Établissement de Communication et de Production Audiovisuelle de la Défense).

86. "De jeunes étudiants peignent sur les murs 'À bas la CIC,'" 1954, 10H, SC 55–177, ECPAD.

87. Miller, *Misalliance*, 141.

88. Ton, *India*, 134.

89. Gerard Daniel Cohen, "The Holocaust and the 'Human Rights Revolution': A Reassessment," in *The Human Rights Revolution: An International History*, ed. Akira Iriye, Petra Goedde, and William I. Hitchcock (Oxford: Oxford University Press, 2012), 53–72; Guy Goodwin-Gill, "The Politics of Refugee Protection," *Refugee Survey Quarterly* 27, no. 1 (2008): 8–23.

90. Meredith Oyen, *The Diplomacy of Migration, Transnational Lives and the Making of U.S.-Chinese Relations in the Cold War* (Ithaca, NY: Cornell University Press, 2016).

Chapter 2

1. "Zhongmei junjian zuo dao basao zailai yibao wansiqianyu" [Eight Chinese and American ships arrived yesterday carrying roughly fourteen thousand righteous compatriots], *Zhongyang ribao*, February 10, 1955, 1. This news report was written in regard to the first and larger group of Dachen refugees in the middle of the evacuation. Thousands more would arrive, especially toward the latter half of February 1955.

2. "Keelung gang zuo chongjian weida changmian Dachen yibao dabu ditai quanguo chaoye relie huanying" [Another great scene was witnessed at Keelung Harbor yesterday: Most of the Dachen righteous compatriots had arrived; The entire nation welcomed them with enthusiasm], *Zhongyang ribao*, February 10, 1955, 1.

3. For the preparation work, see Council for International Economic Cooperation and Development (hereafter cited as CIECD), "Dachen yibao anzhi jihua zongjuan" [The plan to resettle Dachen righteous compatriots, combined volume], 1955–1958, 36-18-004-039, pp. 502, 507–8, 551–54, Institute of Modern History Archives, Academia Sinica, Taipei (hereafter cited as IMHA).

4. The figure of the Dachen migrants given in Chiang's initial radio speech was actually seventeen thousand. There were an additional one thousand residents arriving from the southern island of Nanji (南麂), which was not evacuated until late February 1955.

5. "Guojun zhuanyi zengfang jinma gonggu taipeng zhunbei fangong zongtong wei Dachen chetui bogao quanguo junmin" [The Nationalist army moving from Dachen to reinforce Quemoy and Matsu, bolstering defense for Taiwan and Penghu and preparing for the counterattack: The president's broadcast to the nation's army and people], *Lianhe bao*, February 8, 1955, 1.

6. For photos taken by Nationalist state news agencies at the port that day, see Chen Jen-ho, *Minzhi guiren* [The eighteen thousand freedom seekers] (Taipei: Dachen diqu wenxian weiyuanhui, 1975), 82–89.

7. For notable contributions, see Shu Guang Zhang, *Deterrence and Strategic Culture: Chinese-American Confrontations, 1949–1958* (Ithaca, NY: Cornell University Press, 1992), chap. 7; Robert Accinelli, *Crisis and Commitment: United States Policy toward Taiwan, 1950–1955* (Chapel Hill: University of North Carolina Press, 1996), chaps. 8–11; Chen Jian, *Mao's China and the Cold War* (Chapel Hill: University of North Carolina Press, 2002), chap. 7; Steve Tsang, *The Cold War's Odd Couple: The Unintended Partnership between the Republic of China and the UK, 1950–1958* (London: I. B. Tauris, 2006), chap. 5; Nancy Bernkopf Tucker, *Strait Talk: United States–Taiwan Relations and the Crisis with China* (Cambridge, MA: Harvard University Press, 2011), 13–17; Bruce A. Elleman, *Taiwan Straits: Crisis in Asia and the Role of the US Navy* (Lanham, MD: Rowman and Littlefield, 2015), chap. 5; Hsiao-ting Lin, *Accidental State: Chiang Kai-shek, the United States, and the Making of Taiwan* (Cambridge, MA: Harvard University Press, 2016), 226–40; Pang Yang Huei, *Strait Rituals: China, Taiwan, and the United States in the Taiwan Strait Crises, 1954–1958* (Hong Kong: Hong Kong University Press, 2019), chaps. 5–6.

8. There is some discussion of Dachen migrant experiences in Rebecca Nedostup, "Burying, Repatriating and Leaving the Dead in Wartime and Postwar China and Taiwan, 1937–1955," *Journal of Chinese History* 1, no. 1 (2017): 128–36.

9. Michael Szonyi, *Cold War Island: Quemoy on the Front Line* (Cambridge: Cambridge University Press, 2008); Wei-Ping Lin, *Island Fantasia: Imagining Subjects on the Military Frontline between China and Taiwan* (Cambridge: Cambridge University Press, 2021).

10. Peter Gatrell, *The Making of the Modern Refugee* (Oxford: Oxford University Press, 2015), x.

11. Angelina Y. Chin, *Unsettling Exiles: Chinese Migrants in Hong Kong and the Southern Periphery during the Cold War* (New York: Columbia University Press, 2023), 22.

12. H.-t. Lin, *Accidental State*.

13. While the Nationalist authorities promoted the Dachen migrants as the "righteous compatriots," the Americans intended to make a motion picture about them called *They Chose Freedom*. CIECD, "Dachen yibao anzhi," 36-18-004-039, p. 180. The English term for the Dachen migrants was "the eighteen thousand freedom seekers." See Chen, *Minzhi guiren*, cover page.

14. Nedostup, "Dead in Wartime," 115.

15. See Chi-Kwan Mark, "The 'Problem of People': British Colonials, Cold War Powers, and the Chinese Refugees in Hong Kong, 1949–62," *Modern Asian Studies* 41, no. 6 (November 2007): 1145–81; Glen Peterson, "To Be or Not to Be a Refugee: The International Politics of the Hong Kong Refugee Crisis, 1949–55," *Journal of Imperial and Commonwealth History* 36, no. 2 (July 2008): 171–95; Madeline Y. Hsu, "Aid Refugee Chinese Intellectuals, Inc. and the Political Uses of Humanitarian Relief, 1952–1962," *Journal of Chinese Overseas* 10, no. 2 (November 2014): 137–64; Meredith Oyen, "'Thunder without Rain': ARCI, the Far East Refugee Program, and the US Response

to Hong Kong Refugees," *Journal of Cold War Studies* 16, no. 4 (October 2014): 189–221; Laura Madokoro, *Elusive Refuge: Chinese Migrants in the Cold War* (Cambridge, MA: Harvard University Press, 2016).

16. The figure of one million is a conservative estimate. It is impossible to determine the exact number of mainland Chinese refugees that entered Hong Kong during the Chinese Civil War and following the CCP victory. Hong Kong's total population before the Japanese occupation was roughly 1.6 million. The tiny British colony saw a massive influx of people in 1949 and 1950 when the CCP came to power in China. More than seven hundred thousand entered in the first half of 1950 alone. The total population in the colony reached 2.25 to 2.5 million in the early 1950s. See Peterson, "Refugee," 171–72; Chin, *Unsettling Exiles*, 22–24.

17. It is also impossible to determine the exact number of those involved in the mainland exodus to Taiwan. That said, approximately one million is a fairly reasonable estimate. See my discussion in Dominic Meng-Hsuan Yang, *The Great Exodus from China: Trauma, Memory, and Identity in Modern Taiwan* (Cambridge: Cambridge University Press, 2021), 63–65.

18. This is due to the ways in which historiographies of the Chinese Civil War and modern Taiwan have been shaped by Cold War politics and the development of area studies. Yang, *Great Exodus from China*, 19–24.

19. Joshua Fan's monograph contains many oral history accounts of these experiences. See Fan, *China's Homeless Generation: Voices from the Veterans of the Chinese Civil War, 1940s–1990s* (New York: Routledge, 2011). Also see some of the personal stories in Mahlon Meyer, *Remembering China from Taiwan: Divided Families and Bittersweet Reunions after the Chinese Civil War* (Hong Kong: Hong Kong University Press, 2012).

20. These figures are approximations based on multiple social surveys. Dominic Meng-Hsuan Yang and Mau-kuei Chang, "Understanding the Nuances of *Waishengren*: History and Agency," *China Perspectives*, no. 3 (2010): 110.

21. For more on the 228 Massacre, see Lai Tse-han, Ramon H. Myers, and Wei Wou, *A Tragic Beginning: the Taiwan Uprising of February 28, 1947* (Stanford, CA: Stanford University Press, 1991).

22. Sylvia Li-chun Lin, *Representing Atrocity in Taiwan: the 2/28 Incident and White Terror in Fiction and Film* (New York: Columbia University Press, 2007).

23. "Guojun zhuanyi zengfang jinma."

24. Chen Jen-ho, Ma Chih-chien, and Lin Chih-ming, "Cong Dachen dao Taiwan—Dachen dao de lish yu qianxi" [From the Dachen Islands to Taiwan—the history and migration of Dachen islanders], *Yilan wenxian* 30 (November 1997): 110.

25. The generalissimo felt betrayed when he found out that the Americans, under both international and domestic pressure, were unwilling to put Quemoy and Matsu in the defense treaty or make a public statement guaranteeing their safety. H.-t. Lin, *Accidental State*, 235–37; Chang Mau-kuei, "Chuanyue shiguang: Dachenren de qianxi zhilyu" [Through time: The migration journey of the Dachen people], in *Dachenren zai Taiwan: Dachen qiantai liushi zhounian jinian tekan*, ed. Wang Chuan-ta (New Taipei City: Dachen qiantai jinian weiyuanhui, 2015), 59–64.

26. H.-t. Lin, *Accidental State*, 237.

27. For more, see Huang Hsiang-yu, "Zhiyue junmin zhi jieyun laitai (1949–1953)" [The transportation of the soldiers and civilians from Vietnam to Taiwan (1949–1953)], *Bulletin of Academia Historica* 11 (March 2007): 143–88; Wen-Chin Chang, *Beyond Borders: Stories of Yunnanese Chinese Migrants of Burma* (Ithaca, NY: Cornell University Press, 2014); David Cheng Chang, *The Hijacked War: The Story of Chinese POWs in the Korean War* (Stanford, CA: Stanford University Press, 2020).

28. See Shen Hsing-yi, *Yiwang siqian ge zhengren: Hanzhan shiqi fangong yishi zhi yanjiu* [Fourteen thousand witnesses: A study of the anti-Communist defectors during the Korean War] (Taipei: Guoshiguan, 2013).

29. For more on the geography of the Dachen Islands, see Sun Ching-chiang, *Dachen Jilüe* [The chronicle of Dachen] (Taipei: Minfeng, 1965), 2–3; Chen Ling, *Dachen jiyi: Liangan xinyimin de beihuan* [Dachen memories: Joys and sorrows of new immigrants on both sides of the Taiwan Strait] (Taipei: Shiying, 2015), 1.

30. Xingzhengyuan, "Chin Tung-chang Dachen diqu shicha baogao ji Zhejiang Fangong Jiuguojun zongzhihuibu jianyi shixian" [Report and recommendations from Chin Tung-chang's inspection of the Dachen region and the Zhejiang Anti-Communist Salvation Army headquarters], 1951–1952, 014-010200-0105, p. 20, Academia Historica, Taipei (hereafter cited as AH); Chen, Ma, and Lin, "Cong Dachen dao Taiwan," 111–112.

31. The KMT guerrilla groups occupied a total of twenty-one islands in the region. See Xingzhengyuan, "Chin Tung-chang Dachen diqu," p. 19. Also, see the map in Chen, Ma, and Lin, "Cong Dachen dao Taiwan," 112.

32. Frank Holober, *Raiders of the China Coast: CIA Covert Operations during the Korean War* (Annapolis, MD: Naval Institute Press, 1999).

33. For more on the Zhoushan Islands campaign and the KMT withdrawal operation, see Chen Ling, *Zhoushan chetui jimi dangan: Liushinian qian de yiye cangsang* [Zhoushan withdrawal secret files: A page of history from sixty years ago] (Taipei: Shiying, 2010).

34. Kuo Ting-yee et al., *Wang Wei xiansheng fangwen jilu* [The reminiscences of General Wang Wei] (Taipei: Zhongyangyanjiuyuan jindaishi yanjiusuo, 1996), 125.

35. Kuo, *Wang Wei xiansheng*, 127.

36. Kuomintang, "Yizhou shehui diaocha baogao zhaiyao" [A summary of the weekly investigative report on society], August 30, 1951, C5060607701-0040/zongcai piqian/001/0003/40-0303, p. 3, National Archives Administration, Hsinchuang District, New Taipei City (hereafter cited as NAA).

37. Hu conducted operations in Dachen under the alias of Chin Tung-chang (Qin Dongchang 秦東昌). He authored all the classified war zone reports using this assumed name.

38. Holober, *China Coast*, 108–9.

39. For more on the WEI, see Kuo, *Wang Wei xiansheng*, 122–24; Holober, *China Coast*, 7–8.

40. See documents contained in "Political: Detention of British Crews and Looting

of Personal Property by the Chinese Nationalist Gov. in Formosa," June 16, 1950, to May 23, 1951, HKRS 163-1-1260, Public Records Office, Hong Kong. Great Britain was one of the first Western countries and American Cold War allies to recognize the PRC diplomatically. The China trade was vital for Hong Kong's economy.

41. Elleman, *Taiwan Straits*, 54.

42. Jay Taylor, *The Generalissimo: Chiang Kai-shek and the Struggle for Modern China* (Cambridge, MA: Belknap Press of Harvard University Press, 2011), 456.

43. Chen, Ma, and Lin, "Cong Dachen dao Taiwan," 113; Chen, *Dachen jiyi*, 12.

44. Ho Cheng-che, "Dachen guo Taiwan—1950 niandai xinyimin de gean yanjiu" [From Dachen to Taiwan—a case study of 1950s new immigrants] (MA thesis, Tamkang University, 2005), 13–16; Sun, *Dachen Jilüe*, 12.

45. "Zhejiang shengzhengfu junshichu dangan: Baofang" [Zhejiang provincial government military bureau files: Antiespionage], August 1954, 0042/3-3-3-7/070, NAA; "Chuanbo guanzhi an" [The control of boats], October 8, 1954, to December 29, 1954, 0043/3-3-3-7/226, p. 151, NAA.

46. "Chuanbo guanzhi an," p. 105.

47. "Chuanbo guanzhi an," p. 159.

48. "Chuanbo guanzhi an," p. 163.

49. Chou Hsiu-hui, *Cijin de Dachen xincun—lishi bianqian yu rentong* [The Dachen new village in Cijin—historical transformation and identity] (Kaohsiung: Gaoshi bowuguan, 2018), 60–61.

50. E.g., see Guofangbu junfaju, "Liu Mu-er panluan an" [The treason case of Lu Mu-er], March 22, 1954, to April 28, 1954, 0043/3132348/348, NAA; Guofangbu junfaju, "Yang Lao-er deng panluan an" [The treason case of Yang Lao-er and others], January 28, 1954, 0042/3132328/328, NAA; Guofangbu junfaju, "Chen Fu-lang deng panluan an" [The treason case of Chen Fu-lang and others], October 9, 1954, to December 6, 1955, 0043/3132371/371, NAA.

51. Chang Chih-cheng, "Chang Chi-cheng de jiaoshi mindai shengya" [Chang Chicheng's life and career as a teacher and a people's representative], in Wang, *Dachenren zai Taiwan*, 206.

52. See, e.g., "Feiji zuo chudong yibai jiaci jing rixi Dachen toudan sanbai yu mei pingmin duo shangwang [. . .]" [The bandit air force flew over one hundred sorties yesterday to bomb Dachen in broad daylight resulting in a great number of civilian casualties . . .], *Zhongyang ribao*, January 11, 1955, 1.

53. According to the tally made by the Nationalist staff, a total of 18,261 people (9,763 males and 8,498 females) were included in the Dachen-refugee relief programs. CIECD, "Dachen yibao anzhi," 36-18-004-039, p. 436. For the figure of the military personnel, see ibid., 36-18-004-039, pp. 413–14.

54. CIECD, "Dachen yibao anzhi," 36-18-004-039, pp. 551–56.

55. "Zongtong Jiang Zhongzheng jiejian Dachen chetui laitai yibao daibiao" [President Chiang received representatives from the evacuated Dachen righteous compatriots who arrived in Taiwan], February 26, 1955, 002-050101-00023-212, AH; "Song

Meiling peitong meiguo canyiyuan Shimisi furen canguan Dachen yibao ertong jiaoyang qingxing" [Madame Chiang accompanied US Senator Margaret Chase Smith to visit the education facility for Dachen children], February 21, 1955, 002-050113-00008-154, AH. Also, see Chen, *Minzhi guiren*, 99–103.

56. For the names and locations of these villages, see CIECD, "Dachen yibao anzhi jihua zongjuan" [The plan to resettle Dachen righteous compatriots, combined volume], 1958–1962, 36-18-004-040, pp. 229–32, IMHA.

57. For the vocational-training programs and the funds allotted for these programs, see CIECD, "Dachen yibao anzhi," 36-18-004-039, p. 47.

58. For a list of American aid institutions and the Nationalist bureaus involved in the Dachen-relief work, see CIECD, "Dachen yibao anzhi," 36-18-004-039, p. 52. The ad hoc committee responsible for the new villages and the vocational programs was disbanded by the end of September 1956. Its various tasks were turned over to roughly a dozen Taiwan provincial government (TPG) bureaus and offices. See ibid., 36-18-004-039, pp. 137–38.

59. For an overall assessment of the problems associated with the programs, see CIECD, "Dachen yibao anzhi," 36-18-004-040, pp. 128–42.

60. E.g., see the petition letter submitted by residents of an agricultural labor village in Pingtung County in CIECD, "Dachen yibao anzhi," 36-18-004-040, pp. 76–79.

61. CIECD, "Dachen yibao anzhi," 36-18-004-039, p. 180.

62. CIECD, "Dachen yibao anzhi," 36-18-004-039, p. 38.

63. The US financial support included direct funding, which accounted for 51.7 percent of the entire Dachen-assistance budget. The agriculture-development projects sponsored by the Sino-American Joint Commission on Rural Reconstruction contributed roughly another 8 percent. See CIECD, "Dachen yibao zhuzhai xingjian jihua" [The community housing construction project for the Dachen righteous compatriots], 1955–1963, 36-18-004-045, pp. 28–29, IMHA.

64. CIECD, "Dachen yibao shougongye jihua" [Dachen righteous compatriots handicraft industry plan], 1958–1967, 36-18-004-044, pp. 19–48, IMHA.

65. The contributions were recorded in the new Taiwan dollar (NTD). The calculation is made based on the exchange rate of USD 1 = NTD 40. See CIECD, "Dachen yibao zhuzhai," pp. 28–29.

66. Reports filed by local KMT officials and refugee petition letters needed to be translated into English for the reviews and comments by the US aid officials.

67. For the relief and resettlement by ARCI, see Hsu, "Aid Refugee Chinese Intellectuals"; Oyen, "Thunder without Rain."

68. Initially, the Americans specified that most financial-assistance programs to the Dachen refugees were loans. The refugees needed to earn a living and pay these government loans back. It was only after seeing the failure of the vocational-training projects that the US administrators agreed to turn the loans into nonrepayable grants. E.g., see the switching of Dachen housing expenses from loans to grants in CIECD, "Dachen yibao zhuzhai," pp. 13–15.

69. CIECD, "Dachen yibao anzhi," 36-18-004-039, p. 46; Chou, *Cijin de Dachen xincun*, 77–80.

70. Dominic Meng-Hsuan Yang, "The Displacement and Relief of Chiang Kai-shek's 'Righteous Compatriots' in the Global Cold War," *Historical Journal* (forthcoming).

71. Many of the Dachen new villages were also built on rugged terrain and on lands that were susceptible to constant flooding. See Ho, "Dachen guo Taiwan," 105–8.

72. CIECD, "Dachen yibao anzhi," 36-18-004-039, p. 54.

73. CIECD, "Dachen yibao anzhi," 36-18-004-039, p. 55.

74. For the dispute involving this overseas Chinese entrepreneur, see CIECD, "Dachen yibao shougongye jihua" [Dachen righteous compatriots handicraft industry plan], 1955–1958, 36-18-004-043, pp. 223–25, 237–38, 253–59, IMHA.

75. See the petition letter in CIECD, "Dachen yibao shougongye jihua," 36-18-004-043, pp. 343–45.

76. CIECD, "Dachen yibao anzhi," 36-18-004-039, p. 55.

77. For the structure and mission statement of the CAARC, see CIECD, "Dachen yibao anzhi," 36-18-004-039, pp. 517–19. The name of the committee was later changed to Employment Assistance Committee for the Righteous Compatriots Coming to Taiwan from the Dachen Region (Dachen diqu lai Tai yibao jiuye fudao weiyuanhui 大陳地區來台義胞就業輔導委員會).

78. For a list of government institutions and officials that participated in the Dachen-relief work, see CIECD, "Dachen yibao anzhi," 36-18-004-039, p. 336.

79. CIECD, "Dachen yibao anzhi," 36-18-004-039, pp. 139–40.

80. CIECD, "Dachen yibao anzhi," 36-18-004-039, p. 54.

81. Liu Wen-hsin, "Taitung Fukang Xincun Dachen yibao shenghuo fangshi de bianqian" [The changing lifestyle of Dachen righteous compatriots in Taitung's Fukang New Village], *Taitung wenxian* 5 (May 1999): 14.

82. For the twelve fishing villages, see Ho, "Dachen guo Taiwan," 194–96.

83. CIECD, "Dachen yibao zhuzhai," p. 42.

84. Chen, Ma, and Lin, "Cong Dachen dao Taiwan," 119; Chang Lien-ping, "Dachen qilao zuotanhui jilu" [Oral history records of Dachen elders], *Yilan wenxian* 30 (November 1997): 132. Also, see Ho, "Dachen guo Taiwan," 120–21.

85. Ko Kai-pei, "Dachencun wenhua: Xingcheng shenghuo jingyan yu jiti jiyi" [Dachen village culture: Formation, lived experience, and collective memory], in *Fusanghua yu jiayuan xiangxiang*, ed. Chang Han-pi (Taipei: Qunxue, 2011), 153.

86. Liu, "Taitung Fukang Xincun," 14–15.

87. Chen, Ma, and Lin, "Cong Dachen dao Taiwan," 119.

88. CIECD, "Dachen yibao anzhi," 36-18-004-039, p. 54.

89. Xingzhengyuan, "Gaishang Dachen yibao shenghuo ji jiuye fudao jihua an" [The plans for improving the life and employment of the Dachen righteous compatriots], October 30, 1964, to February 25, 1995, 0053/3-8-1-2/6/0001, pp. 0017–0018, 0022–0023, NAA; CIECD, "Dachen yibao anzhi," 36-18-004-039, p. 54.

90. CIECD, "Dachen yibao shougongye jihua," 36-18-004-044, p. 471.
91. CIECD, "Dachen yibao shougongye jihua," 36-18-004-044, pp. 469–70.
92. Xingzhengyuan, "Gaishang Dachen yibao," 0053/3-8-1-2/6/0001, p. 0023.
93. Xingzhengyuan, "Gaishang Dachen yibao," 0053/3-8-1-2/6/0001, p. 0022
94. Xingzhengyuan, "Gaishang Dachen yibao," 0053/3-8-1-2/6/0001, p. 0023.
95. Xingzhengyuan, "Gaishang Dachen yibao," 0053/3-8-1-2/6/0001, pp. 0022–0023.
96. See the investigation and the report in CIECD, "Dachen yibao nongken jihua" [Dachen righteous compatriots agricultural-reclamation plan], 1958–1962, 36-18-004-042, pp. 249–56, IMHA.
97. CIECD, "Dachen yibao nongken jihua," p. 219.
98. CIECD, "Dachen yibao nongken jihua," pp. 220–21.
99. CIECD, "Dachen yibao nongken jihua," p. 223.
100. CIECD, "Dachen yibao nongken jihua," p. 222.
101. Xingzhengyuan, "Gaishang Dachen yibao," 0053/3-8-1-2/6/0001, pp. 0144–0145, 0004–0006.
102. Ho, "Dachen guo Taiwan," 131–32.
103. Xingzhengyuan, "Gaishang Dachen yibao," 0053/3-8-1-2/6/0002, p. 0196.
104. Xingzhengyuan, "Gaishang Dachen yibao," 0053/3-8-1-2/6/0002, p. 0197.
105. Chou, *Cijin de Dachen xincun*, 95–99; Xingzhengyuan, "Gaishang Dachen yibao," 0053/3-8-1-2/6/0005, n.p.
106. Xingzhengyuan, "Gaishang Dachen yibao," 0053/3-8-1-2/6/0005, n.p.
107. Xingzhengyuan, "Gaishang Dachen yibao," 0053/3-8-1-2/6/0005; Chou, *Cijin de Dachen xincun*, 168; Ho, "Dachen guo Taiwan," 132.
108. Ho, "Dachen guo Taiwan," 132–33.
109. Chou, *Cijin de Dachen xincun*, 11.
110. Ho, "Dachen guo Taiwan," 136.
111. For the oral history accounts, see Chou, *Cijin de Dachen xincun*, 167–201; Ho, "Dachen guo Taiwan," 136–38.
112. These are the Wuhe New Village (Wuhe xincun 五和新邨) in New Taipei City and the Shijian New Village (Shijian xincun 實踐新村) in Kaohsiung City.
113. For more on the CCP resettlement, see Chen, *Dachen jiyi*, chaps. 4–5.

Chapter 3

1. This project on North Korean refugees began in 2010, when I interviewed several individuals, including Yu In-bŏm (a pseudonym), who migrated from the Soviet-occupied zone to South Korea between 1945 and 1949. Since then, I have greatly benefited from the feedback received during lectures at various universities and conferences. My research on North Korean refugees expanded to explore similar phenomena across Asia, leading to the organization of a conference panel with Dominic Meng-Hsuan Yang, Phi-Vân Nguyen, and Sabauon Nasseri. This panel was accepted for the 2021 Annual Meeting of the American Historical Association.

Amid the challenges of the pandemic, I hosted an online workshop titled "Cold War Refugees in Asia" in March 2021 at Stanford. I extend my sincere thanks to the workshop participants, particularly Odd Arne Westad, Dafna Zur, Alyssa Park, and my PhD students, who critically reviewed the papers and provided invaluable comments for their improvement. Additionally, I presented a revised draft of this chapter at a workshop hosted by the Asia Center at Seoul National University in July 2022. I am especially grateful to Beom-Shik Shin and Heonik Kwon for hosting the event, as well as to Yong Chool Ha and Song Ha Joo for their engaged discussions of my draft.

2. Yu In-bŏm, in discussion with the author, July 27, 2010, Seoul, South Korea. The name has been modified to protect his identity.

3. The *Intelligence Summary Northern Korea*, dated March 20, 1946, states, "Political enemies of the Communists in North Korea cannot legally be arrested on charges of being 'reactionary,' therefore they are reportedly charged with being 'Anti-Soviet elements' and are handed over to the Soviet Authorities in accordance with an implied understanding between the Soviets and officials of the People's Committees." See United States Army Forces in Korea, *Intelligence Summary Northern Korea* (hereafter cited as *ISNK*), no. 8 (March 20, 1946): 11. I use the volumes printed by Hallim Taehak Asia Munhwa Yŏn'guso in 1989, but the page numbers of the citations in this chapter are original to *Intelligence Summary*.

4. Yu, discussion. Yu said that the northern youth groups had disagreements about the idea of going to Cheju. According to Yu, he did not support the idea and proposed to the group that if they went, they should build a place for settlement. Yu said that several of his friends were killed in Cheju.

5. Kim Sŏng-bo et al., "Wŏlnammin kusul saengaesa chosa yŏn'gu," Hangukhak Chungang Y'ŏn'guwŏn, accessed February 9, 2025, http://waks.aks.ac.kr/rsh/dir/rdir.aspx?rshID=AKS-2014-KFR-1230004.

6. Kim Chae-ung, "Pukhan ŭi wŏlgyŏng t'ongje wa wŏlnam wŏlbuk ŭi yangsang," *Han'guk minjok undongsa yŏn'gu*, no. 87 (2016): 189–232; Yi Tong-wŏn, "Wŏlnam ŭl sŏnt'aek han saramdŭl: Wŏlnam tonggi wa idong kyŏnno iyagi," *Naeil ŭl yŏnŭn yŏksa* 79 (December 2020): 420–43; Yun Chŏng-nan, "Wŏlnam sŏpuk chiyŏkmindŭl ŭi yŏksajŏk chŏngch'esŏng chaehwangnip kwa kanghwa, 1960s–1970s," *Hangnim* 42 (2018): 139–80; Han Sŏng-hun, "Wŏlnam chisigin ŭi chŏngch'esŏng: Chŏngch'i sahoe pyŏndong kwa chagi kyŏlchŏngsŏng," *Tongbang hakchi*, no. 180 (September 2017): 99–139; Chŏng Chu-a, "Wŏlnam chakka wa 'chŏngch'ijŏk nanmin ŭi chonjae pangsik," in *Han'guk hyŏndae munhakhoe haksul palp'yohoe charoyjib*, ed. Han'guk Hyŏndai Munhakhoe (South Korea: Kat'ollic Taehakkyo, Puch'ŏn, 2014), 180–88.

7. Yun Il-yŏng, in discussion with the author, July 27, 2016, Seoul, South Korea.

8. Ch'oe Ŭn-bŏm, in discussion with the author, July 27, 2016, Seoul, South Korea.

9. Department of State, Special Committee on Migration and Resettlement, *Displaced Populations and Groups in Korea*, RG 165, Civil Affairs Division General Records, Security Classified General Correspondence, 1943–July 1949, box 140, sec. 3: Refugees, National Archives and Records Administration, College Park, MD (hereafter cited as NARA).

10. Department of State, Special Committee on Migration and Resettlement, "Recommendations to Military Authorities with Respect to Displaced Groups in Korea (October 26, 1944)," RG 165, box 140, sec. 3: Refugees, NARA.

11. Headquarters, United States Army Military Government in Korea, Foreign Affairs Section, "Repatriation: From 25 September 1945 to 31 December 1945" (Seoul, Korea), box 4, p. 3, Walter E. Monagan Papers, Hoover Archives, Stanford University (hereafter cited as "Repatriation").

12. "Repatriation," 3–4.

13. "Repatriation," 4. On the role of social groups in refugee relief, see Alyssa Park, "Making 'Refugees': Repatriates, Migrants, and Institutions of Care in Liberated South Korea, 1945–1950," *Seoul Journal of Korean Studies* 36, no. 2 (2023): 621–54.

14. "Repatriation," 4.

15. *ISNK*, no. 2 (December 17, 1945): 3.

16. *ISNK*, no. 2, 3.

17. *Intelligence Summary North Korea* was a confidential publication meant for the US government. The editors of *Intelligence Summary* exercised caution to verify the reliability of information obtained from northern refugees, as the report aimed to provide an analysis rather than propaganda.

18. *ISNK*, no. 1 (December 1, 1945): 6.

19. *ISNK*, no. 6 (February 18, 1946): 3.

20. *ISNK*, no. 6, 5; emphasis added.

21. *ISNK*, no. 8, 12.

22. *ISNK*, no. 42 (August 1–15, 1947): 4.

23. Anju Chŏngch'i Powibu, *Ilban pumun t'ujaeng taesangja myŏngbu*, comp. North Korean Political Security Bureau (January–June 1950), RG 242, container 873, SA2010, box 3, item 105, NARA (hereafter cited as *Myŏngbu*).

24. Yi Sang-ch'ŏl, in discussion with the author, July 27, 2016, Seoul, South Korea. Yi was then the chair of Ilch'ŏnman Isangajok Wiwŏnhoe (Committee for Ten Million Separated Families).

25. Thomas Nail, *Theory of the Border* (New York: Oxford University Press, 2016), 4.

26. *ISNK*, no. 1, 1.

27. *ISNK*, no. 1, 4.

28. *ISNK*, no. 2, 1.

29. *ISNK*, no. 2, 3.

30. "Samp'alsŏn ibuk unhaeng chungdan," Ch'ŏlto T'onghap Yŏnp'yo, August 24, 1945, https://www.kric.go.kr/jsp/railplaza/rhp/intergrateTableDetail.jsp?board_seq=688&q_frdate=1800-01-01&q_todate=1949-12-31&q_relline=&q_relstation=.

31. *ISNK*, no. 2, 2–3.

32. *ISNK*, no. 2, 3.

33. *ISNK*, no. 2, 3.

34. *ISNK*, no. 3 (January 2, 1946): 2–3.

35. The Soviet consulate in Seoul first broached the subject of evacuating Japanese residents directly from Russian-occupied territory to Pusan, the southern port close to

Japan, and US headquarters expressed willingness to cooperate with the Soviet forces on mutual interests, including the direct evacuation of Korean repatriates from Pusan to North Korea. *ISNK*, no. 3, 1.

36. *ISNK*, no. 5 (February 5, 1946): 3–4.

37. *ISNK*, no. 5, 9.

38. Michael Lee, "North Korean Food Shortages, 1945–1946" (MA thesis, Stanford University, 2017); Yumi Moon, "Imperial Shift: Rice and Revolution in Transwar Korea, 1939–1949," in *Transwar Asia: Ideology, Practices, and Institutions, 1920–1960*, ed. Reto Hofmann and Max Ward (London: Bloomsbury Academic, 2022), 17–48.

39. *ISNK*, no. 5, 2.

40. United States, *Weekly Military Occupational Activities Report (Areas Reported On: Districts of Koyang, Pochon, Kapyong, Yangju, Yangpyong and Kwangju, All in Kyong Gi Do, Covering the Week Ending 2400, Saturday, 18 May 1946)* (Seoul: Kuksa P'yŏnch'an Wiwŏnhoe, Migunjŏnggi Kunjŏngdan-kunjŏnggi Chungdae Munsŏ, 1946), Database of Korean History, accessed February 20, 2021, http://db.history.go.kr/id/pm_004_1180 (hereafter cited as *18 May 1946*).

41. *ISNK*, no. 42, 4.

42. *ISNK*, no. 43 (August 16–31, 1947): 9.

43. After the Korean War, the border line moved, placing more counties in the North. The counties in the South were within the demilitarized zone area and shut down in 1972.

44. Changdan Kunji P'yŏnch'an Wiwŏnhoe, *Changdan kunji chŭngbop'an* (1980; repr., Chongno: Changdan Kunminhoe, 2009), 191–92.

45. According to *Changdan kunji chŭngbop'an*, the incident occurred in June 1947. See Changdan Kunji P'yŏnch'an Wiwŏnhoe, *Changdan kunji chŭngbop'an*, 191–92. But the newspaper articles of the time reported the same case with some different details. Following the newspapers, I cited that the incident occurred in March 1947. See "Sobyŏng samp'alsŏn wŏlgyŏng," *Kyŏnghyang Sinmun*, March 20, 1947.

46. Changdan Kunji P'yŏnch'an Wiwŏnhoe, *Changdan kunji chŭngbop'an*, 192–93.

47. Despite this verdict, violence continued in Changdan. Soviet soldiers killed a young man who was weeding ancestral graves and shot to death a middle school student returning home. Changdan Kunji P'yŏnch'an Wiwŏnhoe, *Changdan kunji chŭngbop'an*, 194.

48. "Kyŏngmubu 38 sŏn wŏlnamja rŭl ch'ep'o suyong choch'i palp'yo," *Kyŏnghyang Sinmun*, April 18, 1948; *Sŏul Sinmun*, April 20, 1947, cited in Kuksap'ŏnch'an Wiwŏnhoe, ed., *Charyo taehanmin'guksa* (Seoul: Kuksap'ŏnch'an Wiwŏnhoe, 1968–2008), 29 vols., vol. 4, Database of Korean History, accessed February 20, 2021, http://db.history.go.kr/id/dh_004_1947_04_18_0010. The chief of the South Korean police, Cho Pyŏng-ok, declared in September 1947 his plan to enhance the police force along the parallel. Mentioning that North Korean gangs and security guards occasionally cross the border and threaten border security, he promised a comprehensive measure to increase the number of police guards, police station branches, and other facilities and to

reinforce the transportation and arms capability of the police guarding the border. "Cho Pyŏng-ok, 38 sŏn pugŭn sich'al sogam p'iryŏk," *Tonga Ilbo* (hereafter cited as TI), September 17, 1947, cited in Kuksap'ŏnch'an Wiwŏnhoe, *Charyo taehanmin'guksa*, vol. 5, Database of Korean History, accessed February 9, 2025, https://db.history.go.kr/contemp/level.do?levelId=dh_005_1947_09_17_0120.

49. *ISNK*, no. 35 (April 30, 1947): 15; *Intelligence Summary Korea*, no. 139 (May 14, 1948): 24.

50. United States Army Forces in Korea, *South Korean Interim Government Activities*, no. 30 (March 1948): 6–7, box 2, Walter E. Monagan Papers, Hoover Archives, Stanford University.

51. "Kwihwan ibaekyŏmyŏng, wŏlnamja nŭn paeksasimman," *Chayu Sinmun*, September 10, 1948.

52. Ibuk Odominhoe, *Wolnam pansegi* (Seoul: Ibuk Odowiwŏnhoe, 1995), 79.

53. Kang Chŏng-gu, "Haebang hu wŏlnamin ŭi wŏlnam tonggi wa kyekŭpsŏng e kwanhan yŏn'gu," in *Han'guk chŏngjaeng kwo han'guk sahoe pyŏndong*, ed. Han'guk sahoehakhoe (Seoul: P'ulpit, 1992), 96–99; Kang Chŏng-gu, *Pundan kwa chŏnjaeng ŭi han'guk yyŏndaesa* (Seoul: Yŏksa Pip'yŏngsa, 2008), 278–80, 282–87.

54. Kwon Tai Hwan, "Population Change and Its Components in Korea, 1925–66" (PhD diss., Australian National University, 1972), 247, 267; Kim Kûi-ok, *Wŏlnamin ûi saenghwal kyônghôm kwa chôngch'esông* (Seoul: Seoul National University, 1993), 1:33.

55. United States Army Forces in Korea, *Republic of Korea: Economic Summation*, no. 36 (November–December 1948): 4.

56. That one was Ch'oe Ŭn-bŏm, although he did not enter a quarantine camp or a settlement center. I received his paper "Na ŭi isan kajoksa 70 nyŏn ŭi hoego" during my interview with Ch'oe in the summer of 2016. He said that on March 15, 2016, he presented it at the Geneva conference on the separated Korean families. Ch'oe Ŭn-bŏm, discussion. One interviewee said that he had heard about the existence of refugee-relief camps but understood that the people who stayed in them only did so because they had no acquaintances in the South. Yun Il-yŏng, discussion.

57. "Wŏlnamja 140 man myŏng, kwihwan tongp'o 200 man myŏng tŭng ijaemin silt'ae," *Taehan Ilbo*, September 11, 1948, cited in Kuksap'ŏnch'an Wiwŏnhoe, *Charyo taehanmin'guksa*, vol. 8, Database of Korean History, accessed February 9, 2025, https://db.history.go.kr/contemp/level.do?levelId=dh_008_1948_09_11_0130.

58. Ibuk Odominhoe, *Wolnam pansegi*, 81.

59. Ibuk Odominhoe, *Wolnam pansegi*, 77.

60. Kim Kûi-ok, *Wŏlnamin ûi saenghwal kyônghôm*.

61. This calculation is only approximate because I could account for neither the deaths of northern refugees during the Korean War nor the potential migration from North Korea to the South between 1953 and 1961. The latter's case was seemingly minimal because the establishment of the demilitarized zone after the Korean War impeded border crossing between the two Koreas.

62. Ibuk Odominhoe, *Wolnam pansegi*, 74–75.
63. South Korea claimed that defectors from the North Korean Army reached 1,300 in June 1949. "1947 nyŏn 6 wŏl irae pukhan inmingun kwisunja nŭn ch'ong 1,300 myŏng," *Yŏnhap Sinmun*, June 3, 1949, cited in Kuksap'ŏnch'an Wiwŏnhoe, *Charyo taehanmin'guksa*, vol. 12, Database of Korean History, accessed February 9, 2025, https://db.history.go.kr/contemp/level.do?levelId=dh_012_1949_06_03_0010.
64. "1948 nyŏn 12 wŏl–1949 nyŏn 10 wŏl kkaji ŭi wŏlnamja hyŏnhwang," *Sŏul Sinmun*, November 1, 1949, cited in Kuksap'ŏnch'an Wiwŏnhoe, *Charyo taehanmin'guksa*, vol. 14, Database of Korean History, accessed February 9, 2025, https://db.history.go.kr/contemp/level.do.
65. *ISNK*, no. 38 (June 15, 1947): 16–17.
66. *ISNK*, no. 2, 3.
67. *ISNK*, no. 3, 3.
68. Kim T'aenam, "Samp'alsŏn ibuk t'alch'ulgi," *Ibuk T'ongsin* (hereafter cited as *IB*), June 1946, 45–50.
69. Ibuk Odominhoe, *Wolnam pansegi*, 75–78.
70. "Kyŏlsajŏk ŭro hoedŭkhan kŭkpi munsŏ," *IB*, August–September 1947, 16–17.
71. "Igŏsi nugu ŭi choeinga?," *IB*, August–September 1947, 22–23.
72. "Untitled Memorandum on the Political and Morale Situation of Soviet Troops in North Korea and the Economic Situation in Korea," trans. Gary Goldberg, January 11, 1946, op. 480, 29, st. 5, p. 2, pa. 21, k. 35, Archives of the Russian General Staff, Digital Archive, Wilson Center, Washington, DC, https://digitalarchive.wilsoncenter.org/document/114893.
73. *ISNK*, no. 41 (July 15–31, 1947): 3–4.
74. *ISNK*, no. 50 (December 1–15, 1947): 26–27.
75. *ISNK*, no. 50, 28; *ISNK*, no. 3, 422.
76. "T'ŭkpo: Pukchosŏn e Hwap'ye Kaehyŏk Pŏmnyŏng Kongp'o," *IB*, January 1948, 36–38.
77. Chŏn Hyŏn-su, "1947 nyŏn 12 wŏl, Pukhan ŭi Hwap'ye Kaehyŏk," *Yŏksa wa Hyŏnsil* 19 (1996): 186.
78. "T'ŭkpo: Pukchosŏn," 38, 37.
79. *Myŏngbu*.
80. The total printed in the document is 103,626. But the combined number obtained by adding up all the figures from occupational categories is 103,628. This suggests an error in one of the two totals. I use 103,628 for my analysis of the data.
81. United States Army Forces in Korea, *South Korean Interim Government Activities*, no. 27 (December 1947): 7. Kim Chae-ung used a similar record—*Chosŏn kyŏngje yŏnbo*, published in 1948—in his article. Kim also used an Anju record created during the first week of the Korean War (June 23–30, 1950), but it is different from *Myŏngbu*. Kim Chae-ung, "Pukhan ŭi wŏlgyŏng t'ongje," 201–2.
82. United States Army Forces in Korea, *Interim Government Activities*, no. 27, 7.
83. In the Anju records, more than 75 percent of refugee families were from the middle class rather than the class of landlords or poor peasants.

84. Kang In-suk, *Sŏul, haebang konggan ŭi p'ungmulji* (P'aju: Pakha, 2016), 19–34.
85. "Salin kangdoful sinmak poansŏ," *IB*, June 1946, 30–31.
86. Kim T'aenam, "Samp'alsŏn ibuk t'alch'ulgi," 49–50.
87. "Kumyŏngdae," *IB*, June 1946, 31.
88. E.g., a refugee published a description of an incident involving multiple deaths that had occurred when he crossed the border in January 1948. He chose Sunday to cross the parallel because fewer Russian soldiers patrolled it on that day. About thirty minutes from the South, his group of men and women, six in total, were caught by North Korean guards. He ran, hearing gunshots behind him. After a while, he found a young man from the group rolling on the ground, crying, and screaming, "My wife got killed. The others were all gunned down!" Bemoaning the sufferings of the young man, the author attributed such tragedies to "evil deeds of the partition" that resulted from "Soviet tricks." He ended the report with a note that all the dead people in his group came from Kanggye, North P'yŏngan. He asked people from Kanggye to visit the *Ibuk T'ongsin* office to check on the identities of the dead. "Hwap'ye kaehyŏk ihu sich'e ro makhin samp'alsŏn," *IB*, February 1948, 21–23.
89. "Kang In-dŏk," in Kim Sŏng-bo et al., "Wŏlnammin." A similar episode is found in "Kang Hyŏn-du," in Kim Sŏng-bo et al., "Wŏlnammin."
90. Ch'oe Ŭn-bŏm, discussion.
91. "Repatriation," 17–18.
92. United States, *Weekly Military Occupational Activities Report (Covering Week Ending 2400 Saturday 27 Apr 46) (Area Reported Hong Chon and Chun Gun)* (Seoul: Kuksa P'yŏnch'an Wiwŏnhoe, Migunjŏnggi Kunjŏngdan-kunjŏnggi Chungdae Munsŏ, 1946), Database of Korean History, accessed February 20, 2021, http://db.history.go.kr/id/pm_002_0290 (hereafter cited as *27 Apr 46*).
93. *27 Apr 46*.
94. United States, *Weekly Military Occupational Activities Report (Covering Week Ending 2400 Saturday 22 June, 1946)* (Seoul: Kuksa P'yŏnch'an Wiwŏnhoe, Migunjŏnggi Kunjŏngdan-kunjŏnggi Chungdae Munsŏ, 1946), Database of Korean History, accessed February 9, 2025, https://db.history.go.kr/common/imageViewer.do?levelId=pm_002_0370.
95. United States, *Weekly Military Occupational Activities Report (Areas Reported On: Districts of Koyang, Pochon, Kapyong, Yangju, Yangpyong and Kwangju, All in Kyong Gi Do, Covering the Week Ending 2400, Saturday, 20 July 1946)* (Seoul: Kuksa P'yŏnch'an Wiwŏnhoe, Migunjŏnggi Kunjŏngdan-kunjŏnggi Chungdae Munsŏ, 1946), Database of Korean History, accessed February 9, 2025, https://db.history.go.kr/contemp/level.do?levelId=pm_004_1270 (hereafter cited as *20 July 1946*).
96. *18 May 1946*.
97. *20 July 1946*.
98. "Namtchok ch'ajŏon pukchosŏn tongp'o maeil p'yŏnggyun 5 paekmyŏng [*sic*] ŭl tolp'a," *TI*, March 28, 1947.
99. "Namha hanŭn ibuk tongp'o wihae kukyŏng kuho kŏmyŏkso sŏlch'i," *TI*, March 30, 1947.

100. "38 sŏn nŏmŏon tongp'o e paengmi somaek tŭng taeryang kŭbyŏ," *TI*, May 7, 1947.

101. "Wŏlnam taebi 38 sŏn pugŭn e 4 kae oemuch'ŏ ch'ulchangso kaesŏl," *Sŏul Sinmun*, May 6, 1947, cited in Kuksap'ŏnch'an Wiwŏnhoe, *Charyo taehanmin'guksa*, vol. 4, Database of Korean History, accessed February 9, 2025, https://db.history.go.kr/contemp/level.do?levelId=dh_004_1947_05_06_0100.

102. "Ibuk sŏ on ijaemin maeil 150 myŏng suyong," *TI*, May 16, 1947.

103. "Namha hanŭn tongp'o wihae kakto e chigyŏng suyongso sŏlch'i," *TI*, May 21, 1947.

104. "Wŏlnamja ŭi chŭngga ro singnyang paegŭp ŭi pyŏn'yŏng silsi," *Sŏul Sinmun*, May 7, 1947, cited in Kuksap'ŏnch'an Wiwŏnhoe, *Charyo taehanmin'guksa*, vol. 4, Database of Korean History, accessed February 9, 2025, https://db.history.go.kr:443/id/dh_004_1947_05_01_0050.

105. "Wŏlnam tongp'o swaedo ro singnyang paegŭmnyng kamso," *TI*, May 31, 1947.

106. "Ibuk Sosik," *IB*, July–August 1947, 17.

107. "Sŏbuk haksaeng e hakcha myŏllyŏn pihaengtaewŏn migŏ," *TI*, December 18, 1945.

108. "Panghak e sŏbuk tapsa sŏbuk haksaeng ch'inhwahoe rŭl kyŏlsŏng," *TI*, December 15, 1945.

109. "Sŏbuk tongp'o wiro ŭi pam," *TI*, March 12, 1946.

110. "Nangwan t'agae kiro haktotŭl chasin i sŏbuk haksaeng wŏnhohoe chojik," *TI*, April 1, 1946.

111. *Iibuk odo 30 nyŏnsa* (Seoul: Ibuk Odo Wiwŏnhoe, 1981), 279, 338.

112. "Sŏbuk haksaeng e onjŏng," *TI*, April 12, 1947.

113. "Chŏn'guk haksaeng taehoe," *TI*, December 13, 1945.

114. "Sŏbuk haksaeng hŭisaengja ch'udohoe rŭl gŏhaeng," *TI*, December 30, 1945.

115. "Chosŏn minjudang ŭn pulhapchak," *TI*, January 13, 1946, Database of Korean History, https://db.history.go.kr/common/imageViewer.do?levelId=npda_1946_01_13_x0002_0100.

116. "38 changpyŏk tolp'ahal uri son ŭro tŏen kikwanch'a haebang 1 ho," *TI*, January 10, 1946; "Yŏngyŏl toen nambuk ŭi t'ongsinmang," *TI*, January 10, 1946.

117. "Sŏbugin taehoe kich'ŏnggwan esŏ," *TI*, May 21, 1946.

118. "Uri hyŏlmaek mangnŭnja nugu," *TI*, May 22, 1946.

119. "Hyŏllu ro tongnip chŏnch'wi rŭl chŏlgyu," *TI*, May 13, 1946.

120. "P'amyŏl ŭi wigi, kkŭnŏra, kyosu ŭi samp'alsŏn," *TI*, May 13, 1946.

121. The aforementioned Yu In-bŏm told me that Kim Sŏng-su gave an office in the *Tonga Ilbo* Building to Yu's organization, the Northwestern Student Association. Yu, discussion.

122. "Chaju tongnip kwa samp'alsŏn ch'ŏlp'ye," *TI*, May 23, 1946; emphasis added.

123. "Sŏbuk haksaeng ch'ongyŏnmaeng kyŏlsŏngsik," *TI*, June 17, 1946.

124. "Sŏbuk haksaeng yŏnmaeng sŏngmyŏng," *TI*, August 5, 1947.

125. "Choguk chaegŏn ŭi yŏkkun ŭro illo yŏnjin," *TI*, November 30, 1946; "7 gae

ch'ŏngnyŏn tanch'e haptong onŭl sŏbuk ch'ŏngnyŏnhoe kyŏlsŏng," *TI*, December 1, 1946.

126. "Sŏbuk ch'ŏngnyŏnhoe sangim wiwŏn sŏnjŏng," *TI*, December 12, 1946.
127. "Wŏlnam tongp'o ŭi annaeso sŏlch'i," *TI*, June 15, 1947.
128. "Kang Ch'ang-jin," in Kim Sŏng-bo et al., "Wŏlnammin."
129. Kim Chin-sŏp, in discussion with the author, July 27, 2016, Seoul, South Korea.
130. "Ibuk kyŏngbidae ka wŏlgyŏng, sŏbuk ch'ŏngnyŏn ŭl napch'i," *TI*, August 27, 1947.
131. "Ibuk kyŏngbidae wŏlgyŏng sŏbuk ch'ŏngnyŏn 20 myŏng napch'i," *TI*, September 6, 1947.
132. "Sŏbukchŏng kyŏngbiwŏn ch'oe kit'ae kun p'isŭp chŏlmyŏng," *TI*, January 10, 1948.
133. Yu, discussion.
134. After the Korean War, he ran a newspaper called *Chungang Ilbo*, but he was jailed after being accused of corruption. After the government thwarted Yi Puk's efforts to save himself, arresting both his wife and lawyer on charges of bribing police and prosecutors, Yi Puk died suddenly in jail with brain damage. *Tonga Ilbo* covered his death in several articles and hinted at his conflicts with Syngman Rhee's Liberal Party, which had tried to place party associates in the newspaper's editorship. "Ŏllon chayu ch'imhae han kongboch'ŏ," *TI*, September 30, 1954.
135. "Tokcha hŏewŏn mojip," *IB*, June 1946, 15.
136. "T'ŭkpo: Sowi p'yŏngyang esŏ samangja p'albaegyŏmyŏng," *IB*, August–September 1947, 40.
137. "Kŭnha sinnyŏn: Tokchasu ilman ŭl tolp'a han idae chisa," *IB*, January 1948, 33. It is unclear if ten thousand "readers" in the text refers to the magazine subscribers or the sales of copies.
138. "Kang Ch'ang-jin," in Kim Sŏng-bo et al., "Wŏlnammin." It appears that *Ibuk* is an abbreviation of *Ibuk T'ongsin*.
139. "P'amyŏl ŭi wigi."
140. This term was not invented by the editor but had been alluded to in the northerners' assembly in May 1946, as reported by *Tonga Ilbo*. "Samp'al kyosŏn: Ibuk t'ongsin ŭl kanhaenghamyŏ," *IB*, June 1946, 1–2.
141. "Hambuk ch'ŏngjin ŭi chunggongŏp sisŏl panch'ul mokkyŏkki (ki il)," *IB*, March 1947, 14–17, 17; "Hambuk ch'ŏngjin ŭi chunggongŏp sisŏl panch'ul mokkyŏkki (ki i)," *IB*, April 1947, 21–23 (hereafter cited as "Ki i").
142. "#rön yŏja pyŏngdae e puttŭllyŏga," *IB*, August–September 1947, 27–34, 26.
143. "P'yŏnjip hugi," *IB*, September 1948, 39; "Tongji hoeramp'an," *IB*, September 1948, 39.
144. When the magazine published a series of articles on heavy-industry factories in the North and the Russian transfer of their equipment, the editors mentioned that they had translated these articles and a confidential report into English and submitted them to the US State Department, General Douglas MacArthur, and Ambassador Edwin W.

Pauley on the Allied Reparations Committee. "Hambuk ŭi chunggongŏp banch'ul mokkyŏggi (ki ol)," *IB*, April 1947, 23.

145. "Ki i," 21.

146. "Amhŭgŭi pukchosŏn," *IB*, October 1947, 24–27.

147. "Samp'alsŏn nŏmŏon tongp'odŭlŭi anwi," *IB*, October 1947, 9.

148. "Tongji hoeramp'an," *IB*, March 1947, 35.

149. "T'ŭkpo pant'ak siwi sagŏn ŭi chinsang palp'yo," *IB*, August–September 1947, 40.

150. An Min-se, "Taehan min'guk kŏnsŏl ŭi kusang," *IB*, October 1948, 4–5.

151. Kim Sam-gyu, "Kukhoe ŭiwŏn ege koham," *IB*, June 1948, 8–9.

152. Ko Chae-uk, "Taehan min'guk kŏnsŏl ŭi kusang," *IB*, October 1948, 9.

153. Kim Tong-ni, "Munhwa chŏngch'aek ŭi ch'aengmu," *IB*, September 1948, 7.

154. Kim Kwang-sŏp, "Munhwain ui hyŏngsŏng," *IB*, June 1948, 11.

155. On the state ideology of postcolonial South Korea, see Sungik Yang, "Korea's Fascist Moment: Liberation, War, and the Ideology of South Korean Authoritarianism, 1945–1979" (PhD diss., Harvard University, 2023).

156. Bruce Cumings, *The Origins of the Korean War* (Princeton, NJ: Princeton University Press, 1981); emphasis original.

157. Louise Althusser, "Contradiction and Overdetermination," in *For Marx*, trans. Ben Brewster (New York: Pantheon, 1969), 87–128.

Chapter 4

1. M. Ijlal Muzaffar, "Boundary Games: Ecochard, Doxiadis, and the Refugee Housing Projects under Military Rule in Pakistan, 1953–1959," in *Governing by Design: Architecture, Economy, and Politics in the Twentieth Century*, ed. Aggregate Architectural History Collaborative (Pittsburg: University of Pittsburg Press, 2012), 147–75.

2. Constantinos Doxiadis, letter to Colonel Nasser Humayune, the military director of the National Housing and Settlement Agency, and Harry Case, the Ford Foundation representative in Karachi, 1959, ser. 1959, General Correspondence, Central Index, Ford Foundation Records, Online Collection and Catalogue, Rockefeller Archive Center, Sleepy Hollow, NY, https://dimes.rockarch.org/objects/cChTYbgGeFM8i4D4UQfdFY, microfilm.

3. Anna Lowenhaupt Tsing, *Friction: An Ethnography of Global Connection* (Princeton, NJ: Princeton University Press, 2011), 6.

4. For a discussion of these other schemes, see Muzaffar, "Boundary Games."

5. This shift was most prominently marked by the establishment of the United Nations Human Settlements Programme (UN-Habitat) in 1978 after the first United Nations Conference on Human Settlements in Vancouver in 1976. But the transformation was already underway after large-scale projects of the so-called first development decade failed to take root—a change reflected in the titles of prominent economic and planning books, like Ernst Schumacher's *Small Is Beautiful: A Study of Economics As If People Mattered* (London: Blond and Briggs, 1976); and Charles Abrams's *Man's Struggle for Shelter in an Urbanizing World* (Cambridge, MA: MIT Press, 1964).

6. Doxiadis coined the term "ekistics" in 1942 to designate what he called "the science of human settlements," comprising basic elements of "man," "society," "shell," "nature," and "networks." These elements, when connected with each other according to ekistics principles, would generate, Doxiadis asserted, a worldwide future global city, or "Ecumenopolis," that stretched across continents and eschewed political borders. See Panayiota Pyla, "Planetary Home and Garden: Ekistics and Environmental-Developmental Politics," *Grey Room*, no. 36 (Summer 2009): 6–35. The term "ekistics" was adopted as the title of a long-running journal as well that came out of Doxiadis's office.

7. No one really knows the origins of the saying, but, attributed to an unknown bureaucrat, it is repeated in numerous publications from edited volumes, such as Christophe Jaffrelot, ed., *Pakistan at the Crossroads* (New York: Columbia University Press, 2016), to newspaper articles, like Isaac Chotiner, "An Army with a Country," *Wall Street Journal*, August 14, 2016, https://www.wsj.com/articles/an-army-with-a-country-1471208655.

8. Vazira Zamindar, *The Long Partition and the Making of Modern South Asia: Refugees, Boundaries, Histories* (New York: Columbia University Press, 2010).

9. Joya Chatterji, "The Fashioning of a Frontier: The Radcliffe Line and Bengal's Border Landscape, 1947–52," *Modern Asian Studies* 33, no. 1 (1999): 185–242; Sumanta Banerjee, "Indo-Bangladesh Border: Radcliffe's Ghost," *Economic and Political Weekly* 36, no. 18 (2001): 1505–6. The most salient accounts of the repercussions of Radcliff's decisions, however, are perhaps recorded in the short fiction stories of Sadat Hasan Manto, tried for indecency in Pakistani courts after the partition but now hailed as one of the most poignant portrayals of the violence of displacement. See Tarun K. Saint, "The Long Shadow of Manto's Partition Narratives: 'Fictive' Testimony to Historical Trauma," *Social Scientist* 40, no. 11–12 (2012): 53–62.

10. Debdatta Chowdhury, *Identity and Experience at the India-Bangladesh Border: The Crisis of Belonging* (Taylor and Francis, 2018), map 3.1. For the map, see also T. J., "The Land That Maps Forgot," *The Economist*, February 15, 2011, https://www.economist.com/banyan/2011/02/15/the-land-that-maps-forgot.

11. "The Forgotten Hero," *Dawn*, August 2, 2009, https://www.dawn.com/news/826674/the-forgotten-hero. Also, see Mitha's own autobiography, Aboobaker Osman Mitha, *Unlikely Beginnings: A Soldier's Life* (Karachi: Oxford University Press, 2003).

12. Constantinos Doxiadis, "Progress Report on Korangi, 1959," ser. 1959, General Correspondence, Central Index, Ford Foundation Records, Online Collection and Catalogue, Rockefeller Archive Center, Sleepy Hollow, NY, https://dimes.rockarch.org/objects/cChTYbgGeFM8i4D4UQfdFY, microfilm.

13. Doxiadis, "Progress Report on Korangi."

14. Doxiadis, "Progress Report on Korangi."

15. Shahana Rajani and Shayan Rajani, "Making Karachi," *Tanqeed*, May 2016, https://www.tanqeed.org/2016/05/making-karachi/.

16. Rajani and Rajani, "Making Karachi."

17. Peter Hopkirk, *The Great Game: The Struggle for Empire in Central Asia* (New York: Kodansha International, 1990).

18. Khushwant Singh, *Train to Pakistan*, 50th anniversary ed. (1956; New Delhi: Roli, 2006). The new addition includes sixty-six of Margaret Bourke-White's partition photographs.

19. Laurent Gayer, "The Battle for Karachi: Changing Patterns of a Permanent Civil War," in *Pakistan's Political Labyrinths: Military, Society and Terror*, ed. Ravi Kalia (London: Routledge, 2016), 106–24. Also, see Gayer, *Karachi: Ordered Disorder and the Struggle for the City* (New York: Oxford University Press, 2014).

20. Abira Ashfaq and Nausheen Anwar, *Understanding Urban Resilience: Migration, Displacement, and Violence in Karachi* (Karachi: Karachi Urban Lab, 2019), http://karachiurbanlab.com/assets/downloads/Understanding_Urban_Resilience_Migration_Displacement_&_Violence_in_Karachi.pdf. Also, see Nausheen H. Anwar et al., *Land, Governance and the Gendered Politics of Displacement in Urban Pakistan* (Karachi: Karachi Urban Lab, 2021), http://karachiurbanlab.com/assets/downloads/IDRC_Report.pdf.

21. For a detailed history of Karachi's land organization, see the seminal study Arif Hasan et al., *Karachi: The Land Issue* (Karachi: Oxford University Press, 2015).

22. These include Operation Enduring Freedom (2001–2002), Operation Al Mizan (2002–2006), Operation Zalzala (2008), Operations Sher Dil, Rah-e-Haq, and Rah-e-Rast (2007–2009), and Operation Rah-e-Nijat (2009–2010). See Zahid Ali Khan, "Military Operations in FATA and PATA: Implications for Pakistan," *Strategic Studies* 31–32, nos. 4–1 (Winter–Spring 2011–2012): 130, https://www.issi.org.pk/wp-content/uploads/2014/06/1339999992_58398784.pdf. Also, see D. Suba Chandran, "Violence against Women in Swat: Why Blame Only Taliban?," *IPCS Issue Brief*, no. 97 (April 2008): 1–4, https://www.files.ethz.ch/isn/98731/IB97-Suba-WomenSwat.pdf.

23. It was the military government of General Zia-ul-Haque, which passed the Sindh Katchi Abadi Act of 1987 to provide "a comprehensive legal and administrative framework for the process of regularization" to counter the wide support of MQM in Karachi and PPP in Sindh. See Haris Gazdar and Hussain Bux Mallah, "The Making of a 'Colony' in Karachi and the Politics of Regularisation," in "Rethinking Urban Democracy in South Asia," ed. Stéphanie Tawa Lama-Rewal and Marie-Hélène Zérah, special issue, *South Asia Multidisciplinary Academic Journal*, no. 5 (2011), https://doi.org/10.4000/samaj.3248. Also, see Ashfaq and Anwar, *Understanding Urban Resilience*; Anwar et al., *Politics of Displacement*.

24. Recently, land allocation was reverted back to the provincially controlled board of revenue, which has allocated land to Pakistan Railways, the Port Qasim Authority, the Karachi Port Trust, the Defence Housing Authority, the government of Pakistan, the cantonment boards, the Sindh Katchi Abadi Authority, new developments such as Education City and Textile City, the Lyari Development Authority, Sindh Industrial Trading Estate, the government of Sindh, the Malir Development Authority, and the Karachi Metropolitan Corporation. See Arif Hasan et al., "Land Ownership, Control and Contestation in Karachi and Implications for Low-Income Housing" (Urbanization and Emerging Population Issue Working Paper No. 10, International Institute for

Environment and Development, Human Settlement Group, United Nations Population Fund, March 2023), 5.

25. Hasan et al., "Land Ownership," 3–5.

26. ANP and other new political parties, like the PTI (Pakistan Tehrike Insaf), had their strongholds along the Lyari River, which cut through Doxiadis's Korangi, while MQM, supporting settlements, occupied the areas around the Gujjar Nala.

27. Duniya Aslam Khan, "UNHCR Looks at the Economic Contribution of Afghan Refugees in Pakistan," UNHCR, January 18, 2011, https://www.unhcr.org/hk/en/10385-unhcr-looks-at-the-economic-contribution-of-afghan-refugees-in-pakistan.html; Agence France-Presse, "Afghan Scavengers in Karachi Crosshairs," *Dawn*, August 2, 2012, https://www.dawn.com/news/739147/afghan-scavengers-in-karachi-crosshairs.

28. See, e.g., Hunain Ameen, "Karachi Garbage Story 2: Government and Mafia," *ARY News*, May 9, 2022, https://arynews.tv/karachi-garbage-story-2-government-mafia/.

29. Oonib Azam, "Heavy Toll of Development Frenzy on Karachi Coast," Third Pole, August 5, 2022, https://www.thethirdpole.net/en/livelihoods/heavy-toll-of-dha-phase-8-development-karachi/.

30. Bashir Lakhani, "How DHA Built Its Stormwater Drainage System," interview by Mahim Maher, *Aaj News*, last modified July 18, 2022, https://www.aajenglish.tv/news/30292656/how-dha-built-its-stormwater-drainage-system.

31. The damage was so widespread that the Sindh High Court had to approve the petition filed against DHA for using landfills to build commercial real estate, declaring it illegal and threatening the city's ecological survival. See Naeem Sahoutara, "Fighting for Amenity: Petitioner Wins Plea against DHA's Commercialization," *Express Tribune*, December 4, 2013, https://tribune.com.pk/story/641130/fighting-for-amenity-petitioners-wins-plea-against-dhas-commercialisation.

32. See Fizza Qureshi and Amar Latif Qazi, *Short Report on Gujjar Nala Demolitions* (Karachi: Karachi Bachao Tehreek, 2020), https://karachibachaotehreek.org/docs/gujjar-nala-report.pdf.

33. Aquila Ismail, "The Technical Training Resource Center (TTRC): Building Community Architects," *Environment and Urbanization* 23, no. 1 (April 2011): 183–93, https://journals.sagepub.com/doi/pdf/10.1177/0956247810396057.

34. Arif Hasan, "The Judiciary and the Poor," Arif Hasan (website), June 26, 2021, http://arifhasan.org/development/the-judiciary-and-the-poor.

35. Arif Hasan, "How Community Mapping of Storm Water Drains Is Fighting Evictions in Karachi's Informal Settlements," International Institute for Environment and Development, March 24, 2021, https://www.iied.org/how-community-mapping-storm-water-drains-fighting-evictions-karachis-informal-settlements.

36. Arif Hasan, "Expressway Concerns," *Dawn*, March 27, 2022, https://www.dawn.com/news/1682058/expressway-concerns. Also, see Hasan et al., "Land Ownership."

37. Sobia Ahmad Kaker and Nausheen H. Anwar, "From One Flooding Crisis to the Next: Negotiating 'the Maybe' in Unequal Karachi," *Geographical Journal* 190, no. 1 (2022): e12498, https://doi.org/10.1111/geoj.12498.

Chapter 5

1. Rupert Colville, "The Biggest Caseload in the World," *Refugees Magazine*, June 1, 1997, https://www.unhcr.org/en-us/publications/refugeemag/3b68ofbfc/refugees-magazine-issue-108-afghanistan-unending-crisis-biggest-caseload.html.

2. Alessandro Monsutti, *War and Migration: Social Networks and Economic Strategies of the Hazaras of Afghanistan* (Abingdon: Routledge, 2016), xiii. For more details, see Gilles Dorronsoro, *Revolution Unending: Afghanistan, 1979 to the Present* (London: Hurst, 2005), 169–72. On the policies of the governments of Pakistan and Iran, see Maliha Safri, "The Transformation of the Afghan Refugee, 1979–2009," *Middle East Journal* 65, no. 4 (Autumn 2011): 587–601; and on intraopposition violence and the manipulation of refugee flows by mujahideen commanders and Pakistani authorities, see Michael Pohly, *Krieg und Widerstand in Afghanistan: Ursachen, Verlauf und Folgen seit 1978* (Berlin: Das Arabische Buch, 1992). On Pakistani policies and the experiences of Afghans in Peshawar and Karachi, see Sanaa Alimia, *Refugee Cities: How Afghans Changed Urban Pakistan* (Philadelphia: University of Pennsylvania Press, 2022).

3. Note the similarities with the politics of later African refugee camps, where, as Liisa Malkki argues, the authorities sought "to depoliticize the refugee category and to construct in that depoliticized space an ahistorical, universal humanitarian subject." See Malkki, "Speechless Emissaries: Refugees, Humanitarianism, and Dehistoricization," *Cultural Anthropology* 11, no. 3 (1996): 378.

4. See Pohly, *Krieg und Widerstand*, 387–431.

5. Pierre Centlivres and Micheline Centlivres-Demont, "The Afghan Refugee in Pakistan: An Ambiguous Identity," trans. Mary Ellen Chatwin, *Journal of Refugee Studies* 1, no. 2 (1988): 146. See also M. Nazif Shahrani, "Afghanistan's *Muhajirin* (Muslim 'Refugee-Warriors'): Politics of Mistrust and Distrust of Politics," in *Mistrusting Refugees*, ed. E. Valentine Daniel and John Chr. Knudsen (Berkeley: University of California Press, 1995), 187–206.

6. Helga Baitenmann, "NGOs and the Afghan War: The Politicisation of Humanitarian Aid," *Third World Quarterly* 12, no. 1 (January 1990): 62–85.

7. Safri, "Afghan Refugee," 589–90. In Pakistan, official use of *muhajir* (or *mohajer*) was limited to Muslims who migrated from India after partition of the subcontinent in 1947. In 1993, Iran shifted to calling Afghans there refugees. See ibid., 592. See also Alimia, *Refugee Cities*.

8. Telegram from the embassy in Pakistan to the Department of State (Islamabad, January 17, 1980), in *Foreign Relations of the United States: 1977–1980*, vol. 12, *Afghanistan* ([Washington, DC]: Office of the Historian, Foreign Service Institute, US Department of State, n.d.), https://history.state.gov/historicaldocuments/frus1977-80v12/d171.

9. Michael T. Kaufman, "Mrs. Thatcher Visits Afghans on the Frontier," *New York Times*, October 9, 1981, https://www.nytimes.com/1981/10/09/world/mrs-thatcher-visits-afghans-on-the-frontier.html.

10. Mohsen M. Milani, "Iran's Policy towards Afghanistan," *Middle East Journal* 60, no. 2 (2006): 235–56.

11. See, e.g., Mohammad Tahir Aziz Gumnam, *Kandahar Assassins: Stories from the Afghan-Soviet War*, ed. Alex Strick van Linschoten and Felix Kuehn (Berlin: First Draft, 2013), 128. See also Sayyid Muḥammad ʿAlī Jāvīd, *Khāṭirāt-i man: Barahah-yī ḥassāsī az tārīkh* (Kabul: Nashr-i Nigar, 2017).

12. Safri, "Afghan Refugee," 589. On tensions between Afghan refugees and the political parties charged with administering camp life, see, e.g., David B. Edwards, *Before Taliban: Genealogies of the Afghan Jihad* (Berkeley: University of California Press, 2002), esp. 158–61, 267–68.

13. Gumnam, *Kandahar Assassins*, 118.

14. Shahrani, "Afghanistan's *Muhajirin*," 194.

15. Aleksandr Liakhovskii, *Tragediia i doblest' Afgana* (Yaroslavl': Nord, 2004), 492.

16. Liakhovskii, *Tragediia i doblest' Afgana*.

17. "Haq Nawaz: Zia Misuses Afghan 'Refugees' as Means for Prolonging His Rule," *Kabul New Times*, May 16, 1983, 1–2. It should also be noted that DRA authorities sometimes used the discredited "refugee" label euphemistically to describe forced disappearances and executions: enemies simply "escaped to Pakistan."

18. Burhanuddin Hassas, in discussion with Sabauon Nasseri, July 31, 2021, Lakeville, MN. Dr. Hassas was teaching at Kabul University when Nur Muhammad Taraki and Hafizullah Amin led the revolutionary government in 1978 and 1979.

19. "Afghan 'Refugees' in Pak Respond to RC Decree," *Kabul New Times*, September 11, 1982, 1. In a similar vein, in 1982, Asadullah Habib, rector of Kabul University, published a novella in which he distinguished between "good" and "bad" mujahideen. The bad were "gang members" (*ashrar*) or "Reagan's spawn," while the good could be reformed once the revolutionaries had shown them what Islam and the revolution were about. Representing Kabul's official line, Habib and various DRA-affiliated newspapers left out the strife within the government and society at large. They minimized the ever-intensifying war that consumed all his compatriots, reducing the mujahideen to ineffective groups of bandits and ignoring that these groups had become a formidable force with the backing of regional and global powers. Habib, *Dās-hā wa dast-hā* (Kabul: Matboʿā-e dowlatī, 1983), 20.

20. "New Kabul-Soviet Moves," *Afghan Information Centre Monthly Bulletin*, no. 70 (March 1987): 4.

21. Chris Sands and Fazelminallah Qazizai, *Night Letters: Gulbuddin Hekmatyar and the Afghan Islamists Who Changed the World* (London: Hurst, 2019); V. S. Khristoforov, *Afganistan: Voenno-politicheskoe prisutstvie SSSR, 1979–1989 gg.* (Moscow: Institut rossiiskoi istorii RAN, 2016); Vladimir Plastun, *Iznanka Afganskoi voiny, 1979–1989 gg.: Dnevnikovye zapisi i kommentarii uchastnika* (Moscow: IV RAN, 2016); Vasiliy Mitrokhin, "The KGB in Afghanistan," rev. ed. (Cold War International History Project Working Paper 40, Woodrow Wilson International Center for Scholars, July 2002; July 2009), https://www.wilsoncenter.org/sites/default/files/media/documents/publication/WP40-english.pdf.

22. Abdul Salam Zaeef, *My Life with the Taliban* (Oxford: Hurst, 2010), 32.

23. A. Rasul Amin, ed., *Life in Refugee Camps* (Peshawar: [Writers Union of Free Afghanistan], 1985), 15.

24. Amin, *Life in Refugee Camps*, 49.

25. Amin, *Life in Refugee Camps*, 62.

26. See, e.g., 'Ayn Omid and Mohammad Zahir, "Pādshāh-e sābeq cha naqsh-ye rā mytawānad barā-ye rasīdan-e harcha sarī'tar ba sulah bāzi konad?," *Akhbār-e Hafta*, no. 1 (December 1988): 5; Ẓ. Shamshād, "Mohammad Zahir Shah mytawānad ba 'inwān-e mīyānjī tarafîn rā ba mayn-e muzākera bekashānad," *Akhbār-e Hafta*, no. 38 (September 1989): 3.

27. Sayyid Bahauddin Majrooh, "What Do the Afghan Refugees Think? An Opinion Survey in the Camps," *Afghan Information Centre Monthly Bulletin*, no. 76 (July 1987): 2–8.

28. Sayyid Bahauddin Majrooh, "'Political Solution' for Afghanistan: Soviet Tactics of Diversion?," *Afghan Information Centre Monthly Bulletin*, no. 73 (April 1987): 3–4.

29. Majrooh, "'Political Solution' for Afghanistan," 4.

30. Sayyid Bahauddin Majrooh, "Political Events of the Month," *Afghan Information Centre Monthly Bulletin*, no. 74 (May 1987): 4–5.

31. Anthony Hyman, "Reading Afghan Public Opinion: Voices from the Camps," *Central Asian Survey* 9, no. 2 (1990): 113–23.

32. Hyman, "Reading Afghan Public Opinion," 117–18.

33. Hyman, "Reading Afghan Public Opinion," 121, 119.

34. Hyman, "Reading Afghan Public Opinion," 121, 122.

35. Liakhovskii, *Tragediia i doblest' Afgana*, 492; Zaeef, *My Life*, 15. Roger Trask, a foreign correspondent for the *Morning Star*, claims that Pakistanis, specifically in Pashtun areas (parts of Waziristan and Quetta), did not want "counterrevolutionary" Afghans in their territories, preferring better relations with Kabul. He claims that there were antirefugee demonstrations and that the Pakistani Army would disperse them, often injuring and killing demonstrators in the process. See Trask, *Afghanistan: Grasping the Nettle of Peace; An Eye-Witness Account*, *Morning Star* pamphlet, January 1987, box 7, folder 36, School of Oriental and African Studies Library, University of London.

36. Bernt Glatzer, *Return to Kunar? An Enquiry among Refugees from Kunar in Bajaur* (Peshawar: Danish Committee for Aid to Afghan Refugees, March 1990).

37. The case of the family of Dr. Sherhasan Hasan from Kunar fits a broader pattern. When Taraki came to power, his uncle and cousins left for Pakistan, some for Bajaur, to join the mujahideen. But he and his brother remained in Kunar, joined the PDPA, and fought against the mujahideen. The cousins retain relations to this day but don't agree on politics. According to Hasan, the war drew everyone in. It became impossible not to take sides. Kunar was also the first site of the attacks by the mujahideen. Hasan, in discussion with Sabauon Nasseri, April 8, 2019, Moscow, Russia.

38. Zuzanna Olszewska, "If We Do Not Write Poetry, We Will Die: Afghan Diasporic Social Media Poetry for the Fall of Kabul," in *The Routledge Handbook of Refugee Narratives*, ed. Evyn Lê Espiritu Gandhi and Vinh Nguyen (New York: Routledge, 2023), 142–43.

39. On the history of the cassette and related sound technologies in Afghanistan, see Mejgan Massoumi, "The Sounds of Kabul: Radio and the Politics of Popular Culture in Afghanistan, 1960–79" (PhD diss., Stanford University, 2021).

40. Sayd Bahodine Majrouh, ed., *Songs of Love and War: Afghan Women's Poetry*, trans. Marjolijn de Jager (New York: Other Press, 2003), 41.

41. Zuzanna Olszewska, "'A Desolate Voice': Poetry and Identity among Young Afghan Refugees in Iran," *Iranian Studies* 40, no. 2 (2007): 208.

42. Majrouh, *Songs of Love and War*, 41.

43. See, respectively, Majrouh, *Songs of Love and War*, 49, 52, 60, 55.

44. See, respectively, Majrouh, *Songs of Love and War*, 55, 54.

45. Benedict Anderson, "Long-Distance Nationalism," in *The Spectre of Comparisons: Nationalism, Southeast Asia and the World* (New York: Verso, 2002), 60.

46. Hadi Arussang, in discussion with Sabauon Nasseri, October 25, 2019, Nijmegen, the Netherlands. See also the poems in Bilqis Jafari Alawi, *Bāznumā'ī-yi mohājarat wa mohājar dar āhanghā wa ash'ār-i 'āmiyāna-yi Afghānhā* (Kabul: Markaz-i Manba'-i Ma'lumāt-i Afghānistān dar Pūhantūn-i Kābul, [~2018–2019]), Global Change Research Fund, City University of London, Economic and Social Research Council, https://doi.org/10.29171/azu_acku_risalah_hv640_5_a28_jeem77_1397; Mohammad Nasīr Mahrīn, ed., *Taranahā-yi ghorbat* (Peshawar: Markaz-i nashrātī ārash, 2000).

47. See, e.g., the poems in Mahrīn, *Taranahā-yi ghorbat*, 26–28, 162–68, 181–85. The anthology features the work of twenty-seven Afghans residing in Germany.

48. Rolf Bindemann, "Kunst in Widerstand: 'Revolutionäre' und 'nationale' Lieder der Hazara," in *Neue Beiträge zur Afghanistanforschung*, ed. Erwin Grötzbach (Liestal: Stiftung Bibliotecha Afghanica, 1988), 95; ellipses original. See also Rolf Bindemann, *Religion und Politik bei den schi'itischen Hazara in Afghanistan, Iran und Pakistan* (Berlin: Verlag das Arabische Buch, 1987).

49. Zuzanna Olszewska, *The Pearl of Dari: Poetry and Personhood among Young Afghans in Iran* (Bloomington: Indiana University Press, 2015), 57–58.

50. Hadi Arussang, "Dar Sowg-i edālat" (unpublished manuscript, November 28, 2010), Microsoft Word file.

51. Olszewska, "Write Poetry."

52. Parvin Faiz Zadah Malal [Parween Faiz Zadah Malaal], "Hate," trans. Anders Widmark, Words without Borders, May 1, 2011, https://wordswithoutborders.org/read/article/2011-05/hate/.

53. Malal, "Hate."

54. Parween Faiz Zadah Malaal, "Like a Desert Flower," trans. Dawood Azami, Poetry Translation Centre, accessed January 9, 2025, https://www.poetrytranslation.org/poem/like-a-desert-flower/#translated-poem.

55. Olszewska, "Desolate Voice," 208.

56. Sosan Firoz, quoted in Alawi, *Bāznumā'ī-yi mohājarat wa mohājar*, 25.

57. Anonymous, quoted in Alawi, *Bāznumā'ī-yi mohājarat wa mohājar*, 27.

58. Edwards, *Before Taliban*.

59. "Afghanistan Situation," Operational Data Portal, UNHCR, accessed January 10, 2025, https://data.unhcr.org/en/situations/afghanistan.

60. On Iranian authorities' violence against Afghan refugees, see, e.g., Charlotte Greenfield and Mohammad Yunus Yawar, "UN Seeks Probe into Reported Mass Killing of Afghans Migrating to Iran," Reuters, October 17, 2024, https://www.reuters.com/world/un-seeks-probe-into-reported-mass-killing-afghans-migrating-iran-2024-10-17/. On shifting Pakistani policies, see Alimia, *Refugee Cities*.

61. Former president Hamid Karzai, e.g., lobbied the US government to come to power and remained in in his post without any danger to his immediate family. See, e.g., Matthew Rosenberg, "With Bags of Cash, C.I.A. Seeks Influence in Afghanistan," *New York Times*, April 28, 2013, https://www.nytimes.com/2013/04/29/world/asia/cia-delivers-cash-to-afghan-leaders-office.html. In present-day Washington, some Afghans who have lived most of their lives outside of Afghanistan have formed an anti-Taliban lobbying group. See Kenneth P. Vogel, "Struggle for Control of Afghanistan Comes to K Street," *New York Times*, September 15, 2021, https://www.nytimes.com/2021/09/15/us/politics/afghanistan-taliban.html. Followers of the late Afghan leader Ahmad Shah Massoud (1953–2001) established a foundation in his name, with offices, e.g., in the United States and Australia. It is largely run by Afghans born in the United States or by those with dual citizenship. "Foreign Offices," Massoud Foundation, accessed December 12, 2021, https://massoudfoundation.org/foreign-offices/ (site discontinued). For the Taliban leadership's long-distance politics, see Ahmed Rashid, *Taliban: Militant Islam, Oil and Fundamentalism in Central Asia* (New Haven, CT: Yale University Press, 2010).

62. The quote is from Benedict Anderson, who presents a similar argument in the context of Southeast Asia. See Anderson, "Long-Distance Nationalism," 74. This especially holds true for many Afghan politicians today, from the Taliban in Pakistan to diaspora activists in Iran, India, and the United States.

Epilogue

1. For long, historians have given several names to this emergence of a common world bound by overlapping webs of colonial jurisdictions and institutions. "Globalization" is one such descriptive notion, among others. See, e.g., Jean L. Cohen, *Globalization and Sovereignty: Rethinking Legality, Legitimacy, and Constitutionalism* (Cambridge: Cambridge University Press, 2012).

2. For important exceptions, see Susan Buck-Morss, *Hegel, Haiti, and Universal History* (Pittsburg: University of Pittsburg Press, 2009); and the more recent Elizabeth R. Anker, *Ugly Freedoms* (Durham, NC: Duke University Press, 2022).

3. James Baldwin, "Black English: A Dishonest Argument," in *The Cross of Redemption: Uncollected Writings*, ed. Randall Kenan (New York: Vintage, 2010), 156.

4. For a sensitive articulation of this problem, see Vinh Nguyen, *Lived Refuge: Gratitude, Resentment, Resilience* (Berkeley: University of California Press, 2023).

5. For a powerful examination of this nexus, see Étienne Balibar and Immanuel Wallerstein, *Race, Nation, Class: Ambiguous Identities* (London: Verso, 1991).

6. See, e.g., Alan Weisman, *World without Us* (2007; New York: Picador, 2022); Eugen Thacker, *After Life* (Chicago: University of Chicago Press, 2010).

7. "In some ways the most extreme defenders of negative liberty in our history were the slave-owning planters of the pre–Civil War era," Shklar writes, reconstructing this founding irony in her essay "Conscience and Obligation." "*Rights* was their favorite word." Of course, slavery "was the specter that haunted them all, but which also defined their liberty." Slavery not only was to remain indissociable from claims of political freedom in the South, it also came to define the meanings and limits of human freedom (and its withholding) in liberal thought at large. Even and especially because of her profound liberalism, Shklar does not flinch from the consequence of such an origin. "The chief use of negative liberty was to enslave the black population." See Shklar, *On Political Obligation*, ed. Samantha Ashenden and Andreas Hess (New Haven, CT: Yale University Press, 2019), 11.

8. For the ethical stakes for life at this extremity, see Judith Butler and Frédéric Worms, *The Livable and the Unlivable* (New York: Fordham University Press, 2023).

9. One example of fearlessly staring back at this moral inversion that I have in mind here, which recenters human *temptation*—as opposed to human *nature*—at the core of a world turned into an unlivable hole of oblivion, appears in the final passage of the ninth chapter of Hannah Arendt's *Eichmann in Jerusalem*, under the timeless title "Duties of a Law-Abiding Citizen." An "overwhelming majority" of Germans, Arendt writes there, "must have been tempted *not* to murder, *not* to rob, *not* to let their neighbors go off to their doom . . . not to become accomplices in all these crimes by benefiting from them. But, God knows," she concedes as she finishes the paragraph and chapter, "they had learnt how to resist temptation." Arendt, *Eichmann in Jerusalem: A Report on the Banality of Evil* (New York: Penguin, 1963), 150.

10. In trying to understand how global political thought might succeed in "putting cruelty first" and what such a radical liberalism might look like, I draw from Judith N. Shklar, *Ordinary Vices* (Cambridge, MA: Harvard University Press, 1984).

11. Hannah Arendt, "Freedom and Politics: A Lecture," *Chicago Review* 14, no. 1 (Spring 1960): 29.

12. Walter Benjamin, "Critique of Violence," in *Reflections: Essays, Aphorisms, Autobiographical Writings* (1921; New York: Schocken Books, 1978), 277–300.

13. Hannah Arendt, *The Origins of Totalitarianism* (New York: Harcourt, Brace, 1948), 287.

14. "U.N.: Over 2,500 Migrants Have Died or Gone Missing This Year Trying to Cross the Mediterranean," Democracy Now!, September 29, 2023, https://www.democracynow.org/2023/9/29/headlines/un_over_2_500_migrants_have_died_or_gone_missing_this_year_trying_to_cross_the_mediterranean.

15. For an examination of the landscape of postwar liberal democratic legalism, which has only deepened the theological strains of modern judicial and extrajudicial practice, see Aishwary Kumar, "A Jurisprudence of Neglect: Arendt, Ambedkar, and the Logic of Political Cruelty," in *Faith in the World: Post-secular Readings of Hannah Arendt*, ed. Ludger Hagedorn and Rafael Zawisza (Chicago: University of Chicago Press, 2021), 2023–32.

16. The classic here is Michel Foucault, *The Birth of Biopolitics: Lectures at the College de France, 1978–79*, trans. Graham Burchell (New York: Palgrave, 2008). See also the more recent Achille Mbembe, *Necropolitics*, trans. Steven Corcoran (Durham, NC: Duke University Press, 2019).

17. It is no coincidence that among all the parts of Hobbes's *Leviathan*, it is the chapter on punishment that the Indian moral philosopher and constitutional theorist Bhimrao Ambedkar trains his eyes on as he sets out to deconstruct the intricate juridical logic of caste and its indivisible, invisible sovereignty beyond social norms and the law.

18. On some of these issues inflected through the Roman political and imperial tradition, see David Armitage, *Civil War: A History in Ideas* (New York: Alfred Knopf, 2017).

19. Thus, in his classic work on postwar Europe, James J. Sheehan legitimately asks, "Where have all the soldiers gone?" See Sheehan, *Where Have All the Soldiers Gone? The Transformation of Modern Europe* (New York: Mariner, 2009), front matter. The postwar reduction of the military footprint as a sign of European peace—or, even relatively speaking, of Europe's decreasing dependence on war—seems nonetheless out of joint with the reality of the twentieth century. Beginning with the brutal "counterinsurgency" operations that European powers undertook in midcentury Asia and Africa, followed by the revolutionary (civil) wars in which first the European states and then the United States actively participated, sometimes despite international condemnation and often on dubious legal grounds, most soldiers were already not in or from Europe. And the millions who fought a few decades earlier on behalf of European colonial powers during the two world wars—which also were essentially colonial wars waged for colonial possessions—did not come from the continent either. Over 1.5 million Indian soldiers are reported to have fought as part of the British effort in the Great War alone, spanning theaters across the Middle East, North Africa, and Asia.

20. The expression "global civil war" is Giorgio Agamben's. See Agamben, *Stasis: Civil War as a Political Paradigm* (Stanford, CA: Stanford University Press, 2015), 2.

21. Hannah Arendt, *On Revolution* (New York: Penguin, 1963), 8.

22. Frantz Fanon, *The Wretched of the Earth*, trans. Richard Philcox (1961; New York: Grove Press, 2004), 3.

23. Francis Fukuyama, *The End of History and the Last Man* (New York: Free Press, 1992), front matter. I return below to the tragic salience of the figure of the "last man," which we nonetheless must subject to a closer reading today, if only for its inverted relevance to the philosophy of planetary history.

24. Samuel Moyn offers a strong counterhistory of this turn in American political thought. See Moyn, *Liberalism against Itself: Cold War Intellectuals and the Making of Our Times* (New Haven, CT: Yale University Press, 2023). But even in Moyn's iconoclastic retelling, the question of the color line and of civil rights—which was to emerge as the most formidable site of American racial reckoning at home at the height of its criminal misadventure abroad—does not get a central place. I am not sure it is Moyn's

focus on Jewish liberals that leads him to this silence on civil rights; if anything, the exact opposite should have been the case. The point is these two movements are philosophically indissociable: Cold War liberalism, even though it dissociates itself from the savagery abroad and even makes concessions for it—this is Moyn's signal insight—could not have acquired its structure and form without being profoundly affected by Black thought. Even if they take incommensurable forms, examples of this influence on structure—and the place of the South—in the intellectual trajectories of Judith Shklar and Hannah Arendt, abound. Others, like Isaiah Berlin, chose a closely cultivated ignorance of their own country's barbarities—one whose silent legacy is to be found more recently in the work of Quentin Skinner. For a rare examination of this moment in the itinerary of liberal constitutionalism as one whole, see Aziz Rana, *The Constitutional Bind: How Americans Came to Idolize a Document That Fails Them* (Chicago: University of Chicago Press, 2024).

25. On the institution of the modern citizen-subject, see Étienne Balibar, *Citizen-Subject: Foundations for Philosophical Anthropology* (New York: Fordham University Press, 2016).

26. Marc Crépon, *Murderous Consent: On the Accommodation of Violent Death* (New York: Fordham University Press, 2019).

27. Arendt, *Origins of Totalitarianism*, 296.

28. Paul Rabinow, *French Modern: Norms and Forms of Social Environment* (Chicago: University of Chicago Press, 1995).

29. Grégoire Chamayou, *Manhunt: A Philosophical History* (Princeton, NJ: Princeton University Press, 2012), front matter.

30. Arendt, *Origins of Totalitarianism*, 294.

31. Arendt, *Origins of Totalitarianism*, 297.

32. On contemporary forms of this economy, for which he uses this term, see Yanis Varoufakis, *Technofeudalism: What Killed Capitalism* (New York: Melville House, 2024).

33. Carl Schmitt turns the German term *Großraum* into a category for theory of international law. See Schmitt, *Nomos of the Earth in the International Law of the Jus Publicum Europaeum*, trans. G. L. Ulmen (1950; New York: Telos Press, 2003).

34. Fukuyama, *End of History*.

35. For Africa, this continuum of colonial darkness—despite the redemptive interregnum of decolonization—is made graphically salient in Achille Mbembe, *Out of the Dark Night: Essays on Decolonization* (New York: Columbia University Press, 2021).

36. James Baldwin, "On Being White . . . and Other Lies," in *The Cross of Redemption: Uncollected Writings*, ed. Randall Kenan (New York: Vintage, 2011), 169.

37. Tony Judt, *Postwar: A History of Europe since 1945* (New York: Penguin, 2005).

38. On this deep history, see Thomas Nail, *The Figure of the Migrant* (Stanford, CA: Stanford University Press, 2015).

39. Hannah Arendt, *The Human Condition* (Chicago: University of Chicago Press, 1958), 6.

40. On this history of islands and waste, see Lauren Hirshberg, *Suburban Empire: Cold War Militarization in the US Pacific* (Berkeley: University of California Press, 2022).

41. Judith Shklar, "The Liberalism of Fear," in *Liberalism and the Moral Life*, ed. Nancy Rosenblum (Cambridge, MA: Harvard University Press, 1989), 24.

42. On this hemispheric tradition, see, most recently, Murad Idris, *War for Peace: Genealogies of a Violent Ideal in Western and Islamic Thought* (New York: Oxford University Press, 2018). The legal and liberal democratic scaffolding for war—while scrupulously preserving its autonomy from the law as such—is thoroughly scrutinized in Christopher Kutz, *On War and Democracy* (Princeton, NJ: Princeton University Press, 2016).

43. Arendt, *Origins of Totalitarianism*, 296–97.

44. Arendt, *Origins of Totalitarianism*, 293. On this surreptitious distinction between the rightless and stateless, see Yumi Moon's unsparing chapter on the moral and military tragedy of the Korean peninsula in this volume.

45. On the moral and political implications of this moment, see Aishwary Kumar, *Radical Equality: Ambedkar, Gandhi, and the Risk of Democracy* (Stanford, CA: Stanford University Press, 2015). Despite Judith Shklar's powerful opening three decades ago in "The Liberalism of Fear," we are yet to fully mine the implications of caste law for liberal jurisprudence (and for neoliberal planetarity itself).

46. Arendt, *Origins of Totalitarianism*, 295–96.

47. Carl Schmitt, *Land and Sea: A World-Historical Meditation*, trans. Samuel Garrett Zeitlin (New York: Telos Press, 2015), 25. For a phenomenological reading of this view, see Daniel Heller-Roazen, *The Enemy of All: Piracy and the Law of Nations* (Cambridge, MA: MIT Press, 2009).

48. Aurora Levins Morales, "Red Sea: April 2002," Aurora Levins Morales (website), April 2002, http://www.auroralevinsmorales.com/red-sea.html.

49. Terisa Siagatonu, "Atlas," *Poetry*, April 2018, https://www.poetryfoundation.org/poetrymagazine/poems/146222/atlas-5aa944cf31dad. As Arendt writes at a searing moment in her examination of the ultranationalist production of stateless populations, leading up to the catastrophic disposal (and disposability) of the *idea* of the human itself,

> new refugees were persecuted not because of what they had done or thought, but because of what they unchangeably were—born *into* the wrong kind of race or the wrong kind of class or drafted by the wrong kind of government (as in the case of the Spanish Republican Army).
>
> The more the number of rightless people increased, the greater became the temptation to pay less attention to the deeds of the persecuting governments than to the status of the persecuted.

See Arendt, *Origins of Totalitarianism*, 294; emphasis added.

50. For this other defining and damning fold of penal power—*paperwork*—as it

functions on the idea of the human, see Daniel Heller-Roazen, *Absentees: On Variously Missing Persons* (Cambridge, MA: MIT Press, 2021).

51. Stephen Castle, "UK Moves First Group of Asylum Seekers onto Barge," *New York Times*, August 7, 2023, https://www.nytimes.com/2023/08/07/world/europe/uk-migrant-barge.html

52. Varoufakis, *Technofeudalism*.

53. Jacques Derrida, "Faith and Knowledge: The Two Sources of 'Religion' at the Limits of Reason Alone," in *Acts of Religion*, ed. Gil Anidjar (New York: Routledge, 2002), 1–39.

54. Mbembe, *Necropolitics*, 42–65 passim. The provocative power of Mbembe's critique comes from the attention he pays to the place of movement—which is to say, of *repetitive displacement*—in the consolidation of older colonial apartheids in contemporary global and neocolonial forms. Less through fixing and detention of populations, it is now by raising collective panic around the specter of unstable marauders, invaders, pirates, and abductors—around visions of a volatile, destabilizing movement of the stateless, who are, by their very *birth*, criminals—that nationalist and religious rhetorics of immigration in liberal democracies today take shape. As Nasseri and Crews trace in their sensitive counternarrative of Afghan globality in this volume, however, nomadic movement (as opposed to *fratricidal stasis*) and transnational travel (as opposed to *national territory*) have also emerged, for better or worse, as the new crucible of moral and revolutionary claims of civic belonging, conflict, and identity.

55. Mike Davis, *The Planet of Slums* (London: Verso, 2006), front matter. It is illuminating how little room there is for the poor, the migrant, and the refugee in the comforting liberal talk of the "planetary age," which sees in the inauguration of the Anthropocene the dissolution into irrelevance of all existing categories of thought produced by capitalism, its conception of humanity now hinged upon an abstract common future that binds all of humanity into one equally imaginary whole. See Dipesh Chakrabarty, *The Climate of History in the Planetary Age* (Chicago: University of Chicago Press, 2021).

56. Arendt, *Human Condition*, 6.

57. James Baldwin, *Nothing Personal* (Boston: Beacon Press, 2021), 50.

Index

Page numbers in italics denote figures, and endnotes are indicated by "n" followed by the endnote number.

228 Massacre, 51

'Abd-al Rahman, Amir, 153
"absentee persons," 189
Afghanistan, 1, 124, 127
Afghan refugees: 1979 Soviet invasion, 135–36; as critics and activists, 146–50, *147, 148,* 181, 234n61; definitions and portrayals of, 16, 137–40; exclusion from political participation, 20–21, 136–37, 230n3; in ideological narratives, 140–43, 231n19; legacies of displacement, 153–57; music, poetry, and prose, 150–53; refugee camp as catalyst, 143–46
agency: centrality of, 4; criticism and activism, Afghanistan, 146–50, *147, 148,* 181, 234n61; definitions of "refugees" and, 15; in motivations for migration, 11; organizations and activism, Korea, 74–76, 99–104; refugee petitioning, Dachen Islands, 49–50, 65–71; in self-identification, 138, 157; through music, poetry, and prose, 150–56, 187, 188–89
Aid Refugee Chinese Intellectuals Inc. (ARCI), 60
Althusser, Louis, 109
Ambedkar, Bhimrao, 183, 184, 186, 236n17
Amnesty International, 1
An Chae-hong, 107
Anderson, Benedict, 152, 234n62
Anderson, Charles A., 97
Anju County, North P'yŏngan Province, 89–93, *91*
antirevolutionary pressure, 168–69
Anwar, Nausheen H., 133
archipelagos of inequality, 190

241

Arendt, Hannah: on confronting moral inversion, 165, 235n9; on expulsion, 174, 175–76, 183; on meaning of "refugee," 15; on neglect, 191; *The Origins of Totalitarianism*, 158, 166, 176, 183; on paramilitary logic, 166; *On Revolution*, 161; on rightlessness, 173; on statelessness, 168–69, 238n49; on world alienation, 180
Army of the Associated State of Vietnam, 27
Arnold, Archibold V., 77
Aron, Raymond, 39
art, 150–56, 187, 188–89
Arussang, Hadi, 154
Associate State of Vietnam (ASV), 25–26, 27, 28, 41
authoritarianism, 111, 114
Awami National Party (ANP), 124–25, 127–28, 229n26

Baldwin, James, 160, 178, 194–95
Bandung Conference (1955), 44
Bảo Đại, 28
Bascara, Victor, 2
Benjamin, Walter, 191
Berlin, Isaiah, 236n24
Berry, G. A., 97
Bombay Presidency (anticaste movement), 186
Bourke-White, Margaret, 121–22, *122*, *123*
Britain, 23, 41, 55, 115, 120–21, 127, 128
Bureau of Planning (US), 77
Burma, 35

Cairo Declaration (1943), 6
Cambodia, 25, 26, 35
The Cambridge History of the Cold War (Leffler and Westad), 2, 197n5
Canada, 32, 37, 208n63
Cao Đài (religious group), 26
capitalism, 33, 176, 190

Case, Harry, 110
caste, 183–84, 186, 236n17
Centlivres, Pierre, 138
Centlivres-Demont, Micheline, 138
Central Intelligence Agency (CIA), 54, 55–56, 60
Chamayou, Grégoire, 174
Chang, David, 11
Cheju Island uprising (1948), 74
Cheondoism, 90
chhits (boundary enclaves), 115–16
Chiang Kai-shek, 44, 46, 47, 49, 50–53, 55, 73, 212n25
Chin, Angelina Y., 46
China: 1949 mainland exodus, 50–51, 212n17; Communist revolutionary movement, 25; "Free China"-"Red China" divide, 47; US guidelines on displaced persons and, 5–8, 198n14. *See also* Dachen refugees; Kuomintang (KMT) government
Chinese Civil War (1945-1949), 46, 51, 62, 212n16
Chinese Communist Party (CCP), 44, 50, 51–52, 212n16
Ch'oe Ŭn-bŏm, 75, 95–96, 221n56
Cho Mansik, 100
chŏnjaemin (war refugees), 79
Cho Pyŏng-ok, 85
Chosŏn Democratic Party, 85, 87, 101
Christianity, 90
city planning. *See* spatial politics
class composition of refugees, 89–93, *91*
climate change, 165, 180, 192–93
Cohen, Gerard Daniel, 9
Cold War: as counterpart to colonialism, 166, 168, 170, 176–78; Indochina War and, 24–26; military withdrawal, 181–86, *185*; paramilitary logic, 166–68; rhetorical fallacy of, 170; as war over space vs. territory, 17–18, 112–13

Cold War humanism: being human without land, 186–91; cruelty and transcendence, 171–75, 194–95; extraterrestrial flight, 192–93; inequality and violence, 165; neglect and freedom, 166–70; neodemocratic condition, 165–66; new segregation, 178–81; oligarchic escape, and equality vs. extinction, 175–78; planetarity vs. equality, 163–64; segregation and statelessness, 161–63; southern theory of political freedom, 158–60; violence without legal theory, 181–86, *185*

Cold War refugees: as "anticitizens," 176; class composition, North P'yŏngan, 89–93, *91*; differential representations of, 31–32, 48; as enemies, 112, 114, 119; exemplify the "mutation in the human," 165; as helpless subjects, 121–24, *122*, *123*, 136–37, *138*; ideological framings of, 29–32, 48, 136–37, 139, 140–43, 156–57; invisibility of, in Cold War studies, 1–2; language barriers, 65; partitions and artificial borders, 3–4; as politically influential, 45, 157; refugee agency and experiences, 4; "refugees," "violence," and "refugeetude," 12–18; as source of labor, 9, 49, 61–62, 200n26; text overview, 19–21; trans-Asian connections, 3; unequal protections for, 42; US guidelines on displaced persons, 5–8, 76–77; US refugee administration in Asia, 8–11. *See also* Afghan refugees; Cold War humanism; Dachen refugees; northern Korean refugees; partition of Vietnam; spatial politics

colonialism: Cold War as counterpart to, 166, 168, 170, 176–78; enduring impacts of, 158–59, 163; provisions for land acquisition, 120; refugee experiences and, 104; white fear and, 178. *See also* decolonization; imperialism

Committee for Assisting Anti-Communist Righteous Compatriots, 63–64

Communism: anti-Communist activism, Korea, 102–4, 106–8; anti-Communist propaganda, 43–44, 47, 51–52, 58, 139, 211n13; Chinese movement in Vietnam, 25; depoliticization of Vietnamese migration and, 37–39; US response to Vietnamese partition, 28, 29–32

counterrevolutionary pressure, 168–69

cultural production, 150–56, 187, 188–89

Cumings, Bruce, 108

currency reform, North Korea, 88–89

Czechoslovakia, 10

Dachen refugees, *72*, *73*; anti-Communist propaganda, 43–44, 51–52, 211n13; Cold War Taiwan, 50–51; failed KMT-US resettlement efforts, 48–49, 58–65; Korean War coastal raids, 54–58; refugee petitions and seamen training, 49–50, 65–71; in refugee scholarship, 48; as "righteous compatriots," 43–47, 52–53

Dachen xincun 大陳新村 ("Dachen new villages"), 49, 58–59, 61–64, *73*

Đại Việt (political party), 26

Darkwater (Du Bois), 163

decolonization: Cold War as extension of, 166, 168, 170, 176–78; India's role in, 32–35, 38–39, 41–42; paramilitary logic and, 166–67; partition of Vietnam and, 23, 24–28, 41–42. *See also* colonialism

Defense Housing Association (DHA), 129–32, 229n31

Deliver Us from Evil (Dooley), 31

democracy and dispossession, 165
Democratic People's Republic of Korea (DPRK), 86, 88
Democratic Republic of Afghanistan (DRA), 138, 140–42, 143, 145–46, 231n17
Democratic Republic of Vietnam (DRV), 24–29, 34, 36, 37–41
denialism, 158
Departures (Espiritu et al.), 2
"dependent mentality" (*yilai xinli;* 依賴心理), 66, 68, 71
Derrida, Jacques, 191
displaced persons (DPs): definitions of, postcolonial Korea, 76–80; legacies of displacement, 153–57; "refugees" vs., WWII, 13–14; as source of labor, 9, 49, 61–62, 200n26; strategic mobilization of, 118–19, 126–27; US guidelines on, post-Japanese Empire, 5–8, 76–77; US vs. European classifications, 9–10
Displaced Persons Bureau (US), 77–78, 96
Dooley, Thomas A., 31
Doxiadis, Constantinos, 110–12, 114, 116, 118, 121, 227n6
Dubnov, Arie M., 23
Du Bois, W.E.B., 158, *162*, 163, 170, 180–81
Dulles, John Foster, 52
Duong, Lan, 2
Dutch East Indies, 5, 6–8, 199n17

economic hardship, as migrant motivator, 87, 88–89
Eichmann in Jerusalem (Arendt), 175, 235n9
"ekistics" (science of settlement), 167, 173, 227n6
Elusive Refuge (Madokoro), 2
Enders, Gordon B., 77
The End of History and the Last Man (Fukuyama), 177

Espiritu, Yen Le, 2
exile: exiles vs. refugees, 15; expulsion, 174, 175–76, 183; in poetry and music, 150–56, 187, 188–89

Fanon, Frantz, 169
February 28 Massacre, 51
First Indochina War (1946–1954), 22–23, 24–28
First Taiwan Strait Crisis (1954–1955), 4, 19, 44–45, 57. *See also* Dachen refugees
food shortages, as migrant motivator, 87, 88
forcible displacement, 12–13
Ford Foundation, 110, 116
France: criticisms of, post-partition, 40; First Indochina War, 22–23, 24–28; response to ICC position, Vietnam, 38
French Modern (Rabinow), 173
French Union Forces, 22, 24–27, 39
Friendly Society of Northern Students, 99
Fukuyama, Francis, 169, 177

Gane, William J., 77
garbage, covert mobilization of, 130–33
Gatrell, Peter, 5, 14, 45
Geneva Accords (1954): complications in execution of, 11, 36, 38, 39–40; negotiations, 25–28, 35; provisions of, 22–24, 30
Germany, 9, 14, 30, 31
Glatzer, Bernt, 150
"global civil war," 168–70, 174
global color line, 163, 164, 170, 180–81, 236n24
Gorbachev, Mikhail, 145
The Great Exodus from China (Yang), 16
Great Korean Progress Youth Association [Taehan Hyŏksin Ch'ŏngnyŏnhoe], 103

Gul, Momin, 135
Gumnam, Mohammad Tahir Aziz, 140

Habib, Asadullah, 231n19
Hakka-speaking ethnic Chinese, 51, 60
Hamlin, Rebecca, 12
Han Kyŏngjik, 99
Hasan, Arif, 132
"Hate" (Malal), 154–55
Hatton, Nigel, 2
Hazara people, 153
Hekmatyar, Gulbuddin, 147
Heller-Roazen, Daniel, 189
Hòa Hảo (religious group), 26
Hobbes, Thomas, 167, 186, 194, 236n17
Ho Chi Minh, 24, 26, 28, 34, 35
Hodge, John, 84
Hok-lo-speaking ethnic Chinese, 51, 60
Hong Kong: 1949 mainland exodus to, 3, 50, 212n16; in extant refugee scholarship, 48
Hopkirk, Peter, 120
Hsu Nai (Xu Nai 徐鼐; 1910–1992), 69–70
human rights, 114, 163, 165, 169, 183–84
Humayune, Nasser, 110
Hu Tsung-nan (Hu Zongnan 胡宗南; 1896–1962), 55
Hwanghae Association (Hwanghaehoe), 100
Hwanghae Youth Association [Hwanghae Ch'ŏngnyŏnhoe], 103
Hyman, Anthony, 147–48

Ibuk Odominhoe (Association of the People from Five Northern Provinces), 86
Ibuk T'ongsin magazine, 76, 87, 88, 94–95, 99, 104–8
identity, 6–7, 15, 138, 144, 194
immigration: forced vs. voluntary, 12; "jumping ship," 71; nation-state interests in, 46; post-2021 policies on Afghan refugees, 156–57; post-WWII migration control, 10–11; Western positions on Asian immigration, 2
imperialism, 5, 8, 39, 142, 158–59, 169. *See also* colonialism
India: caste and rightlessness, 184; characterizing Vietnamese migration, 16; in evacuation of Vietnam, 24, 36–40, 41–42; as intermediary in Vietnam, 32–36, 207n52
indifference, 21, 181–82
"Indo-European," 7
Indonesia, 33, 35
inequality: archipelagos of inequality, 190; exacerbated by climate change, 192; kinship between violence and, 165; planetarity vs. equality, 163–64; white fear and, 178
"In Mourning for Justice" (Arussang), 154
Intelligence Summary North Korea (intelligence report), 78, 79, 81, 218n3, 219n17
internally displaced persons, 14
International Control Commission (ICC), 24, 32, 36–38, 40
International Refugee Organization, 48
Iran, 137–38, 139–40, 141, 151, 156–57
isan kajok ("separated families"), 80
Islam, 139, 140, 145, 148
islands, 176, 186–91

Japan: colonial rule over Taiwan, 51; end of Korean occupation, 74–75; prioritization of Japanese DPs, 9; repatriation of DPs from North Korea, 82; US guidelines on DPs in Japan-occupied regions, 5–8, 76, 199n17, 200n26
Jewish refugees, 8, 15
Jinnah, Muhammad Ali, 118
Judt, Tony, 179

246   Index

"jumping ship" (illegal immigration), 71
"jurisprudence of neglect," 165–70

Kaker, Sobia Ahmad, 133
Kamal, Mustafa, 125, 127, 128
Kang Ch'ang-jin, 103, 105
Kang Chŏng-gu, 85
Kang In-dŏk, 95
Kang In-suk, 94
Karachi, Pakistan. *See* spatial politics
Karachi Bachao Tehreek (Save Karachi Movement), 133
Karachi Development Authority (KDA), 130, 132
Karachi Urban Lab, 133
Kazemi, Mohammad Kazem, 153–54
KGB (Soviet State Security Committee), 74
Khalis, Yunus, 150
Khan, Ayub, 110, 114, 118, *119*, 124–25
Khomeini, Ruhollah Musavi, 139, 149
Kim Chihwan, 101
Kim Chin-sŏp, 103
Kim Dae-jung, 95
Kim Il Sung, 104, 109
Kim Kûi-ok, 85
Kim Kwang-sŏp, 107, 108
Kim Sam-gyu, 107
Kim Sŏng-su, 102
Kim T'aenam, 87, 94–95
Kim T'aesŏng, 101
Kim Tong-ni, 108
Ko Chae-uk, 107
Korean Armistice Agreement (1953), 57
Korean War (1950–1953): coastal raids on Dachen Islands, 47, 54–58; evacuation from Hŭngnamu Harbor, 1; India's involvement in arbitration, 33–34; number of south-bound refugees, 85; prisoner repatriation, 10–11; US influence in, 108. *See also* northern Korean refugees

Kuomintang (KMT) government: 1949 collapse of, 50, 54; coastal raids on Dachen Islands, 54–58; facilitating migration from Zhejiang islands, 43–44, 52–53, 210n4; failed Dachen-resettlement efforts, 48–49, 58–65; frustrations with Dachen refugees, 66, 68–69; rule in postwar Taiwan, 51–52
Kwŏn T'ae-hwan, 85

labor, displaced persons as source of, 49, 61–62, 200n26
Lakhani, Bashir, 131
land-acquisition, covert, 120–21, 126–32
Land Acquisition Act (1894), 120–21
Land and Sea (Schmitt), 186
language barriers, 65
Laos, 25, 26, 35
law: Cold War as legal fantasy, 170; Cold War in restructuring of, 169; statelessness, segregation and, 21, 161–63, 174; violence without legal theory, 182–86; water as analogue of lawlessness, 173, 186–91
Leffler, Melvyn P., 2, 197n5
Leviathan (Hobbes), 194, 236n17
Liakhovskii, Aleksandr, 141
"The Liberalism of Fear" (Shklar), 158
Life in Refugee Camps (pamphlet), 144–45
"Like a Desert Flower" (Malal), 155
Lin, Hsiao-ting, 46

Madokoro, Laura, 2
Majruh, Sayyid Bahauddin, 143, 144, 145–47, 149, 151
The Making of the Modern Refugee (Gatrell), 45
Malal, Parween Faiz Zadah, 154–56
Malkki, Liisa, 20–21, 230n3
Manchuria, Korean migrants from, 86–87
Manto, Sadat Hasan, 227n9

Mao Zedong, 1, 3, 55
Matsu Islands, 19, 45, 52, 212n25
Mbembe, Achille, 191, 239n54
Mendès France, Pierre, 28
Menon, V. K. Krishna, 35, 39
Mitha, Aboobaker Osman, 116
"mnemonic regimes," 16
mohajer/mujahed ("two-fold" person), 138
Morales, Aurora Levins, 187
Moyn, Samuel, 236n24
mujahideen (holy warriors), 124, 136–37, 138, 140, 143–44
Musharraf, Pervaiz, 124, 125
music, 151, 153, 156
Muttahida Qaumi Movement (MQM), 124–25, 127–28, 129, 133, 229n26

Nail, Thomas, 80
Najibullah, Mohammad, 146
nationalism: anti-Communist activism, Korea, 102–4, 106–8; anti-trusteeship activism, Korea, 100–102; influence of refugees on nation-states, 45
Nationalist Party of China. *See* Kuomintang (KMT) government
nationality, as criterion for repatriation, 5, 6–7, 8, 76–78
"native Taiwanese," 51
Nawaz, Haq, 141–42
Nedostup, Rebecca, 47–48
negative liberty, 235n7
neglect, 166–70, 190–91
Nehru, Jawaharlal, 33, 35–36
"neocolonial atlas," 188–90
neodemocratic condition, 165, 167, 172
Neutral Nations Repatriation Committee (NNRC), 33
Ngô Đình Diệm, 23, 28, 30, 36, 39–40
Nguyen, Vinh, 16–17
Northern Academic Society (Sŏbuk Hakhoe), 100

Northern Association (Sŏbuk Hyŏphoe), 100
northern Korean refugees: border-crossing experiences, 94–99; defining "displaced persons" and "refugees," 76–80; interweaving factors in, 108–9; journalistic narratives, 104–8; motivations of, 87–89; occupation and border-making, 80–84; organizations and activism, 74–76, 99–104; refugee numbers and routes, 84–87, 221n61; refugees in media coverage, 31; social characteristics, 89–93, *91*; US guidelines on displaced persons in, 5–6, 76–77, 199n17. *See also* Korean War (1950-1953)
Northern Student Self-Help Organization, 99
North Hamgyŏng Youth Association [Hambuk Ch'ŏngnyŏnhoe], 103
North Korean Revolution (1945-1950), 92, 93, 102, 109
North Korean Youth Association [Puksŏn Ch'ŏngnyŏnhoe], 103
Northwestern Student Association (Sŏbuk Haksaeng Yŏnmaeng), 74, 102
Northwestern Youth Association (Sŏbuk Ch'ŏngnyŏndan), 75, 90, 103–4
North-West Frontier Province (NWFP), 120–21
"Nothing Personal" (Baldwin), 195

Olszewska, Zuzanna, 150–51
On Revolution (Arendt), 161
Operation Auvergne (1954), 27, 29
Operation Passage to Freedom (1954), 30
Orange Pilot Project, 132
The Origins of the Korean War (Cumings), 108
The Origins of Totalitarianism (Arendt), 158, 166, 176, 183

Paek Namhong, 101
Pakistan: Afghan-refugee experiences in, 137–38, 151; British establishment of Karachi, 127; civilian impacts of partition, 34; instrumentalization of Afghan refugees, 139, 141–42; post-2021 policies on Afghan refugees, 156–57. *See also* spatial politics
Pakistan Defence Officers Cooperative Housing Society (PDOCHS), 129
Pakistan People's Party's (PPP), 128, 129, 133
Panchsheel Agreement on Tibet (1954), 33
paramilitary logic, 166–68, 173–74
partitioning: border-making, Korea, 80–84; as deliberately ambiguous, 114–16, *115*; political advantages to, 28–32, 41
partition of Vietnam: conflicting definitions of displaced persons, 16; decolonization and Cold War divisions, 24–28; India as intermediary, 32–36, 207n52; India's technical population transfer, 36–40, 41–42; political advantages of partition, 28–32, 41; provisions of, 22–24
passivity, 21, 181–82
penal logic, 166–68, 173–74, 193
People's Army of Vietnam, 22, 24–26, 27
People's Democratic Party of Afghanistan (PDPA), 141
People's Liberation Army (PLA), 44, 54, 57
People's Republic of China (PRC), 46, 50, 54–55
People's Volunteer Army (PVA), 53, 55
"petition and snitch" (*chenqing gaozhuang;* 陳情告狀), 67–68
Philippines, 5, 199n17
planetarity, 163–64, 181, 184, 192

poetry, 150–56, 187, 188–89
Poland, 32
Political Security Bureau (Chŏngch'i Powibu), 89–92
propaganda: anti-Communist, 43–44, 47, 51–52, 58, 139, 211n13; in portrayals of Afghan refugees, 140–43
prose, 154–55
Protocol Relating to the Status of Refugees (1967), 12
P'yŏngan Youth Association [P'yŏngan Ch'ŏngnyŏnhoe], 103

quarantine centers, Korea, 97–98
Quemoy (Kinmen) islands, 45, 52, 212n25

Rabinow, Paul, 173
race: exclusionary border practices, 48; global color line, 163, 164, 170, 180–81, 236n24; racialized segregation, 173–74; US approach to displaced persons and, 7
Radcliffe, Cyril, 115, 227n9
Rajani, Shahana, 118, 120
Rajani, Shayan, 118, 120
Refugee Convention (1951), 12, 16
refugees, defined, 12–16, 76–80. *See also* displaced persons (DPs)
"refugeetude," 16–17
religion, 90–91, 139, 140, 145, 148, 175, 191, 192
Republic of China (ROC), 46, 51–52
"Return" (Kazemi), 153–54
Rhee Syngman, 10–11, 106, 107, 108, 109
rightlessness, 173, 174, 183–84
Robson, Laura, 23
Romulo, Carlos, 33, 38
Ryu Ch'ŏl, 101

Said, Edward, 15
samp'al tojuja ("runaways to the South"), 80

samp'al ttaraji ("leftovers of the thirty-eighth parallel"), 80
Sarkhosh, Sarwar, 153
Saur Revolution (1978), 153
Sayaf, Abdul Rasul, 147
Schmitt, Carl, 173, 186
segregation: inequality and, 178–81; logic of paramilitary law, 173–74; statelessness and, 21, 161–63
Sharif, Lila, 2
shelter without amnesty, 183
Shklar, Judith, 158, 164, 169, 181, 183, *185*, 235n7
Siagatonu, Terisa, 188–89, 190, 191, 192
silhyangmin ("people who lost homes"), 80
Sindh Katchi Abadi Act (1987), 228n23
Sindh Katchi Abadi Authority (SKAA), 128
Sindh Local Government Ordinance (SLGO), 128
Singh, Khushwant, 121
Sino-American Mutual Defense Treaty (1954), 57
Sinŭiju massacre (1945), 100
Sirajuddin, Muhammad, 132
Skinner, Quentin, 236n24
slavery, 164, 235n7
"the society of enmity," 191
The Souls of Black Folk (Du Bois), 158, 163
Southern Wind (Namp'unghoe) organization, 105
South Korea: Cheju Island uprising (1948), 74; nationalism in, 100–104, 106–8; North Korean POW release, 10–11. *See also* Korean War (1950–1953); northern Korean refugees
South Korean Workers' Party, 89, 90, 103, 106
sovereignty: independence of paramilitary forces, 166–67; refugee protection vs., 42; segregation and, 173–74; use of migrants in state-formation, 46
Spain, 13
spatiality vs. territoriality, 17–18, 112–13
spatial politics: covert land-acquisition and management, 126–34; covert urban planning, 114–21, *115*, *117*, *119*; encroachment and conflict, 121–26, *122*, *123*, *126*; space vs. territory, 112; strategic advantages to instability, 20, 110–13, *111*
Special Committee on Migration and Resettlement, 5–7, 76–77, 198n14, 199n17, 200n26
Special Services Group (SSG), 116
Stalin, Joseph, 26
statelessness: colonial geographies and, 189; defining "refugees," 12–16, 17, 76–80; juridical color line and, 183–84; jurisprudence of neglect and, 166–70; segregation and, 21, 161–63
State of Vietnam (SVN), 23, 30, 31, 35, 38, 40
"stay-behind" warfare strategy, 114, 116, 119, 121
surveillance, 112–13, 166, 193

Taiwan: changing refugee recollections, 16; First Taiwan Strait Crisis, 4, 19, 44–45, 57; as "Free China," 46, 47, 51–52; mainland exodus to, 50–51, 212n17; US guidelines on displaced persons in, 5–6, 198n14, 199n17. *See also* Dachen refugees
Taliban movement, 156
Technical Training and Resource Center (TTRC), 132–33
technology: mobility and, 193–94; techno-feudalism, 176–77, 190–91; theological-technological bonds, 175, 191
Thailand, 26

250 Index

Thatcher, Margaret, 139
Thimayya, K. S., 34
Tonga Ilbo newspaper, 98, 102
Train to Pakistan (Singh), 121
Transportation Bureau (US), 77, 96
Treaty for the Relinquishment of Extraterritorial Rights in China (1943), 6
Tsing, Anna Lowenhaupt, 112

Um, Khatharya, 2
United Kingdom, 6, 100, 190
United Nations High Commissioner for Refugees (UNHCR), 12, 48
United Nations Refugee Agency, 167
United Nations Relief and Rehabilitation Administration (UNRRA), 9, 33, 48
United States: Afghan-refugee allies, 157; anti-Communist propaganda, 43–44, 47, 58, 211n13; CIA-funded operations on Dachen Islands, 54, 55–58; Dachen Islanders' displacement and, 52, 212n25; "displaced persons" vs. "refugees," WWII, 13–14; failed Dachen-resettlement scheme, 48–49, 58–65, 215n63, 215n68; funding of first Afghan war, 129; funding of French Union Forces, 25; guidelines on displaced persons, 5–8, 76–79, 198n14, 199n17, 200n26; illegal immigration to, 71; influence in Pakistan, 114; influence on Korea War, 108–9; invasion of Afghanistan, 156; joint trusteeship over Korea, 100–101; Korean occupation, 80–84; politicization of Afghan refugees, 139; refugee administration, 8–11, 96–98; response to ICC position, Vietnam, 38; response to Vietnamese partition, 23, 24, 28, 29–32; withdrawal from Afghanistan, 182

United States Agency for International Development (USAID), 119, 125
Universal Declaration of Human Rights, 169
urban planning. *See* spatial politics
urban segregation, 173–74
USSR (Union of Soviet Socialist Republics): 1979 invasion of Afghanistan, 135–36; administration of Korean migrants, 86–87; joint trusteeship over Korea, 100–101; Korean occupation, 74–75, 78–79, 80–84; North Korean currency conversion and, 89; post-WWII conception of Soviet refugees, 10; support for Chinese Communist movement, 25; US administration of wartime refugees and, 10–11; violence toward Korean refugees, 94–95, 105, 220n47, 223n88; withdrawal from Afghanistan, 145, 146, 153. *See also* Afghan refugees

Vang, Ma, 2
Varoufakis, Yanis, 190
Vietnam. *See* partition of Vietnam
Việt Nam Quốc Dân Đảng (political party), 26

War on Terror, 113, 156
Warren, George L., 8
"wartime developmentalist logic," 61
waste management, Karachi, 130–33
watan ("home village" or "home country"), 152
water, as analogue of lawlessness, 173, 186–91
Watt, Lori, 5, 9, 199n17
Welfare Quarantine Camp (US military), 97
Westad, Odd Arne, 2, 18, 197n5
Western Enterprises Inc. (WEI), 55, 57

"White Terror," 51
wŏlnamja ("person crossing thirty-eighth parallel"), 79, 80
women: as artists, 151–52, 154–55; as critics and activists, 149–50; feminized representations of refugees, 140
Working Committee on Displaced Persons, 9
World War II, 5–11, 13, 168
Writers Union of Free Afghanistan, 144–45

Yainsidae (*Rustic Period;* television series), 104

Yangho League [Yanghodan], 103
Yi Puk, 104, 107, 225n134
Yŏngnak Presbyterian Church, 99
Yun Il-yŏng, 75

Zaeef, Mullah Abdul Salam, 143–44
Zahir Shah, Mohammad, 146–49
Zamindar, Vazira, 114
Zhejiang Anti-Communist National Salvation Army (ZANSA), 55–57
Zhejiang Province, 43–44, 54. *See also* Dachen refugees
Zia-ul-Haque, Muhammad, 129, 228n23

The authorized representative in the EU for product safety and compliance is:
Mare Nostrum Group
B.V Doelen 72
4831 GR Breda
The Netherlands

www.ingramcontent.com/pod-product-compliance
Lightning Source LLC
Chambersburg PA
CBHW022004220426
43663CB00007B/955